Life Reborn

JEWISH DISPLACED PERSONS 1945–1951

CONFERENCE PROCEEDINGS

Life Reborn

JEWISH DISPLACED PERSONS 1945–1951

CONFERENCE PROCEEDINGS

WASHINGTON, D.C.
JANUARY 14–17, 2000

Edited with an Introduction by MENACHEM Z. ROSENSAFT
Preface by RABBI IRVING GREENBERG

ROMANA STROCHLITZ PRIMUS
Conference Chairperson
ROSITTA EHRLICH KENIGSBERG
Chairperson, Second Generation Advisory Group

A project of the United States Holocaust Memorial Museum and
its Second Generation Advisory Group in association with
The American Jewish Joint Distribution Committee

Publication of this volume was made possible through special grants from the Theodore and Renee Weiler Foundation, Inc., and the Jewish Community Endowment Fund of the Jewish Community Federation of San Francisco, the Peninsula, Marin and Sonoma Counties.

Some Hebrew, Yiddish, and German terms and phrases italicized in the text are defined in the glossary on p. 139.

Copyright © 2001 Menachem Z. Rosensaft

Library of Congress Cataloging-in-Publication Data

Life reborn: Jewish displaced persons, 1945–1951: conference proceedings, Washington, D.C.
      January 14–17, 2000 / edited with an introduction by Menachem Z. Rosensaft.
      p. ; cm.
      Includes bibliographical references.
      ISBN 0-89604-706-7 (cloth)—ISBN 0-89604-707-5 (pbk.)
      1. Holocaust survivors—Germany—Congresses. 2. Refugees, Jewish—Germany—
Congresses. 3. Children of Holocaust survivors—United States—Congresses.
      4. Refugee camps—Europe—Congresses. I. Rosensaft, Menachem Z., 1948–

D804.18 .L54 2001
940.53'18—dc21
                                                      00-012326

Printed in the United States of America

For Jodi,

for Richard, Ida, Lisa, Aryeh, and Jacob,

for David, Tamara, and Max,

for Jessica and Stephanie,

for Adam,

and for all our children and grandchildren

Contents

Monday, January 17, 2000

PREFACE

Rabbi Irving Greenberg
Chair, United States Holocaust Memorial Council

Although the Nazi "Final Solution" ground to a halt in the collapse of the Third Reich, the Holocaust did not end on V-E Day. The organized mass killing stopped, but the dying went on. Out of tragic lack of understanding of the condition of survivors, prisoners in such camps as Dachau were fed food too rich for starvation-reduced stomachs and died. This mishandling reflected Allied ignorance and failure to plan, which in turn mirrored the democracies' lack of concern for the fate of the Jews.

Even in Bergen-Belsen, where the British appointed Dr. Hadassah Rosensaft to lead a team of 28 prisoner physicians and 620 volunteers who desperately worked with military doctors to save as many survivors as possible, "the Holocaust claimed 13,944 additional victims during the two months after the liberation." (Menachem Z. Rosensaft, p. 5) In Kielce, Poland, a local pogrom killed 42 surviving Jews and injured many others—an outburst of hatred that was replicated in individual acts, albeit on a smaller scale, throughout postwar Eastern Europe.

The Nazi torturing stopped, but tragically, the victims continued to suffer. Ignoring the differential Nazi persecution of Jews, the British (on the basis of liberal values) and the Americans (on the basis of efficiency) had decided not to treat the Jews in DP camps separately from other prisoners. As a result, German Jews and other Jews (as well as anti-Nazi nationals) from Axis countries often were classified as enemy nationals and denied privileged rations. Many Jewish survivors were left in camps containing substantial numbers of displaced Volksdeutsche and East European populations that had collaborated with the Nazis and who were themselves deeply antisemitic. The survivors, for their part, insisted that as they were Jewish in fate and identity, they would come together in their own communities and camps and be treated as Jews. (The Americans shifted policy when they realized the suffering they were inflicting on the DPs; the British held out longer.) Initially, many Jews were kept in camps behind barbed wire and were given less food every day than the prisoners of war were given. In many aspects of life, they were treated worse than the prisoners of war. Earl Harrison, appointed by President Truman to investigate conditions in the DP camps, reported, "we appear to be treating the Jews as the Nazis treated them, except that we do not exterminate them." (Quoted by Leonard Dinnerstein, p. 105)

The pattern of callousness was widespread. Where General Patton was in command, Jews continued to be treated more harshly than under other American generals. In America, there was strong resistance to any increase in admission quotas on the grounds that "refugees" were a threat to America's future and economy and culture. The term "refugee" was widely recognized as a thinly veiled euphemism for "Jews." Someday the full record will be laid out for all to see—the priests and religious officials who worked to enable war criminals to flee, while survivors were prevented from going to Palestine; the welcoming absorption of various Nazis into Cold War intelligence services, while over 50,000 Jewish DPs were transshipped and interned in Cyprus by the British after they managed to sail up to the gates of Zion. Add to this tale, widespread postwar unwillingness to hear the stories of survivors and the frequent accusatory questions: "Why did you not fight?" and "What did you do to survive?" The whole adds up to the shameful aftermath of the Holocaust. Someday, if decency prevails, the whole narrative will be documented and reported. Then the world can ponder what this devastating record says about antisemitism and human behavior, about group morality and ethical apathy and indifference.

It follows that Holocaust remembrance and United States Holocaust Memorial Museum programs dare not stop at the date of May 8, 1945. The so-called civilized world's continuation of policies of discrimination and neglect—not to mention business as usual—as well as the incredible survivor response of renewing personal life and re-creating Jewish community and dignity are essential parts of the history and record of the Shoah. As Samuel Norich says in these proceedings, it is a "central mystery" how survivors found the inner strength to pursue such constructive new lives. (p. 53) As Elie Wiesel asks, "How did these men and women, who have seen the absurdity of what we call culture, education—how did they get, where did they get the courage, the imagination, the need to believe in them? . . . How did you, parents, grandparents, manage to behave with so much humanity in spite of the pain that remained in you. . . ?" (p. 84) Part of the response is elemental human behavior. Humans react to the surge of death in wartime by creating new life. There are postwar spikes in childbearing and family formation worldwide. Part of the response is the primordial Jewish religious instinct to choose life and to re-create communities after every destruction. In the end, the inexplicable, but astonishing, credit goes to the survivors' own nature and behavior.

It is still too early for definitive scholarly treatments of this history. For one, the field of Holocaust scholarship is still nascent and is understaffed in this area. The Russian and East European archives are only recently opened and not fully available. And while the survivors have given serious testimony to their fate in the Shoah, they and their children have only begun to open up about postwar life. This conference—*Life Reborn*—is a wonderful down payment, if you will, a first approximation, of the comprehensive portraits that will follow.

This conference gives us a highly useful—nay, inspiring—working model of the tasks before us. It starts with celebration of the survivors and their courage and love in rebuilding life. This includes, and stimulates, reflections on the resilient power of life, even after it was crushed under the heel of the most total, murderous tyranny ever. The record points to the impact of survivors—especially of their refusal to rejoin the European societies that were the cemeteries of their past lives and families, and their insistence on going to live in a Jewish state, yet to be born. This determination cost many of them additional years of displacement and, for some, years of imprisonment in Cyprus. But their courage moved American and, then, world policies. The survivors' fight was essential to winning the right to declare and defend Israel. Their instant creation of Jewish communities and autonomous entities also served as a critical role model, for the nations and for Jewry, of Jewish capacity to take power for the sake of life and morality.

This book is an important compendium of witness by the survivors and by the Second Generation. All wisdom—and morality—starts with witness, which also provides the raw material for the history and analysis that will follow. We are also given an essential instruction that the witness dare not be apologetic or propagandistic; that would cheapen the awesome dignity of this topic. As Thane Rosenbaum warns us, the testimony cannot be all about happy lives and memories—for we are witnesses also to loss, to unhealed wounds, to suffering that goes on and on. (p. 127)

These proceedings also offer important guidelines on the Second Generation's role and responsibilities. As Gary Schiller puts it, the Second Generation's obligation is "to do something concrete with the biologic heritage of transmitted memory." He speaks of the roles of witness and teacher. Pointing to the compelling objective of remembrance, he correctly stresses that it needs no other justifications: "the development of memory is sufficient." (p. 133) He speaks of the task of being Jewish—with a Judaism that is informed by this special heritage of memory. I would add that once remembrance is established and recognized as self-validating, as the human thing to do, then the effort to arouse the conscience of the world to prevent future genocide becomes the final tribute that one pays to the victims. We truly honor the dead when we determine to save lives by our actions and then work to perfect the world in their memory.

Let us, therefore, thank all who labored to create this conference, to carry it out, and now to publish its proceedings. As current chairman of the United States Holocaust Memorial Council, I thank the Second Generation for pushing us to do the right thing. I thank the Museum staff for their valiant extra effort to advance this program. This conference broadened the mission and service of the Holocaust Memorial Museum. We are indebted to you for that.

I shall not repeat our collective thanks to all the co-chairs, planning committee, donors, etc., for they are listed within. I feel a personal gratitude to each and every one.

In one of its darkest moments, the Torah suggests that the suffering of parents will be visited on children to the third and fourth generations. But in facing this depressing and shocking prophecy, the Rabbis snatch at consolation in the jaws of horror. They point out that the kindness and loving memory of Divine Providence stretches 500 times further into future generations. This book proves a parallel proposition. The suffering and pain that is inflicted on the generations of survivors' children and descendants—from which we cannot protect them although we wish we could—is far outstripped by the models of compassion and life affirmation which the Second Generation is given as its inheritance. It is also heartening to discern in the witness contained in this book that while the Second Generation's fate is passed on to them by a kind of "lineal osmosis," they live it out by their own freely given, loving choice.

INTRODUCTION

Menachem Z. Rosensaft

Partner in the law firm of Ross & Hardies; Founding Chairman, International Network of Children of Jewish Holocaust Survivors; member, United States Holocaust Memorial Council

I was born in Bergen-Belsen. My cradle stood only a short distance away from the mass graves in which Anne Frank and tens of thousands of other European Jews lie buried anonymously. More than 2,000 Jewish children were born in the displaced persons (DP) camp of Bergen-Belsen in Germany between 1945 and 1950. What had been one of the most notorious Nazi concentration camps became a sanctuary of life.

While much has been written about the Holocaust, relatively little is known about the years immediately after World War II when the survivors of the death camps returned to life in DP camps throughout Germany, Austria, and Italy. Most people, including most Jews, think of Holocaust survivors as skeletal figures in striped uniforms staring aimlessly into the distance on the day of their liberation. And then they fast-forward 40 or 50 years to somber commemorations at which gray- and white-haired men and women mourn their dead by lighting candles and reciting memorial prayers. But what happened to the victims when they ceased to be victims?

On January 14–17, 2000, in Washington, D.C., *Life Reborn, Jewish Displaced Persons, 1945–1951*—a conference organized by the United States Holocaust Memorial Museum and its Second Generation Advisory Group in association with The American Jewish Joint Distribution Committee (JDC)—shed light on the Jewish DP camps and their unique place in contemporary history. The main purpose of the conference was to expand the historiographical boundaries of the Holocaust to incorporate what the survivors experienced and accomplished once they reclaimed control of their destinies.

On April 15, 1945, when British troops entered Bergen-Belsen, near the German city of Hanover, they encountered a devastation of human misery for which they were utterly unprepared. More than 10,000 bodies lay scattered about the camp, and the 58,000 surviving inmates—the overwhelming majority of them Jews—were suffering from a combination of typhus, tuberculosis, dysentery, extreme malnutrition, and countless other virulent diseases. Most were too weak even to walk.

Brigadier H. L. Glyn-Hughes, the deputy director of medical services of the British Army of the Rhine, appointed my mother to organize and head a group of doctors and nurses among the survivors to help care for the camp's thousands of critically ill inmates. For weeks on end, my mother and her team of 28 doctors and 620 other female and male volunteers, only a few of whom were trained nurses, worked round the clock with the military doctors to try to save as many of the survivors as possible. Despite their desperate efforts, the Holocaust claimed 13,944 additional victims during the two months after the liberation. And those who lived had to face a grim reality. "For the greatest part of the liberated Jews of Bergen-Belsen," my mother later recalled, "there was no ecstasy, no joy at our liberation. We had lost our families, our homes. We had no place to go to, nobody to hug. Nobody was waiting for us anywhere. We had been liberated from death and from the fear of death, but we were not free from the fear of life."[1]

In order to contain the different epidemics that were rampant throughout Bergen-Belsen, the British evacuated the survivors to nearby German army barracks that had previously housed a Panzer training school, and which became the DP camp. On May 21, 1945, when the relocation had been completed, the British set fire to all of the concentration camp's wooden barracks.

Jews from Western European countries returned to their homes as soon as they could, leaving behind primarily those from Poland and Hungary. Within a few weeks, the camp's Jewish population stabilized at around 12,000. Most had lost entire families. On their own, they were now forced to come to terms with their shattered universe.

Millions of uprooted and homeless non-Germans from all over Europe found themselves in Germany at the end of the war. The vast majority was successfully repatriated in a matter of months. Most of the approximately 100,000 Jewish Holocaust survivors from Eastern Europe, however, especially those from Poland, were unwilling to go back to their prewar homes. Having been subjected to widespread antisemitism on the part of their Christian neighbors, both before and during the Holocaust, these Jewish survivors wanted only to begin new lives in countries that were not haunted by bitter memories. Classified as DPs, they were placed in camps under the control of the respective American, British, and French military authorities. At first, they were forced to live alongside non-Jewish refugees, including many from the Baltic States, Ukraine, Hungary, Romania, and elsewhere, who had willingly assisted the Germans, and who did not want to return to their countries of origin for fear of retribution.

The Jewish survivors refused to remain in the midst of Nazi collaborators and other antisemitic DPs. While the American and British military authorities were generally unsympathetic to Jewish concerns, they ultimately were forced to give in, enabling the Jewish survivors to live in separate DP camps.

The population of these camps was constantly shifting. Tens of thousands more Jews from all across Eastern Europe, often fleeing renewed antisemitic persecution, arrived in droves. Jewish Holocaust survivors who had returned to Poland in search of family members and friends were greeted with intense hostility that frequently escalated into violence. The July 1946 pogrom in the city of Kielce persuaded large numbers of Polish Jews to seek refuge in the DP camps of Germany. There, they waited. Prevented from settling in Palestine, the United States, and other Western countries, the Jewish DPs were left in a surreal limbo.

Bergen-Belsen, in the British zone of Germany, was the largest of the DP camps. Most commonly referred to simply as Belsen, it was an autonomous, self-governed, and largely self-contained Jewish community. And then there were Landsberg, Feldafing, Bad Reichenhall, Eschwege, Zeilsheim, Wetzlar, Pocking, and Foehrenwald, to name only eight such camps in the American zone. In short order, they all had their own political administrations, schools, and cultural institutions.

---

[1] *In 1978 President Carter appointed my mother, Dr. Hadassah Bimko Rosensaft, to his Commission on the Holocaust. In 1980 she became a founding member of the United States Holocaust Memorial Council.*

The years the survivors spent in the DP camps were a period of critical transition and resuscitation. As Allied soldiers began to return home in 1945, most Americans wanted only to get on with their lives. So did the British, the Canadians, the French. They did not want to have to think about anything that would distract them from their immediate personal concerns. Jewish military chaplains and a handful of Jewish organizations, principally the JDC—which provided extraordinary assistance—and the World Jewish Congress, took up the cause of the Jewish DPs. Otherwise, the human condition of homeless European Jews was a matter of relative indifference for most Americans, including most American Jews. Thus, the survivors were left to cope as best they could.

They coped by creating life in every meaning of the term. In the aftermath of destruction, the process of both national and individual rebirth took on an almost mystical quality. Left to their own devices, the Jewish DPs tried to replicate the life they had known before the Holocaust. Most importantly, they supported one another physically, emotionally, and spiritually. And so faith and love were able to blossom anew in the shadow of mass graves. Mourning soon gave way to thousands of marriages, and new families emerged from the ashes. Dr. Romana Strochlitz Primus, who chaired the *Life Reborn* conference, tells a wonderful story about her parents during the early months following their liberation. Shortly after they had found each other in the Belsen DP camp, Dr. Primus recounts: "My father borrowed a motorcycle and took my mother for a ride. Once they were on the road, however, he realized that he didn't know how to stop. So they rode the motorcycle until it ran out of gas. But it didn't matter. They rode for the pure pleasure of it, simply because they could. There was no destination. It was purely for joy."

My father, Josef Rosensaft, who headed both the Belsen DP camp's Jewish Committee and the Central Jewish Committee in the British Zone of Germany, used to describe Belsen as the last *shtetl* in Europe. Twenty years later, Elie Wiesel wrote in the *Jewish Daily Forward* of August 13, 1965, that, "Upon the ruins of Europe, on the scorched earth of Germany, yesterday's candidates for death began to build a Jewish future. . . . The people of Belsen chose life."

For five months prior to the liberation, my mother, helped by several other women among the inmates, had managed to keep alive 150 Jewish children, most of them orphans, ranging in age from eight months to 15 years. Of those children, 110 remained in the DP camp. As early as June of 1945, the first school was opened in Belsen, with separate classes in Polish, Romanian, and Hungarian. Other Jewish children from different parts of Eastern Europe soon joined them. In due course, Belsen had a kindergarten, an elementary school, a high school, and a vocational training school run by ORT, the Organization for Rehabilitation through Training, as well as a full complement of Jewish educational institutions. In addition, the camp had a rabbinate, its own Jewish police force, a library, two theater companies, an orchestra, and a host of youth and sports clubs.

Yiddish was the official language of the camp and Zionist politics became the order of the day. The first issue of the Belsen newspaper, *Undzer Shtimme* (Our Voice), handwritten and mimeographed, appeared on July 12, 1945. At first declared illegal by the British military authorities, it soon received official sanction and then regularly appeared in print. The first book published in Belsen on September 7, 1945, was a listing, in English and German, of the camp's Jewish survivors to facilitate the reunification of family members and friends. Some 60 other publications followed, including a religious tract relating to the status of Jewish survivors whose spouses were presumed, but not known to be, dead.

Similar scenarios took place in the other DP camps, resulting in the ultimate irony that the very land that Hitler had wanted to make *Judenrein*—that is, free of Jews—became one of the most vibrant, flourishing centers of Jewish life of all time. Of course, there were tremendous hardships that must not be overlooked or underestimated, but the Jewish DPs overcame them, primarily on their own and thanks to their tremendous collective inner strength.

The survivors' extended stay in the DP camps was dictated primarily by their inability to settle elsewhere. At first, virtually all doors, except to their countries of origin, to which they refused to return, were slammed shut. The British allowed only a trickle of them into Palestine. Beginning in March 1947, for instance, Belsen was allocated between 400 and 500 legal certificates to Palestine a month, which the Central Jewish Committee shared with other Jewish communities and DP centers in the British zone. Those survivors looking to go to the United States, meanwhile, were faced with restrictive immigration laws, including the 1948 Displaced Persons Act which blatantly discriminated against Jewish DPs.

Nevertheless, it is estimated that around 67,000 survivors entered Palestine illegally between 1945 and 1948, and beginning in May 1946, increased numbers of Jewish DPs were admitted into the United States under a special directive issued by President Truman on December 12, 1945. The situation improved dramatically with the establishment of the State of Israel in May 1948. Within less than three years, virtually all the Jewish DP camps were closed as the DP era came to an end.

The *Life Reborn* conference had its origins in a 1995 pilgrimage to Bergen-Belsen by its survivors on the fiftieth anniversary of their liberation. Among the participants were Sigmund Strochlitz, a founding member of the United States Holocaust Memorial Council, and his daughter, Romana Strochlitz Primus. Other sons and daughters of survivors were there as well. "I was struck by the number of children of survivors who knew little about their parents' lives during the DP period," she recalls. "They knew about the prewar years, about the Holocaust, about their parents' lives after immigration, but there was a big hole between liberation and immigration. This is a story that must be told."

Two years later, after she had been appointed to the United States Holocaust Memorial Council, Dr. Primus suggested to Council Chairman Miles Lerman that the United States Holocaust Memorial Museum sponsor a conference about the DP years, and that such a conference would be an ideal initiative for the Council's Second Generation Advisory Group. In December 1997, Mr. Lerman formally proposed the *Life Reborn* conference to the Second Generation Advisory Group, under the leadership of Rositta Ehrlich Kenigsberg, which enthusiastically embraced the project and unanimously affirmed Dr. Primus as conference chair. The story of the Jewish DPs, Rositta Kenigsberg explains, is one "that must be documented and memorialized because it captures the remarkable resurgence and resilience of our parents' human spirit and their yearning to create a new life and a new beginning."

After several brainstorming meetings, the outline of the conference emerged. It was to be an occasion to bring together survivors from the DP camps and their liberators, military chaplains, officials of Jewish organizations active in the camps such as the JDC, and historians of the period, as well as children and grandchildren of survivors anxious to know more about the immediate postwar years. The focus was to be on eyewitness accounts. Specifically, we did not want to create an event where historians lectured survivors about their experiences. Far too often, scholars and academics demonstrate, in the words of novelist Thane Rosenbaum, "an open and unapologetic disdain for those who were direct witnesses to the atrocity." We were determined that at our conference, the survivors and other participants in the DP era would be the educators.

In his keynote address, Nobel Peace Prize laureate Elie Wiesel, the founding chairman of the United States Holocaust Memorial Council, placed the *Life Reborn* conference in perspective. The concept of "displaced persons," he said is "not only a geographical notion; it's also a philosophical notion. One can be displaced not only in space, but also in time, and I think your parents, young people, are displaced, not only geographically. They are displaced in time. Somehow we live in two time zones." Throughout the conference, the survivors conveyed to their children and grandchildren as well as to the other participants not just the facts but also the atmosphere of the DP camps. As Joseph Berger noted in the *New York Times* of January 17, 2000, the conference "teemed with tales, sometimes zany ones, about the resourcefulness of people who were left with nothing and, often, no one."

In addition to the main plenary addresses, the conference featured study sessions and forums on subjects ranging from newspapers, religious observance, education, and artistic creativity in the DP camps to self-government, the relationship between the survivors and American GIs, the respective experiences of child survivors and non-Jewish DPs, the multiple roles of women, and coping with the psychological aftermath of survival. Those smaller, more intimate sessions gave the participants the opportunity to interact with the speakers and each other.

A fusion of music and memory electrified both Friday and Sunday nights of the conference. At the *Oneg Shabbat* on Friday evening, Cantors Moshe Kraus and Isaac Goodfriend shared recollections of the Belsen and Feldafing DP camps. Listening to them, children and grandchildren of survivors learned, some for the first time, of the painful struggle to reconcile faith and tragedy in the immediate aftermath of the Holocaust.

During the DP years, many young Jewish survivors expressed both agony and rediscovered joy through music. On Sunday, May 27, 1945, less than three weeks after V-E Day, Henia Durmashkin, who had been liberated on a death march from Dachau, sang at a concert for the newly free Jewish survivors at the St. Ottilien DP camp. She would later perform ghetto songs at the Nuremberg Opera House before members of the International War Crimes Tribunal, and sing Hebrew songs in Munich to the piano accompaniment of Leonard Bernstein. Leo Spellman composed his *Rhapsody 1939–1945*, which premiered at the Fuerstenfeldbruck DP camp. Henry Baigelman formed a jazz band, The Happy Boys, which toured the DP camps throughout Germany. Other Jewish DPs found refuge in the written word. After surviving the Riga ghetto and the Kaiserwald and Stutthof concentration camps, Susan Strauss Taube began writing what her husband, Herman, calls a "collection of tears." One of her poems, *DP Camp Ziegenhain*, was first published in 1946 in the Munich-area DP newspaper, *Undzer Veg*. On Sunday, January 16, 2000, in Washington, D.C., Henny Durmashkin-Gurko, Leo Spellman, and Henry Baigelman listened proudly while Adrienne Cooper, Zalmen Mlotek, Frieda Enoch, and other members of the post-Holocaust generation performed their music, including the U.S. premiere of *Rhapsody 1939–1945*; and Susan Taube was on stage as Herman Taube recited *DP Camp Ziegenhain* in Yiddish.

This cultural evening was planned by Second Generation Advisory Group Chair Rositta Ehrlich Kenigsberg, the daughter of a survivor of Auschwitz, Majdanek, Buchenwald, and Mauthausen, who was herself born in the Bindermichel DP camp in Austria, and who conducted the program in both English and Yiddish. The concert began with the Robyn Helzner

Trio's rendition of *Vu Ahin Zol Ikh Geyn?* (Where Shall I Go?), introduced by Rositta Kenigsberg as "the DP anthem." Engraved in the subconscious of those of us who began our lives as the stateless children of stateless Jews are its melancholy lyrics: "Tell me, where shall I go? Every door is closed to me." But within minutes, the evening transformed itself in keeping with the spirit of the DP experience. Spontaneously, members of the audience rose from their seats, erupting into communal dance to the upbeat melody and words of another song, *Am Yisrael Khai* (The Jewish People Lives): "The sun shines once again, joy shines through our tears; sisters, brothers, we return to life."

Unfortunately, it is logistically impossible for us to publish the conference proceedings in full. Thus, with one exception and one addition, only the plenary proceedings of the *Life Reborn* conference are included in this volume. The exception is novelist Melvin Jules Bukiet's address, "Nothing Makes You Free," which, to our profound regret, could not be published here because of copyright restrictions. The addition is the paper delivered by Dr. Eva Fogelman at the forum on "Coping with the Psychological Aftermath of Survival and Extreme Trauma." The psychological dimension, while often overstressed, is nonetheless critical to a comprehensive understanding of both the Holocaust and its aftermath. Since the topic was not addressed anywhere in the course of the plenaries, it was deemed appropriate to include Dr. Fogelman's paper.

The *Life Reborn* conference also provided the sons and daughters of survivors an opportunity to reflect on their own distinct identity. On Saturday evening and in the closing plenary on Monday morning, various members of the Second Generation discussed what they believe to be our mission and our imperatives. The diverse perspectives ranged from social and political activism to artistic and literary creativity. This focus was entirely natural and appropriate in the context of a conference on the Jewish DP camps. As Melvin Jules Bukiet pointed out in his address: "If a chasm opened in the lives of the First Generation, they could nonetheless sigh on the far side and recall the life Before, but for the Second Generation there is no Before. In the beginning was Auschwitz. On the most literal level, their fathers would not have met their mothers if not for the huge dislocations that thrust the few remnants of European Jewry into contact with spouses they would never have otherwise encountered except for DP camps or in the twentieth-century Diaspora. The Second Generation's very existence is dependent on the whirlwind their parents barely escaped."

As a group, the sons and daughters of the survivors are also unique in that while we did not experience the Holocaust, we have, thanks to our parents, a particular knowledge of and sensitivity to its significance and consequences. Elie Wiesel fully understood this when, in 1981, he established the original Second Generation Advisory Committee to the United States Holocaust Memorial Council. He wanted our voices heard and our impact felt in the creation of the United States Holocaust Memorial Museum.

To be sure, confronting our collective identity has not been without cost. Far too often, it has resulted in an artificial and counterproductive separateness. We do not share in our parents' exclusivity. They went through the Holocaust. We did not. They saw their families and friends murdered. We grew up in comfort and security. We are not survivors in any sense of the word. They and they alone, are entitled to that designation. Nor do we have any exclusive rights to the survivors' legacy or to the memory of the Holocaust. These belong to the Jewish people and to humankind.

However, while being children of survivors does not give us any privileges, it does impose a far-reaching responsibility. We were given life and placed on earth with a solemn obligation. Our parents survived to bear witness. We, in turn, must be their attestors.

To be even more specific, we are the bridge between our parents and the future. As Melvin Bukiet went on to say at the *Life Reborn* conference: "The Second Generation will never know what the First Generation does in its bones, but what the Second Generation knows better than anyone else is the First Generation. Other kids' parents didn't have numbers on their arms. Other kids' parents didn't talk about massacres as easily as baseball. Other kids' parents had parents." We, and those of our own children who have been fortunate enough to know their grandparents, have absorbed from our parents, from the survivors, an intuitive perspective on the Holocaust that is beyond the reach or grasp of most historians and other scholars. And it is that perspective, I am convinced, which is essential to a true transmission of the Holocaust experience and of the survivors' memories to our and future generations.

Moreover, for most of us our identity is far more than an abstract concept. We understand that it is not enough for us to commemorate the past. We, the sons and daughters of the survivors, have learned from our parents' tragic experiences that indifference to the suffering of others is in itself a crime. Accordingly, we do not have the right to spend our time talking to ourselves about ourselves. Our place at all times must be at the forefront of the struggle against racial, religious, and ethnic hatred of any kind. We must not forget that Jews are never the only victims of evil. The Armenian and Rwandan genocides, the mass murder of the Gypsies by the Nazis, and ethnic cleansing in the former Yugoslavia are but four examples of civilization run amok in the twentieth century alone.

Together with others of our generation and with our own children, we must speak out and act on behalf of all, Jews and non-Jews alike, who are subjected to discrimination and persecution anywhere in the world. We may never be passive, or allow others to be passive, in the face of oppression, for we know only too well that the ultimate consequence of apathy and silence was embodied forever in the flames of Auschwitz and the mass graves of Bergen-Belsen.

The *Life Reborn* conference was also unusual in that it was conceived and implemented by members of the Second Generation Advisory Group with the support of the Museum staff. The outline of the program was shaped by a program committee headed by Sam Norich, and was subsequently fine-tuned by Romana Primus and myself. Rositta Kenigsberg took charge of the Sunday evening cultural program. Felicia Figlarz Anchor, chair of the arrangements committee, coordinated the conference logistics.

Jean Bloch Rosensaft, exhibitions chair for the conference, met with members of the Museum's curatorial staff to discuss the possibility of creating an exhibition on the DP period in conjunction with the conference. A call to survivors for artifacts led to the acquisition by the Museum of thousands of invaluable objects and archives, enabling Museum curators Steven Luckert and Susan Snyder to mount the highly acclaimed *Life Reborn* special exhibition at the Museum. "When we embarked on the *Life Reborn* project," Jean Bloch Rosensaft explains, "the Museum's collections contained minimal holdings of DP materials. Thanks to these thousands of donations from all over the United States and overseas, the Museum now has one of the largest DP collections in the world." She also met with officials of other Washington-area museums and cultural institutions to see if they would join the United States Holocaust Memorial Museum in highlighting the DP era, thereby giving the topic far broader public visibility. As a result, the B'nai B'rith Klutznick National Jewish Museum featured a photo-documentary exhibition, entitled *Rebirth after the Holocaust: The Bergen-Belsen Displaced Persons Camp, 1945–1950,* which was curated by Sam E. Bloch and Jean Bloch Rosensaft. Another exhibition, *Rescue and Renewal: GIs and Displaced Persons,* was on view at the National Museum of American Jewish History. In addition, the National Archives placed selected pages of the 1945 Harrison Report on view in its rotunda as "treasured documents," alongside the Declaration of Independence, and a selection of books on the DP era was prominently displayed in the Library of Congress.

Fund-raising was a highly successful group effort. From the outset, Rositta Kenigsberg and I gave the United States Holocaust Memorial Council's Executive Committee firm assurances that the members of the Second Generation Advisory Group would raise the entire budget required for the *Life Reborn* conference. We were true to our word. Many of the contributions we received came from new donors who had not previously had any involvement with the Museum. Thanks to the interest of Geoffrey J. Colvin, a member of the Executive Committee of the JDC, that relief organization, which had played so critical a role in the DP camps, became an active sponsor of and participant in the conference. Richard Kandel and the Theodore and Renee Weiler Foundation, Inc., generously provided major support for the *Life Reborn* conference early on, and helped make the publication of this volume a reality.

The *Life Reborn* conference would not have been possible without the hard work and commitment of the Museum's staff. Museum Director Sara J. Bloomfield gave the Second Generation Advisory Group every possible support and encouragement. In particular, Director of Communications Mary Morrison, Martin Goldman and Elizabeth Anthony of the Office of Survivors Affairs, Mel Hecker and Mariah R. Keller of the Publishing Division, Dr. Michael Neiditch and Susan Grant of the Development Office, and Conference Coordinator Sylvia Kaye, together with their respective staffs, earned our heartfelt gratitude.

In addition, special thanks and sincere appreciation are due to Mariah Keller and Elizabeth Anthony for their enthusiastic assistance in the preparation of this volume. The *Life Reborn* conference was a prime example of what an institution can achieve when its lay leadership and staff work together as partners.

A final, personal note. My father died more than 25 years ago, on September 10, 1975. At his funeral, Elie Wiesel's eulogy captured the essence of his personality: "I remember our pilgrimage to Belsen—and Kaddish at the graves. I remember evening walks in Jerusalem at the Western Wall. I remember feverish, endless conversations: how to help the survivors and how to defend the honor of the victims. . . . Few sanctified the Holocaust as he did. Few suffered it as he did. Few loved its holy martyrs as he did." During the *Life Reborn* conference, I had the opportunity to pay tribute to my father's historical role and achievements during the DP era. He was born on January 15, 1911. The publication of the Conference Proceedings coincides with what would have been his 90th birthday. As I conclude this introduction, I am reminded yet again how profoundly his spirit, his example, and his memory continue to guide me in everything I do.

FOREWORD

Sara J. Bloomfield

Director, United States Holocaust Memorial Museum

In 1993, the year the United States Holocaust Memorial Museum opened—as over 2 million visitors poured through its doors—we could think of little else than how to ensure that the enormous crowds would have an experience that was intellectually compelling and emotionally unforgettable. Then in 1994, still overwhelmed by the Museum's popularity, we nevertheless thought it important to divert some of our attention from the crowds in order to mount a major exhibition in conjunction with the May 1995 worldwide events that would commemorate the end of World War II.

We knew that especially in light of the end of the Cold War, the world would want to see this as a glorious celebration. We felt it was our obligation to place the meaning of that celebration in perspective. Surely, most of the public would see V-E Day as the end of the fighting against the Germans; some might even think of the liberation of the Nazi death and concentration camps; but who would be thinking of what that day 50 years ago meant for the remnant of European Jewry who had survived the attempt to annihilate them?

The Museum wanted to ensure that as our nation recalled the war's end, both the military war and the war against the Jews would be remembered. Further, it was important to dispel the myth that the end of the military war marked the end of the Holocaust. Certainly in terms of the impact of the lives lost, families destroyed, cultures eliminated, dislocations created, the Holocaust has no ending. But more concretely, the end of the war did not bring an end to the physical and emotional suffering of the Jews. Hadassah Rosensaft, liberated from Bergen-Belsen, said it best: "For the greatest part of the liberated Jews of Bergen-Belsen, there was no ecstasy, no joy at our liberation. We had lost our families, our homes. We had no place to go to, nobody to hug. Nobody was waiting for us anywhere. We had been liberated from death and the fear of death, but not from the fear of life." That poignant quote ended *Liberation 1945*, the somewhat ironically titled exhibition, which the Museum opened on May 8, 1995. The focus of the exhibition was not on the liberation itself, but on that painful first year of "freedom."

Thus began the Museum's ongoing commitment to a careful examination of that critically important immediate postwar period so often ignored in Holocaust courses, books, or films. And one of the most heartrending objects on display in the *Liberation 1945* exhibition represented another significant dimension of the war's aftermath that ultimately became the focus of the institution's next major undertaking on this period. A menorah, handcrafted from scraps of materials with spent cartridges as candle holders, and made for that first Hanukkah in Bergen-Belsen, was a symbol of the survivors' irrepressible yearning to live, to rebuild their sense of community and spirituality. The menorah is a symbol of an outpouring of creativity that marked every aspect of life in the DP camps, from politics to religion, from work to education, from culture to entertainment. But who knew this remarkable story of renewal in the wake of such unimaginable suffering and loss?

And so the *Life Reborn* conference was fittingly conceived and sponsored by the Museum's Second Generation Advisory Group. Created by the Museum's founding chairman, Elie Wiesel, and later reestablished by Chairman Miles Lerman, this advisory group's purpose is to sustain and nurture the legacy of their parents, the survivors. No topic could have been more appropriate for them than the rebirth of Jewish life in the DP camps, the rebirth into which they were born and which defines their sense of this very special legacy. The Museum is deeply grateful for their leadership and their commitment to remember both the destruction and the renewal.

OPENING SESSION

WELCOME

Rositta Ehrlich Kenigsberg

Executive Vice President, Holocaust Documentation and Education Center, Florida International University; Chairperson, Second Generation Advisory Group; member, United States Holocaust Memorial Council

Mr. Chairman, beloved survivors, members of the Second Generation, members of the United States Holocaust Memorial Council, distinguished guests, family, and friends.

As chair of the Second Generation Advisory Group of the United States Holocaust Memorial Council, it is a distinct honor and privilege to welcome you this evening as we officially open this unprecedented international conference, *Life Reborn, Jewish Displaced Persons, 1945–1951.*

It was Elie Wiesel who said, "For a Jew who went through the war to bring a child into this world was a very great act of faith, for we had all the reason in the world to give up on man, on humankind, to give up on civilization, to give up on everything." But our parents, the survivors, did not give up. Instead, in the immediate aftermath of liberation, despite a shattered past and virtually unknown future, and despite being displaced and dispossessed, the survivors took charge of their own lives and their own destinies with tremendous courage and conviction. Once again, they dared to sing, they dared to dance, they dared to laugh, they dared to dream. They even dared to shed tears of joy and happiness. This, the remarkable resurgence and resilience of their human spirit, and their yearning to create a new life and a new beginning is a tribute to their inner strength, perseverance, and determination and most importantly to Jewish continuity and Jewish existence.

As the daughter of a Holocaust survivor, and one who was born in a DP camp in Austria, I am awed and inspired that we have all come together—the survivors, the Second Generation, members of relief organizations, army personnel, chaplains, historians, and scholars—in a unique setting to illuminate, document, and celebrate this wondrous era of rebirth and renewal. We have come together to ensure that this story will be part of our parents' legacy, which is not only about death, but also about life and life reborn.

At this time, I wish to personally thank each and every member of the Second Generation Advisory Group for their efforts and commitment on behalf of this monumental endeavor. In particular, a very, very special thank you to my colleagues and co-principal organizers, Romana Primus and Menachem Rosensaft; to Sara Bloomfield and your wonderful and devoted staff; and to the incredible group of volunteers at the Museum. On behalf of all of us, I wish to extend our sincere gratitude and heartfelt appreciation to all of the donors who have so graciously and generously contributed to this unique and multifaceted project.

On May 5, 1945, when my father was liberated, tragically, everyone and everything he loved and had known were gone forever. Not a mother, father, brother, grandparent, aunt, or uncle had survived. Not even a grave to mark their lives or their deaths. All that is left is my father and his story. And as my father emerged from the Holocaust, he could never have imagined then that the United States of America would one day build a major national museum in the nation's capital, alongside its own monuments to democracy and museums to human achievement, and that it would be the survivors' heart and soul, the survivors' *neshume,* that would be embodied forever within the walls of this museum as a testament to their life, and as a legacy of remembrance for generations to come.

The accomplished and outstanding leader of this compelling institution of conscience, Miles Lerman, whom many of you know as a partisan, spent eight months in the Schlachtensee DP camp with his loving wife, Chris. Mr. Chairman, as you recall, it was your insight and foresight that led to the reestablishment of the Second Generation Advisory Group, a body that you envisioned would one day embrace and enhance the mission of the Museum into the twenty-first century.

Well, Mr. Chairman, it is the beginning of the new millennium, and it is my privilege as the chair of the Second Generation Advisory Group to welcome you this evening.

OPENING ADDRESS

Miles Lerman

Chair Emeritus, United States Holocaust Memorial Council

This is a very special evening for the Museum. This is a special event for you, the descendants of the survivors. It is also an evening of great significance for me personally as chairman of the Council, as a survivor, a father, and a grandfather.

How should I address you?

I feel like addressing you in two ways—as colleagues, and as *meine tayere kinder*. Thank you for inviting me to be with you.

In the days when the Nazi inferno was devouring the Jewish communities of Europe, we stood all alone, isolated and abandoned, and the whole world remained indifferent to our suffering. In the moments of our deepest despair, we clung to hope in spite of hopelessness. We dared to dream without really believing that our dreams could come true.

Who of us would have dared to think in those days that we would survive, let alone prevail, and that one day a Holocaust museum would arise in the heart of our adopted nation's capital—where millions of visitors would come to see and learn what could happen when hatred runs amok? Who would have believed that the remnants of a world so brutally destroyed would have the inner strength to rise from the ashes and rekindle the flame of Jewish life and creativity?

So, perhaps it would be fitting to use this auspicious moment to take stock of our accomplishments of the last 50 years. We came out of the smoldering ruins of Europe—our families murdered, our homes occupied by strangers, and our dreams completely shattered.

We had every reason to feel bitter and distrustful. There were even those who believed the survivors would never be able to readjust to a normal society. We proved them wrong. We mustered the strength to rebuild our lives and raise our children in an environment of love, learning, and *menshlichkeit*. We instilled in them all of the positive characteristics mankind has to offer.

In spite of the fact that many of us missed out on our own education, we understood the need to give our children a love for learning and a desire for excellence that enabled many of them to make impressive contributions to our society today.

Fifty years ago, Ben Meed and Sam Bloch, with a handful of survivors, were hardly able to bring 200 people together for a *yizkor* service in memory of our loved ones. Today there is not a state of the Union that does not have a day of remembrance for the victims of the Holocaust.

I would like to inform you that at the end of this month, leaders of 43 nations will gather in Stockholm to discuss the most effective methods of how to implement a global network of Holocaust education. I am pleased to inform you that the United States Holocaust Memorial Museum is playing a major part in this endeavor, in the same manner as we did in the international conference in Washington on Holocaust-era assets last December.

Five years ago, at a conference of survivors in Miami, I announced my plans to appoint 15 children of survivors to a special advisory committee of the United States Holocaust Memorial Council. Tonight I have the honor of opening a conference which will celebrate the miracle of life reborn in the displaced persons camps.

Although this conference is under the auspices of the United States Holocaust Memorial Museum, I am proud to tell you that this conference has been planned and organized by children of survivors who serve on either the Council or its Second Generation Advisory Group. I must take a moment to salute the organizers of this historic conference for a job extremely well done.

Although we refer to you as children, you are mothers and fathers of your own children. In actuality you are mature adults and accomplished professionals. Many of you are leaders in your communities as well as your respective fields on a national or international level.

As I look around and see the success of your efforts, I am more than ever convinced that the time has come for those of us who have guarded the sacred flame of remembrance for the last 50 years to begin the process of passing the torch to a new generation of leadership, including children and grandchildren of survivors as well as other young people who, although not connected to this cataclysmic event by family tragedy, are deeply committed to the cause of remembrance.

Without the active engagement of you—the sons and daughters of survivors—our task of ensuring Holocaust remembrance in perpetuity cannot be assured.

But you cannot and should not do it alone. The task of teaching the lessons of the Holocaust must be assumed by a broad spectrum of our society—the Jewish community, the spiritual leaders of America, the theologians who are laboring in the vineyard of Jewish and Christian relations, the educators of young America, and above all, those who are on the fore-front of human rights. Indeed, all of you understand that humanity cannot allow the Holocaust to happen again.

But in this partnership of committed individuals, you, the children and grandchildren of survivors, must be the special guardians of the painful, yet sacred, memories of your parents.

Your job will be different from ours. We, your parents, lived the horror and carried with us the trauma of those bitter days. Your parents, many of them active supporters of the United States Holocaust Memorial Museum, have used their pain and suffering to convince the world that it cannot look the other way when murderous crimes against innocent people are being perpetrated.

Your task will be more difficult than ours, but also more important. You will have to ensure Holocaust remembrance when the living witnesses will be gone. Holocaust deniers will challenge you in ways that they cannot challenge us. As the facts and images of the Holocaust become familiar and lose their initial shock value, you will have to battle the fatigue and indifference that may set in. You will have to find appropriate and meaningful ways to talk to your children so that they can speak to their Jewish and non-Jewish friends.

You will not always have us, but you will have history and memory as your allies.

That is why I believe it is time to start the process of turning the reins over to younger generations who share a profound dedication to our noble cause. Because of what the founders of the United States Holocaust Memorial Museum have accomplished, the coalition of new leadership is broader than it has ever been and reaches further than it ever has.

Those of you who are familiar with the Museum know of our extraordinary success—the millions we reach every year not only in Washington, but in cities around the nation and the world. The history and lessons of the Holocaust are becoming embedded in American life.

The Museum is now poised to build on its extraordinary success of expanding its collections and research programs and implementing new technology to make this education accessible by people everywhere.

We are fortunate to have Sara Bloomfield, a deeply committed person, and your contemporary in age, to lead the institution. She knows that as we envision an even more exciting future, we must always be mindful of the sacred task to which the Museum is dedicated.

The future is in your hands. Guard it with care and devotion.

I know you will.

On a personal note . . . I have always believed that a leader who preaches to others and then excuses himself from the obligations of what he preaches is not a very responsible leader.

I want to use this very special event to announce that I have met with President Clinton and informed him of my intention to step down as chairman of the United States Holocaust Memorial Council as soon as he appoints my successor.

This step reflects everything I have said tonight, that if we are serious about our commitment to remembrance in the new century, we must ensure a strong cadre of young leadership who will be prepared to assume the obligation of that commitment.

Therefore, although I am giving up my position as chairman, I fully intend to remain active with the Museum. I am prepared to serve in any capacity that my successor will ask of me. Let me conclude by telling you that I am very proud and pleased that this conference is taking place. I want to assure you that you can always count on my enthusiastic support of all your future endeavors.

Tonight, as we commemorate the fiftieth anniversary of our life reborn, we must bear in mind that this milestone marks a starting point. This is an occasion for new beginnings. We are at a major point of gradual transition.

The torch must begin to be passed, not just from survivors to their children; not just from the old to the young; but from all of us to all of humanity.

Thank you.

RESPONSE

Romana Strochlitz Primus

Clinical immunologist; Chairperson, Life Reborn *Project, Second Generation Advisory Group; member, United States Holocaust Memorial Council*

A gutten Shabbes.

My father is fond of saying, "In life, you never know."

When I first discussed a DP camp project with Miles in September 1997, we certainly did not know that Miles would announce at this conference his plan to relinquish the Council chairmanship. We did not even know that there would be such a conference. And yet, this is a particularly fitting venue.

Miles is a staunch advocate of the recruitment of children of survivors to help ensure the future of Holocaust remembrance and education. Following the pioneering example of Elie Wiesel, who appointed the original Second Generation Advisory Committee to the United States Holocaust Memorial Council, Miles created the Second Generation Advisory Group. He wanted to institutionalize the active participation of children of survivors in Museum affairs. He also hoped that members of the advisory group would become attractive candidates for presidential appointment to the Council itself. And he succeeded. When Miles established the advisory group, only one child of survivors was a Council member: Menachem Rosensaft, the first chair of the Advisory Group. Now six of us sit on the Council.

Miles supported the idea of a DP camp project largely because he thought it would appeal to children of survivors, particularly those born in a DP camp. When I suggested to him that it could become a project for the Second Generation Advisory Group, he enthusiastically agreed. At its next meeting in December 1997, with Rositta Kenigsberg as its new chair, the Advisory Group embraced the project.

Miles' vision in creating the Second Generation Advisory Group and his strong support of the children of survivors in general add a special poignancy to his announcement this evening.

Miles, as you know, we fervently wish you had not made the decision to resign. Under your tenure, the Museum has become a national treasure. *Life Reborn* is only one of many Museum endeavors that would not have been possible without your remarkable leadership. We are somewhat consoled by the fact that you will remain on the Council, where we will all continue to benefit from your vision, your passion, your dedication.

Thank you for your example and for your faith in the Second Generation. We will not let you down.

FRAMING THE CONFERENCE

OVERVIEW

Romana Strochlitz Primus

Our mental libraries are full of facts and images of the Shoah, often ending with Edward R. Murrow's broadcast from Buchenwald or Allied footage of the liberation of various camps. Liberation is usually seen as the end of the Shoah, but it can also be seen as the gateway to the displaced persons (DP) era, an era which forms a critical chapter of Holocaust history.

What happened to those skeletons the Allies liberated? What happened to Jews who survived in hiding, or with the partisans, or in the Soviet Union?

I hope that we will leave this conference with a clearer picture of what lay beyond liberation. I believe that we have a story to tell. It is worth telling for its own sake. It is worth telling for our sake. And it is worth telling for the sake of the lesson that may be taught to the world.

My parents, who had met briefly in Birkenau, were both liberated in Bergen-Belsen. My mother weighed 78 pounds and was delirious with typhus; she barely understood that she was liberated. My father weighed 88 pounds. They had lost their families, their communities, their entire way of life. And yet, I was born in the Bergen-Belsen DP camp less than 15 months after the liberation. I was born into a vibrant, politically active Jewish community with a newspaper, schools, a theater group, concerts, youth groups, and an explosive birthrate.

How did that community arise? Where did the survivors find the strength, the courage to forge new lives?

The Sh'erit ha-Pletah, the Surviving Remnant, our parents, did not succumb to despair. While mourning the murdered and searching desperately for possible living relatives, while living in deplorable housing on inadequate rations, they nevertheless understood the need to build new lives and regenerate the Jewish people. And so they did just that.

The DP camps became centers of Jewish cultural and political life. Their populations swelled as Jews who had returned to Eastern Europe, mostly those who had survived the war in the Soviet Union, fled both antisemitism and Communism—fled to safety, ironically, in Germany. Ultimately, an estimated 300,000 Jewish DPs lived or sojourned in Germany, Italy, and Austria. Of these, as many as 250,000 Jews passed through the DP camps before the last one was closed in 1957—12 years after liberation.

Our parents had help: the Allied armed forces; UNRRA, the United Nations Relief and Rehabilitation Administration; the Jewish Agency for Palestine; the Jewish Brigade; ORT, the Organization for Rehabilitation through Training; HIAS, the Hebrew Immigrant Aid Society;

and most prominently, the Joint, The American Jewish Joint Distribution Committee and its British counterpart. The aid from these agencies was critical, but it could not have succeeded without the indomitable spirit of the Sh'erit ha-Pletah.

Fortunately, there have always been a few distinguished historians who have called attention to the remarkable activities of Jews in the DP camps. We shall hear from them, beginning this evening.

We shall also hear from those who were there.

The survivors will tell us about their theaters and their newspapers, their makeshift sports programs and improvised travel arrangements, their Zionist youth groups and their struggles to get paper and books for their schools. They will tell us about the first emotional Yom Kippur and about Ben Gurion's visit. They will tell us about the military bureaucracy that alternately nourished them and failed them; about boredom, petty indignities, and triumphs in everyday life in Kafkaesque circumstances. They will tell us about living side by side with their former oppressors. And they will tell us about finding mates and starting families.

Former soldiers and welfare workers will tell us about their own roles, their frustrations, and their achievements.

In addition to the scholars who study the era and the people who lived it, a third group of voices will permeate the conference: the voice of the Second Generation, the children of survivors.

I hope that this weekend will bring all of us closer as we explore and document a remarkable period in Jewish history. May we take with us when we return to our homes on Monday a large collection of stories and images, some gray, but most brightly colored, and a solid historical framework on which to pin them.

In the beginning, of course, we start with the word, and tonight the word shall come from one of our most distinguished historians, a man who has devoted his career to the careful, truthful telling of the history of the Shoah.

Professor Yehuda Bauer is well known to all of us here tonight. He is the director of the International Institute for Holocaust Research at Yad Vashem. He has written numerous books about the Holocaust including, *Out of Ashes,* about the DP period.

THE DP LEGACY

Yehuda Bauer

Director, International Institute for Holocaust Research, Yad Vashem

As with all historical problems, the topic of the Holocaust survivors in the immediate postwar period, of the Jewish displaced persons, of the Sh'erit ha-Pletah, is much more complicated than it first appears. Let me therefore survey first of all the situation of the survivors when the war in Europe ended. I estimate that about 200,000 Jews emerged alive from the Nazi concentration and labor camp system. This was a remnant of possibly up to 500,000 Jews who were still alive in these camps towards the end of 1944. The Nazis themselves reported, in January of 1945, that there were 714,000 internees, Jews and non-Jews, in the concentration camp network, but I do not trust these figures, because quite apart from the disorder already reigning in the Nazi empire at that stage, these numbers do not apparently include many labor camps and *Aussenkommandos* exploited by private German firms. The death marches after January 1945 included the vast majority of prisoners, Jewish and non-Jewish, and the Jewish death rate cannot have been much less than 60 percent, and perhaps it was even higher. A first attempt at investigating this is now being made by Daniel Blatman of the Hebrew University and Yad Vashem, and he is still at it, so that I cannot present you with solid results.

Of those 200,000, well over 70,000 returned more or less immediately to Hungary and Romania, and tens of thousands of others returned to Czechoslovakia and Western Europe, or went to their former homes in Poland and the Baltic States to search for relatives. Also, between May and August 1945, 15,000 Jews were smuggled into Italy from Austria and southern Germany by the Jewish Brigade from Palestine. By August 1945, 55,000 Jewish survivors remained in the western zones of Germany and Austria. At that time, there were about 80,000 Jews in Poland, of whom some 13,000 had been in the Polish pro-Soviet armed forces that had participated in the liberation of Poland. Others had come from liberated camps in Germany and Poland itself, or had emerged from hiding or from partisan detachments. If all this is roughly correct, there would have been approximately 120,000 survivors in Germany, Austria, Poland, and Lithuania. In Hungary we are talking of some 180,000 survivors, including the returnees from the camps and the Jewish labor battalions in the Hungarian army, and the survivors from the Budapest ghetto. In Germany and Austria the number of Jewish DPs increased from 55,000 in August 1945, to some 175,000 at the end of 1946. The reason is that in the meantime, there had been a tremendous move of Polish and Baltic Jews—who had fled into the Soviet Union when the Nazis attacked the USSR, and had survived there—back to Poland. About 175,000 had arrived by the late autumn of 1946, and many of them—and of the original number that had been in Poland before that—fled the rising Polish antisemitism and, via the Bricha network, reached the DP camps, especially in the American zones in Germany and Austria. Others joined in 1947. On the other hand, thousands left the so-called DP countries, which included Italy, and immigrated, mostly illegally, to Palestine, or legally to the U.S. and elsewhere. The total number of Jews who passed through the DP countries—not all of them through DP camps—is probably around the 300,000 mark, and that includes survivors from Czechoslovakia, Hungary, and Romania who entered the DP countries in 1947 and 1948.

The conclusion from this first point must surely be that most of the Jewish DPs were not Holocaust survivors, but wartime refugees in the Soviet Union. They arrived from central Asia after years of starvation, typhoid epidemics, and, many of them, from Soviet gulags, but they had not been under the Nazis and most of them came from the USSR in family groups. The survivors of Nazi camps, on the other hand, were traumatized individuals, remnants of murdered families and communities—but they were often the first to leave, whether for Palestine or overseas, so that the makeup of the first waves of immigrants to these countries was largely of actual survivors of the Nazi regime. On the other hand, the communities in most European countries had smaller or larger, or very large components of Holocaust survivors who were not DPs. This is true of Hungary, Czechoslovakia, Italy, and Western Europe, where all Jews had been under direct Nazi rule. Romania is a special case, because remnants of the deportees to Transnistria, the area between the Dniester and the Bug, who had suffered some of the worst vicissitudes of any Jews in Europe at the hands of the Romanian fascists, came back to Romania, only to meet with antisemitism on the one hand, and a speedy takeover by the Communists on the other hand. Jews who had survived the war in Romania itself, in the so-called Regat, had been maltreated, dispossessed, sent to slave labor camps, and were in a sorry state. Most of these later immigrated to Palestine and Israel. Many DPs then, I repeat, were not, strictly speaking, Holocaust survivors, if by that we mean people who had been for an extended period under Nazi rule; many Holocaust survivors were never DPs. And many people who had not been under direct German rule, such as the Jewish refugees in the Soviet Union, suffered terribly because of the Nazis, and it is an open question whether they should not be included in the definition of survivors as well; yet their fate was obviously different from that of their sisters and brothers under Nazi rule.

Let me then define: by DPs I mean the Jewish inmates of postwar camps in Germany, Austria, and Italy, and others who lived outside the camps in these countries but were treated as DPs by the authorities. In this context, several questions need to be discussed: one, the development among the DPs of self-determination, of taking over responsibility over their present and future in impossible circumstances; two, the tremendous impact of the Bricha; three, the impact of Jewish Palestine and of illegal immigration there; four, the impact of the DPs on the major powers, both regarding Palestine, and regarding their own future; five, their postwar story and their impact on Jewish life in Israel and in the Diaspora, especially in the United States.

The first point is perhaps the most important one: The camp survivors organized immediately as groups, despite the tremendous traumatization they had experienced. From the very first, communal life of the survivors in Germany and Austria was established on the basis of a Zionist ideology. In fact, the first Zionist "publication," if that is the right word for a hand-written sheet, was distributed in the subcamps of Dachau *before* liberation. It was called *Nitzotz* (The Spark), and was edited by Shlomo Shafir, now Dr. Shlomo Shafir, a Kovno ghetto survivor, who now edits a magazine called *Gesher* in Israel. Two points require explanation: One is, where did these people get the strength to return to life at such speed, from the realm of death? And the second, why did they choose Zionism as their ideology? I do not know the answer to the first question. I am not a psychologist, and I don't know whether psychologists have the answer. But the fact is that by the early summer of 1945, Jewish committees were organized in almost all liberated camps at the initiative of the survivors, demanding that separate Jewish DP camps be set up, and that the Jews be allowed to immigrate to Palestine. The essential help without which they could not have done what they did was received from three sources. Perhaps the most important one was the Jewish chaplains in the U.S. Army, first and foremost of whom was a young Reform rabbi, Abraham J. Klausner, whose help was decisive in the organization of the first meetings of representatives of survivors in Bavaria, but there were others, some of whom are here tonight. The second were the soldiers of the Jewish Brigade, who in June 1945, came via Austria to Munich and by their insignia and their very presence inspired the survivors, and especially the first elected leaders there; and then, there were sympathetic American officers and soldiers who, despite the hostile attitude of General

Patton, helped the Jews. It has to be said that the American High Command, and especially Generals Eisenhower and Beddell-Smith, his chief of staff (who had Jewish family connections, but these were unknown at the time), was shaken by what they found in the first Nazi camps they uncovered. The support of the higher ranks of the U.S. Army was indispensable, and without it there is hardly any doubt that the survivors could not have succeeded the way they did.

I don't think I have to explain, to this audience, the importance of the Harrison Report. Earl G. Harrison, the University of Pennsylvania law professor, who was sent to the U.S. zone in Germany by President Truman in July 1945, was to investigate the condition of the DPs there, especially the Jewish ones.[1] But what we still do not sufficiently know is the background to that mission—it appears that the White House received many complaints from Jewish officers, chaplains, and soldiers, transmitted via Jewish communities throughout the United States, regarding the pitiable conditions prevailing in the camps where Jews were held, many of them together with antisemitic Poles and Baltics, in preparation for so-called "repatriation" to their homelands. The army was, after all, interested mainly in getting rid of these vast masses of humanity as quickly as possible. The Jews were but a tiny part of the more than 11 million strangers on German soil at liberation, or of the 825,000 or so who had remained there by the summer of 1945. What appears clear is the fact that Truman reacted to a form of Jewish popular protest. We have no documentation that I am aware of that could reliably explain his behavior, but from what followed I think one can conclude that he was motivated by two main considerations—one, a political one, namely that as someone who had to fill the big shoes of Roosevelt, he needed Jewish electoral support in the crucial states of New York, Illinois, Pennsylvania, and California (this consideration will return again and again as the most decisive one in the following three years); and the second, his humanitarian urges, which have neither to be ignored, nor overstated.

Harrison's mission could easily have failed, from a Jewish point of view, because the mid-level army officers who planned his trip wanted to show him things that would make happy reading back in Washington. It is here that Joseph Schwartz of the Joint intervened and made it possible for Klausner to meet with Harrison and decisively influence him. The Harrison Report bears all the markings of Klausner's impact, down to the actual language of the document. The results are well known: Harrison complained bitterly and, one must say, in a vastly exaggerated way, about the treatment of the Jews by the army, and strongly recommended both the establishment of special Jewish camps, and a speedy immigration of 100,000 Jews to Palestine—which had been the demand of the Jewish Agency since late 1944. By the end of August, Eisenhower had been instructed by Truman to implement those parts of the Harrison Report that dealt with the establishment of special Jewish camps and the improvement of living conditions in them, largely at the expense of the German population. On his part, Truman proposed to the British that they accept 100,000 Jews into Palestine.

However, neither the Jews nor the army waited for these instructions: Jewish camps sprang up as a result of Jewish initiative, or in line with orders of certain army officers. A central committee of survivors, first of the Bavarian area, and then of the U.S. zone at large, became active

[1] *Earl Harrison also visited the DP camp of Bergen-Belsen in the British zone of Germany, where he met with Josef Rosensaft and other leaders of the Jewish survivors. Paul Trepman, one of the editors of the Belsen newspaper,* Undzer Shtimme, *later recalled that at this meeting, Harrison "looked at us and chain-smoked as the tears streamed down his face. . . . Finally, he whispered weakly: 'But how did you survive, and where do you take your strength from now?'" From "On Being Reborn," in* Belsen *(Tel Aviv, 1957), 134.*

in Munich. In the autumn, the Joint was at long last permitted to send crews and supplies to the American zone. Food was supplied by the army, which took it from the Germans, and the Joint supplemented this with special needs in food, clothing, education, and religious life.

But the really decisive moment came as a result of the initiative of Ben Gurion in October 1945, when he visited the U.S. command in Frankfurt: He managed to convince Eisenhower and Beddell-Smith to permit the more or less free entry of Jews from Poland into the U.S. zones. Again, we have no documentation to tell us what motivated the Americans to agree, but it is probable, I think, that they feared another Harrison Report if they used force to prevent the Jews from entering—they tried it once, by the way, and it failed. Also, and this is parallel to what I think happened with Truman, they were deeply affected by what they saw in the liberated camps, and genuinely wanted to help if they could. The result was the growth of the Jewish DP population in the American zone into a critical mass. The success of Ben Gurion in concentrating the survivors from Eastern Europe in the U.S. zones with American army acquiescence was probably the most decisive element in enabling the Jewish Agency to press for the establishment of a Jewish state in Palestine. It was the pressure of these DPs on the army, and of the army on the administration, that combined with the impact of American Jewry in pressuring the British. It was this pressure, I think, that was probably the most decisive factor in persuading the British to hand over the combined Palestine and DP problem to the United Nations in January–February 1947.

The situation in the British zone developed differently, and the establishment of a Jewish DP presence there that had to be taken into account was the work, to a large degree, of one man—Yossel Rosensaft. In a sense, this lecture is a homage to him, because he can be seen as the quintessential DP survivor. He became the head of a camp committee immediately upon liberation of Bergen-Belsen, while thousands of Jews were still dying of the effects of hunger and disease following the last tragic weeks of German rule. Yossel demanded recognition by the British of a Jewish camp of survivors in the place. He received some, but very little, help from Jewish bodies in Palestine, the U.S., and Britain, and had to face an overbearing British military more or less by himself, with his colleagues. The British refused, for quite some time, to recognize the existence of a Jewish camp, because they feared that the survivors, who in their majority declared they wanted to immigrate to Palestine, would be a rallying point of opposition to their Middle East policy. They were right. But they failed to appreciate the stamina of the survivors, and in the end had to yield. Yossel Rosensaft, a very ordinary and a very extraordinary Polish Jew, by no means an angel, but a determined defender of his people and their interests, with his Shakespearean Bedzin English, as he used sarcastically to say, gained, single-handedly, the upper hand. In the teeth of British opposition, not at all as in the U.S. zone, education, religious observance, social, economic, and political activity were developed by the survivors themselves. The pressure of the DPs at Bergen-Belsen on Britain was no less effective than that of the much larger DP population in the U.S. zone in Germany.

Parallel policies were pursued by the Americans and the British in Austria, though the Jewish organizations and committees there became less well known.

The reason why the survivors turned, overwhelmingly, to Zionism is not hard to understand. The murder of the European Jews seemed to vindicate the Zionist argument that there was no future for Jews in Europe. America was closed. It was only in 1948, and again in 1950, that the practical possibility emerged to immigrate there in larger numbers. Had such a possibility existed in 1945–47, I would guess that a much larger number, maybe up to two-thirds of the Jewish DPs, would have left the idleness and hopelessness of the DP camps to go to the New World. As it is, roughly two-thirds immigrated to Palestine/Israel.

Our second main theme is the tremendous impact of the Bricha, probably the largest organized, illegal mass movement in Europe in this century, which brought, roughly, some 300,000 Jews from Eastern to Central, southern, and Western Europe, in the space of less than four years. The most important thing to remember about the Bricha is, I think, that even more than the survivors' organizations in the DP countries, it was founded and organized by survivors, and not by outside helpers. In this case it was a small group of partisans and fighters who in the summer of 1944, while the war was still raging, together with the first returnees from Soviet central Asia, organized groups, first in Vilna and Rowno, who tried to reach Romania, from where they hoped to reach Palestine. All of them had been members of Zionist youth movements, or were ex-Communists who had seen what Soviet Russia was like and had become Zionists. In February 1945, they met in Lublin with the survivors of the ghetto rebellions, and founded Bricha, which means "flight," to smuggle their followers into Romania on their way to Palestine. The inspiration, and the initial organization, came from the poet Abba Kovner of Vilna, who had commanded Jewish partisans in the Rudniki forests on the Lithuanian-Belorussian border. Others took over, as the initial group of a few thousand reached Romania. But it soon became clear that the way to Palestine from there was blocked, so they made their way to the Palestinian Jewish soldiers in the British army in Italy.

At a memorable meeting in July 1945, at Tarvisio in northern Italy, the fighters and partisans and the soldiers were combined. But the command of the Bricha remained in Poland, as more and more Jews, at first survivors and then returnees from the USSR, became part of the movement. As Kovner said, "We removed a grain of sand, and we didn't know that the whole mountain would follow." Bricha became a well-organized, though decentralized, mass movement smuggling multitudes of Jews through so-called green borders, or by arrangement with border guards, from Poland into Czechoslovakia. At first the route went via Hungary to Austria, and from there to Italy, to the Mediterranean shores on the way, hopefully, to Palestine. But Italy was soon closed as well, as the British prevented the border crossings. The decision was therefore taken, even before Ben Gurion's visit to Frankfurt, and completely independent of it, to direct the flow of the refugees to the U.S. zones. Now the routes went either via Bratislava in Slovakia to Vienna, and from there to Salzburg in the American zone in Austria, and from there to Bavaria and beyond, or via Sczeczin, then Stettin, to Berlin and the West. Side streams went to the French and even British zones in Austria, or directly from Prague to Bavaria, or in the north into the overfilled Bergen-Belsen camp. Local commands sprang up en route, and were in communication with the Polish center. Soon a coordination group in Bratislava took over to regulate the flow. It was commanded by Levi Argov, now a completely forgotten farmer in an Israeli *moshav*.

In September 1945, the first Palestinian Jewish emissaries from the Haganah arrived in Poland—actually, they were Polish Jews who had immigrated to Palestine just before the war, or even during it, as was the case with Shlomo Netzer, who became the head of the central Polish Bricha committee toward the end of 1945. The move was financed, basically, by the Joint, and by a clever manipulation of currencies, bought cheaply and sold at a large profit. The Joint did not finance the Bricha directly, because of legal considerations, but it paid for the feeding and shelter of the refugees. Money and valuables were transferred for the people across borders and returned to them—in this complicated, illegal procedure there were no complaints by the people. Whenever there was a hint of irregularity, the person under a cloud was immediately removed. There is the wonderful story of Graz, in the British zone in Austria, in the autumn of 1945, where a colorful figure, Pinhas Zeitag, a partisan, known as *Pinye der Geler* (he had blond hair), was suspected of mishandling money. A new Bricha commander was sent there, Israel Eichenwald. When he arrived, the people in the camp assembled and started yelling: *"Avek a ganev, gekummen a ganev!"*[2] But Eichenwald was different, and the trust was soon reestablished.

Bricha was not organized hierarchically. Theoretically at first, and practically only after the big moves were over at the end of 1946, the Haganah in Palestine was the supreme authority, and its branch of the Mossad, short for *Mossad Le'aliya Bet*—Organization for Illegal Immigration (out of which later developed the Israeli intelligence organization)—had its seat in Paris from late 1945 on under the leadership of Shaul Avigur, a Ben Gurion confidant. The idea was that the Bricha, intent on bringing Jews to the Mediterranean harbors, and the Aliya Bet illegal immigrant organization, which organized and operated the ships that tried to bring Jews to Palestine, would be under one direction and be coordinated accordingly. But in fact, Bricha remained independent, and groups of Jews were directed by Polish, and later Hungarian and Romanian Jewish organizers as well in coordination largely through Levi Argov in Bratislava and others in Berlin for the north, into the DP countries. From there they would be taken over, largely by Palestinian emissaries, to go to Italy or France, where Aliya Bet would receive them. Of course there were frictions between organizers, but these were rather minor. There was a bitter struggle in Germany, Austria, Italy, and France, with the right-wing Zionist Revisionists and emissaries of the Irgun, culminating even in a murder of a Haganah man in Austria in 1947. But the Bricha immigration network remained firmly in the hands of the Haganah, and in Poland and some other places as well the Betar-Revisionist groups were part of Bricha leadership.

It is hard to overestimate the importance of Bricha. It was the lifeline that fed into the DP countries, and created the problem for the Western powers that could not be solved unless a home was found for the Jews. The point is that this was done quite consciously, and not just on the part of the Palestinian Jewish leadership, but on that of the survivors and returnees themselves. There is plenty of evidence for that. The argument by some recent writers that the survivors were manipulated by a clever Zionist leadership bent on creating a Jewish state is misleading: the people *wanted* to be manipulated, they wanted to escape from an untenable situation, first in Eastern Europe and then in the DP countries, and Palestine seemed to them to be the only practical way out. They were not necessarily convinced Zionists, nor did they necessarily want to go to Palestine—it simply looked like that was the only option. In the end, as I said before, about a third went elsewhere, including a majority of the leadership of the DP committees in Germany and Austria. But the political pressure that they created on the U.S. and Britain to open up Palestine was their work and their desire.

My third point deals with the impact of Jewish Palestine, and of Haganah and Mossad. It was not until November 1945 that the first official team of Jewish Agency rescue workers arrived in Germany—the reason was that the U.S. Army was not at all eager to have all kinds of political aid workers come into their zone. That applied to the Joint as well, but at least that was an American organization. The agency team were largely teachers and youth leaders, all representatives of political groups and parties, as was the vogue then. They became foci of identification, they became responsible for children's homes, for educational activities, and of course conducted their work in a Zionist spirit. They certainly politicized the DPs even more than they had been already, and a great deal of criticism has been levied against them because of that. But one has to remember that at least as far as the survivors were concerned, and this is partly true for the returnees from the Soviet Union as well, political parties replaced the destroyed families and communities. This was especially true of the youth movements. The almost desperate identification of young people with their group was an essential psychological

[2] *A thief gone, a thief arrived.—Editor's note*

prop for their spirits. The idea of collectives, kibbutzim, took hold even in right-wing and ultraorthodox circles. These were not replicas of Palestinian kibbutzim, but temporary groups of like-minded individuals and families who found support with each other until they would reach a more permanent place of ordinary life.

The soldiers of the Palestinian units in the British army had been of the greatest moral importance in the immediate post-liberation days. They had infused the survivors with hope and pride, and had been instrumental in getting large numbers of them from the liberated camps in the south to Italy. They had played their part in the initial organization of the survivors there, and some of them stayed on, illegally, to become part of the Bricha. As time progressed, their place was taken by Haganah emissaries, who became the real power behind all the others.

The Haganah commander in Germany was Ephraim Frank, a kibbutz member, as most of the central clandestine figures were. He did not appear in public, but all important political and organizational decisions were referred to him for advice, and his advice was usually heeded. He was responsible to Shaul Avigur in Paris. The Central Committee in Munich was of course in daily touch with him—I have not found any significant dissensions between him, as the ultimate authority, and the committee. Again, to say that the Haganah and the agency manipulated the DP representatives, or that there was a strict hierarchical order in the activities, including the organization of political demonstrations or statements by the DPs, would be very misleading. The DPs saw the agency, the Zionist movement, and their representatives in the DP countries as their legitimate authorities; they wanted to be active and be activated for what they saw to be their own interest. In many cases they complained that they were not being used enough, that the agency and the Haganah were not radical enough, that the movement from Germany and Austria to the seashores was too slow, that they wanted more to be done.

When the Israeli War of Independence started at the end of 1947, young people volunteered in masses to go as quickly as possible to Palestine to fight. This does not mean that some were not coerced, that young men who tried to avoid recruitment were not beaten up. But these manifestations of coercion were organized by the DPs themselves, albeit with the support of some Haganah emissaries; they were the expression of internal tensions between different DP factions. At the back of it all stood the decisive fact that since 1939, all the DPs had been either direct victims of Nazism, or had been refugees in the USSR, or had been soldiers and fighters. In their vast majority they had not had a chance of a settled life of productive work. Now, in the DP countries, they had been condemned to a life of enforced idleness. There was very little one could do in the camps, except for exchanging goods on what was called the black market, but which was the predominant feature of life among Germans at the time and in which the DPs, all assertions to the contrary, played but a very minor part. One participated in vocational courses, attended lectures and political meetings, and grumbled. Moods among the DPs went up and down, as chances of immigration to normalcy decreased or increased.

In the summer of 1946, as the British tried to break the Haganah in Palestine by force, and, contrary to their promise, refused to implement the unanimous recommendations of the Anglo-American Committee of Inquiry—which recommended the immediate immigration to Palestine of 100,000 DPs—demoralization became evident in the DP camps. This was a main factor in the decision of the Jewish Agency executive meeting in Paris in early August to in fact climb down from the demand for all of Palestine as a Jewish state, and suggest, in a rather complicated way, that the Jews would accept partition as a way out of the impasse. Most speakers at that meeting said that they could not take upon themselves the responsibility of having the DPs stay in the camps for much longer, and if partition was accepted and implemented, then the problem of what to do with the DPs would be solved. In 1947, again, as the fate of Palestine hung in the balance at the United Nations, JDC representatives reported that the mood of the DPs neared desperation, and that there could be a total collapse of social norms as a result.

From the Palestinian Zionist perspective, the DPs were, on the one hand, one of their strongest political cards, if not the strongest one. On the other hand, demands and pressures of the DPs on the Zionists to get them out of the camps forced the Zionist leadership into actions—sometimes radical ones such as the increase in illegal immigration; sometimes compromises, as in the negotiations about the future of Palestine—that perhaps would not have happened without that pressure. The DPs, in other words, were partners, and as partners they had a voice of their own, which on occasion rang loud and clear. They made their views known to Frank, or to the Haganah commander in Europe, Nachum Shadmi, and to other Palestinian representatives, who reported back to the agency executive. On the other hand, agency members visited the DPs on a fairly regular basis, and there was constant contact between them.

My third topic, illegal immigration, can be dealt with very briefly, because Aliya Bet was a result of DP pressure, and combined with the burning desire of the Palestinian leadership to get as many Jews into Palestine as possible in order to intensify their struggle for a Jewish state. The total number of illegal immigrants seeking to enter Palestine by sea, between 1945 and May 1948, was 69,000; most of them were deported to Cyprus by the British. Well over a half of these came from the DP camps—the others came from Romania, from North Africa, from Sweden, or directly from Poland and other countries. Again, these people not only were not forced to board the ships, but there was tremendous pressure by them to utilize every possible way to reach Palestine. The Mossad had to surmount tremendous difficulties, and the story is too well known to bear repetition here. One difficulty it did not have was to seek passengers for even the most unseaworthy vessels. Men, women—including women in their last months of pregnancy who were expressly forbidden to join the trip by the Haganah people but joined nevertheless—children of all ages, they all did whatever they could to get away from Europe, from the memories of lost lives, of lost communities, and mainly of their lost relatives. The most bitter quarrels among the DPs centered around the lists of those who would be privileged to go on the ships, though they knew very well, after August 1946, that they would land, most likely, in camps in Cyprus. There was no doubt the influence of Zionist ideology, but there was much more than that: there was the necessity to leave Germany and Austria and the camps, the overwhelming yearning for a new life.

The fourth point is the impact of the DPs on the major powers, and chiefly on the United States. The American administration was in a most difficult situation: The Cold War had just begun, and with it the need, as the Americans saw it, to rebuild Germany as an allied political power. This happened in 1946, just as the big waves of Jewish refugees entered the U.S. zones in Germany and Austria. The non-Jewish DPs could be dealt with relatively easily, because the Western powers were willing to accept farmers, miners, and others, and no one asked questions about the political past of these people, most of whom had been Nazi collaborators, or at the very least willing workers in Germany during the war. But nobody wanted to take Jewish tailors who had not worked at their trade in any case for a number of years. American politicians were willing to express sympathy and support, up to a point, for international efforts to aid the Jewish DPs, but they did not want them in the United States. Britain was in the throes of a serious economic crisis and immigration there was out of the question. On the other hand, Truman, as I have said already, needed the Jewish votes, and needed them badly. American Jewry was disorganized, true. But the Zionist movement, led by Abba Hillel Silver of Cleveland—in part copying the tactics of the Irgun ginger group, the Bergsonites that had made a big splash in America during the war and had opposed the official Zionist movement—became a typical American grassroots organization. Organized in neighborhoods, with responsible wardens and regular meetings, they exerted great political pressure on congressmen and senators, some of whom at least tended to be friendly for humanitarian reasons as well. If Truman wanted to survive politically, he could not afford to alienate the Jews and their supporters. What the Zionists wanted was a Jewish state which would absorb, in the first instance, the DPs. I suspect that Jewish leaders in America seem also to have thought that if a majority of DPs went to Palestine, there would be less pressure by them to arrive in the United States. Truman, besieged by the politicians on the one hand and by the army in Germany, which wanted to get rid of the Jews, on the other hand, vacillated. Spokesmen of industry, and conservative politicians in the Democratic Party did not want a Jewish state, and their views were very efficiently expressed by the State Department. To oppose the British, who were indispensable allies in the Cold War, and the Arabs, who sat on the oil that was essential for the United States, as well as on the mainland and sea routes to and through the Middle East, they argued, was madness. Truman was sacrificing vital American interests to satisfy his Jewish voters. Truman did not want to have a Jewish state in Palestine—all he wanted was to have the DP problem solved; as long as he could, he opposed the linkage between the two issues, and when that could not be achieved, he was looking for a compromise solution that would satisfy the British and the Arabs, and not alienate the Jews. However, no such solution could be found. In the end, he was forced, against his will, to recognize Jewish political aspirations as the price for his political survival. The DPs were a main factor in exerting the pressure. Even had the 100,000 originally proposed by Harrison entered Palestine, in 1947 this would not have solved the DP problem, because by that time there was double that number in the DP camps. The DP problem could not be solved without Palestine, and in the end, Truman had to recognize the Jewish state once it was declared. DP pressure was, as I have said, a main factor in that equation.

As for the British, they tried, in a way not unlike Truman, to reach a compromise solution that would satisfy the Arab claim to an independent Arab Palestine, and the Jewish claim to have the DPs immigrate there—all this while keeping British influence as a dominant factor. This, again, was impossible and, in the end, counterproductive from a British point of view. British interest in keeping Palestine for strategic purposes declined dramatically when in 1947 they withdrew from India and, later on, from what is now Sri Lanka. The Suez Canal lost some of its importance for Britain, and the British general staff advised their government that they were no longer interested in keeping bases in Palestine. What motivated the British to hand over the Palestine Mandate to the UN were the pressure of illegal immigration, which they were unable to prevent, and which was the result, mainly, of the DP situation; the guerilla fight of the right-wing Jewish underground in Palestine, at first supported by the Haganah, which later withdrew from these actions; and, mainly, the constant American pressure regarding DP immigration to Palestine. From every point of view, therefore, the DPs were a major factor in the developing policies of the Western powers. For the Soviets, they were a propaganda card to play, and their immigration to Palestine would be, from the Soviet point of view, a destabilizing factor for Britain. The speech by the Soviet ambassador to the United Nations, Andrei Gromyko in April 1947 at the UN, which announced the change in Soviet policy toward a positive stand regarding Jewish aspirations in Palestine, mentioned the situation of Holocaust survivors and argued that in the shadow of what had happened to the Jewish people in World War II, it would be appropriate to accede to the central political demands of the Jewish side.

For the minor powers too, the DPs were of some importance. French officials helped Bricha and Aliya Bet out of an anti-British sentiment, but also because of a real sympathy with the plight of the survivors. The same was true for Poland, and even more so for Czechoslovakia, where the liberals were supportive of Bricha and, after a very interesting internal debate in the Politbureau of the Communist Party, the Communists as well.

My fifth point, in this very brief survey, deals with the fate of the DPs after their emigration from the DP countries. A majority made its way to Palestine/Israel. They joined survivors from Poland, Romania, from Greece, and from other countries. Their numbers, whichever way you calculate it, approached the number of Jews in Palestine before 1945. They settled in houses that were abandoned by the Palestinian Arabs who either fled or were evicted, and created new communities or joined existing ones. For decades, their influence was very much apparent in the political, social, and cultural life of the country. They were not silent, contrary to legend. The laws against Nazi war criminals, the Law of Return, the Yad Vashem Law, the law to equalize the status of wounded in the Shoah to that of soldiers, the law to establish a Holocaust memorial day, and other legislation, were in large part initiated by organizations of survivors. They were, in their majority, very active in opposition to German restitution and to the resumption of diplomatic relations with Germany. If you scan Israeli newspapers in the fifties, you will be surprised at the number of testimonies published there. True, the way the Holocaust was presented was a distortion, to a certain, or a considerable, extent of what we now know as the historical truth, but that is understandable in the hothouse atmosphere of a young state struggling for survival. There was an overemphasis on armed resistance during the Holocaust; the survivors were asked how come they had survived when all their relatives had been murdered; how come they had not resisted, and so on. Many withdrew into bitterness and silence; but silence was also due simply to the fact that many survivors could not talk about what they had experienced, so that it was not just a reluctance by the others to listen, but also a reluctance to talk. And nevertheless, many did talk, and thousands of testimonies at Yad Vashem originated in the fifties. The accusations hurled against the survivors stemmed from guilt feelings of older established Israelis, most of whom had lost all their families in Europe, and I am certainly not arguing that these guilt feelings, for supposed lack of action on the part of the *Yishuv* during the Holocaust, were objectively justified. But the accusations were a form of defense mechanism to cover those feelings of guilt.

As time went on, there was an emigration of survivors from Israel. There are no statistics, and I can only argue for a hypothesis for which I have no solid documentation—namely, that a disproportionate number of survivors spent a certain time in Israel, and then immigrated, largely to North America, but elsewhere as well. I think this was largely due to a desire to leave a crisis situation and settle in a more comfortable and seemingly more secure place. Many young Israeli soldiers were to fall in battle between 1948 and the present, and many survivor parents lost their sons in this most tragic way. But survivors' sons also served in the U.S. Army in Vietnam, and there were casualties there as well. However, it was the very harsh security and economic situation in Israel in the fifties that motivated many to leave, along with an even larger number of Israeli-born.

It is only now, after the last Israeli election, that the number of survivors in the Knesset has been drastically cut, for simple biological reasons I suppose. It is perhaps symbolic, that the speaker of the previous Knesset was a survivor, Professor Shevach Weiss, whereas the present one, Avraham Burg, is the son of a Polish-German Jew and a major Israeli politician, the late Dr. Yosef Burg, who was the chairman of Yad Vashem. Survivors and their children are today a most central and active element in Israeli life, from industrialists and financiers to writers and journalists, to local government officials, to ordinary business people, kibbutz and moshav members, and manual workers.

The situation in North America is somewhat different. The numbers of DPs who immigrated here was relatively smaller, and smaller still was their proportion among North American Jews. The silence imposed on them by their Jewish and non-Jewish environment was more oppressive than the parallel situation in Israel. The stamina and courage in facing this situation was even more challenging, I think, than the situation in Israel where, after all, the Holocaust, from the early fifties on, became part of the national consciousness. Their achievements in the U.S. and Canada had to be first of all in the realm of the rebuilding of their personal life. This involved the building of an economic foundation for their existence, and in the North American situation this was neither easy nor quick. It took time, and their integration into Jewish community life, for those who wanted it, was not simple either. They had to fight their way up the ladder of economic and social stratification in both the general and the Jewish society. The surprising thing is that they succeeded beyond any reasonable expectation. The psychological reasons for that have not really been properly examined, but it seems to me that the determination to survive during the Holocaust trauma must have played a central part in this success. I don't have to tell this audience what the achievements were and are—the very fact that you are sitting here, people who succeeded in business, in academic life, in the social sphere, and elsewhere, speaks for itself.

However, this picture may be somewhat misleading—not everyone made it. Many are the survivors who were caught in post-Holocaust traumata, sometimes many years after their arrival, here and in other countries, whose lives were permanently and sometimes completely destroyed by the aftereffects of what they went through, or who led or lead lives of bitterness and maladjustment that is sometimes covered up by external success. I do not know the divorce rate of Holocaust survivors; it may actually be lower than that of other groups in Jewish society. But quite a number of marriages, so some psychologists tell us, were entered into in the DP stage when people were desperately eager to resume family life. The stories about the huge number of weddings, and of the amazing baby boom that resulted from that, are well known. It appears that a proportion, and I do not have any figures, went sour, without necessarily being dissolved, because dissolution would have been another unbearable trauma. People carry on living with partners to whom they no longer have anything to say, and what they say is accompanied by a hidden bitterness. On the other hand, marriages were concluded after the Holocaust that rescued people from exactly that kind of traumata, and that are harmonious exactly because of shared experiences and mutual trust. Hence also, the divergence in the stories of what is inaccurately known as the Second Generation—inaccurately, because Holocaust experiences were so different from each other, and hence the transmission to the next generation also differed as between different cases. But these are problems that I was not asked to discuss this evening, and they belong to another chapter.

The story of the Jewish displaced persons is a very unusual story. The survivors of ghettos, camps, or hiding places are living testimonials to the tragedy of the Jewish people, and living documents of the most decisive failure of civilization we know. More importantly, ex-DPs are human beings of the Jewish kind who not only survived, but who organized in near-impossible situations, hurting, suffering, but not giving up, who formed a transitory society of people who wanted to leave a cursed continent in order to find a new life that would be a successful continuation of their struggles. The DPs and the survivors generally are, to my mind at least, the quintessential Jews of this century, living symbols of the unshakable will of Jews to survive as individuals and as communities. They quarreled and continue to quarrel with each other as all Jews do; they faced and are facing tremendous problems in their personal lives. But they are survivors, and they act accordingly.

THE JOINT DISTRIBUTION COMMITTEE IN THE DP CAMPS

INTRODUCTORY REMARKS

Jonathan W. Kolker

President, The American Jewish Joint Distribution Committee

I wish to commend the United States Holocaust Memorial Museum, on behalf of The American Jewish Joint Distribution Committee, for its vision in producing this important conference and its attendant exhibition on the emotion-laden theme of the DP camps.

The role of JDC is central to understanding developments in this period. I say this because JDC was not only "the overseas arm of North American Jewry," as we are commonly known, but also its heart, manifesting deep feelings of Jewish identity and unity. In the camps run by UNRRA and the Allied occupation authorities, JDC staff provided kosher food and clothing, health and vocational training, and helped with religious and cultural needs. JDC also enabled many to emigrate, cooperating with the Jewish Agency in its own heroic efforts.

In this conference we give witness to the courage and resilience of those who suffered the horrors of Nazi persecution and the destruction of their families and communities. We honor the survivors themselves and their life-affirming spirit. Edward Warburg, one of my predecessors as head of JDC said in 1947: "Without the heroic spirit and sense of purpose of the survivors, our accomplishments would be meaningless. They regard us as partners in the challenging adventure of rebuilding Jewish life."

At this session, we will pay tribute to Dr. Joseph Schwartz, who was perhaps the greatest American Jewish professional leader of the twentieth century. As overseas director of JDC, he led the efforts to aid the survivors of the Nazi horror and brought many scores of trained professionals to serve in the support of DPs in or out of the DP camps.

Let me just add that there is another momentous challenge in Jewish life today, and that is the restoration of the three or more million Jews of the former Soviet Union to the Jewish people. We draw upon the inspiration of our postwar experience to seize this historic opportunity. The roots of our efforts lie in the deliberations of this conference.

And now to our program. We begin with a tribute to Dr. Joseph Schwartz, given by the executive vice president of JDC, Michael Schneider. Michael follows in the tradition of Dr. Schwartz as a great and caring Jewish communal servant. He was JDC director for Israel,

Europe, and during the Cold War for Hungary, Czechoslovakia, and Yugoslavia. His initiation into JDC was as director in Iran when the revolution took place.

All this was good preparation for the critical role he played in coordinating the American responses in the rescue of Ethiopian Jewry, as well as his current leadership role in the rescue of Jews from other areas of distress, and directing JDC's relief and Jewish cultural activities in over 50 countries.

Following Michael's presentation, we will hear two brief personal histories of life in the DP camps from Ted Feder and Isaac Norich.

Ted Feder served as deputy director of JDC's DP program in the American zone from 1946–1952. From 1952–1960 he directed JDC services for DPs in Vienna. He subsequently worked in over 30 countries, including Israel (as director of the JDC office), and he remains a valued member of our staff to this very day.

Isaac Norich is a survivor of the Lodz ghetto and Auschwitz/Dachau. From 1945–1951 he worked with UNRRA in the DP camp Feldafing, and from 1951–56 he was JDC assistant director in camp Foehrenwald.

We will bring this session to a close with remarks by Ted Comet, who has been representing JDC on this conference's planning committee and is responsible for the JDC components at this conference. From 1946–48 he was a student volunteer in a JDC-funded program for the rehabilitation of war orphans in France. During his 23-year tenure as director of international affairs at the Council of Jewish Federations, he was concerned with Jewish needs overseas. Ten years ago he returned to JDC as associate executive vice president.

TRIBUTE TO
DR. JOSEPH J. SCHWARTZ

Michael Schneider

Executive Vice President, The American Jewish Joint Distribution Committee

It's a great privilege for me, as the latest in a long line of the Joint's professional leaders, to pay tribute to Joe Schwartz, an authentic hero of the Joint and of the Jewish people.

And it is most appropriate that I do so in front of you, whose lives were shattered over five decades ago—you, who found respite in the displaced persons camps of Europe.

And who managed somehow, against all odds, to find the strength, resilience, and courage to rebuild your lives in new and faraway places. Your children, and your children's children, are the best evidence of the triumph of the human spirit, of Jewish survival, and of the ultimate defeat of the forces of evil in the middle of this century.

But, as we have learned since, evil still lurks in dark corridors. And there have been new murderers. Ever since our own tragedy, every victim of Stalin, Pol Pot, every Moslem killed in Bosnia, every Kosovar body in a mass grave, and every Rwandan chopped down with a machete, is also an affront to our Jewish people and an attack on humanity. And that's why the Joint also helps other nationalities and faiths when such outrages occur.

Joe Schwartz was an outstanding professional leader of his time and of this passing century. He started life as a rabbi from Baltimore and taught government at the American University in Cairo. He led the Joint during the Holocaust, became head of the United Jewish Appeal, and finally, assumed the post of director of Israel Bonds.

But none of his later achievements exceeded his role at the Joint, rescuing Jews from Europe and meeting the huge demands of the aftermath.

Leading the Joint through World War II

Schwartz joined the Joint's Paris office in 1940. Under the protection of his American citizenship when the United States was not yet at war with Germany, he became head of JDC operations in Europe. When the Germans were at the gates of Paris, the Joint offices were evacuated and staff retreated in the opposite direction to other safe havens.

Schwartz established a new office in Lisbon. He arranged legal and illegal escape routes from Vichy France and the Balkans. Refugees were helped via Portugal and Spain to get to Morocco, Cuba, and Turkey. Some were allowed into Switzerland and any other country that would accept Jews. At that time, very few were willing to do so. Six thousand were allowed into Cuba before the doors closed. Ships were chartered to take Jews to Palestine.

Under Joe Schwartz's inspired leadership, heroic efforts were undertaken by the Joint's staff members.

Under him, Laura Margolis received and cared for 23,000 refugees who crossed Russia and Siberia into Shanghai. Herb Katzki and Mel Goldstein arranged shipping of supplies behind Nazi lines.

Emmanuel Ringelblum served in Warsaw until he was executed by the Nazis. Saly Mayer, in neutral Geneva, dealt with financial transactions and negotiations with third parties for the rescue of Jews.

In Budapest, Schwartz's staff indirectly funded some of the efforts of Raoul Wallenberg and worked with Charles Lutz, the Swiss consul. Twenty thousand Swiss and Swedish papers were issued to get Jews out of Hungary.

JDC sent vital funds to the Jews of the Warsaw ghetto through the Polish underground and rescued Jewish children in France through the French Resistance. In France, JDC maintained 7,000 Jewish children who were hidden by Gentile foster parents.

Schwartz himself traveled ceaselessly to bypass the Nazi stranglehold, to find corridors of rescue. He made frequent trips to Istanbul where Jews from the Balkans were led to boats headed for Palestine.

The problem was that there were not enough places to send them to.

Despite opposition by some of the Joint's leaders in New York, Joe Schwartz insisted that the Joint should fund underground escape routes to Palestine, notwithstanding the British restrictions. And he got his way.

His legacy lives on in the current policies of the Joint. To this day, when Jews are in harm's way or hostages to criminal regimes, to this day, we will not hesitate to take all measures, legal or otherwise, to save them. In this way, we have redeemed Jewish hostages from Syria, Yemen, Iran, Ethiopia, and continue to monitor the situations in other countries of potential duress.

By the time the war broke out, over 400,000 Jews had been rescued by the Joint and other organizations. Many thousands were saved during the war. Most notably, 119,000 Jews in Hungary survived the Shoah.

And when it ended, 300,000 survivors were put in displaced persons camps.

We managed to save lives but, of course, not enough. The Joint did what it could with what it had. Were some mistakes made? Of course! But they were human mistakes, and the adversities were immense.

As Professor Yehuda Bauer has pointed out in his histories, while the Allies were single-mindedly intent on ending the war as soon as possible and did not adequately address the Jewish issue, the Joint and other organizations were left to face, alone, the armed might of a powerful and evil sovereign state.

Joe Schwartz reshaped the Joint to meet the overwhelming challenges of the time, with lasting effects on its policies during the 55 years since. Our top priority, to this day, is the saving of Jewish life. Our humanitarian mission is to feed destitute victims of Nazi persecution. Our future goal is to rebuild Jewish life in communities devastated by political events.

Preparing to Aid Jewish Survivors

Well before the war ended, Schwartz began the recruitment of personnel to help manage the aid that would be needed afterwards. When he finally returned to Central Europe, he was graphically exposed to the enormity of the catastrophe and the task of healing that lay ahead.

Survivors, among them perhaps some of those present this afternoon, were streaming into JDC offices everywhere, pale ghosts of their former selves. They traveled from Russia, the Balkan States, by foot, by boat, by train. They straggled, homeless and dispirited, across Western Europe.

Jews also streamed in from Poland, Hungary, and Romania to Austria, Germany, and Italy to seek haven from antisemitism, as was the case after the massacre of Jews in Kielce in 1946. They had no homes, no communities to return to, no means to feed and clothe themselves. Many spirits were broken beyond repair; others like yourselves were able to survive this devastating disaster.

Despite the chaotic conditions and initial lack of organization among the authorities in the DP camps, Schwartz was able to bring in supplies of food and clothing, provided Jewish education and health care, and, through ORT, vocational training; and he mounted a huge immigration program for movement to the free countries of the world.

He worked closely with the Jewish Agency, preparing youth for eventual immigration to Israel.

Displaced persons camps established by the occupying armies were dismal, and their inmates were often treated like criminals. Most shocking was the antisemitism of non-Jews in the camps.

Schwartz and Earl Harrison, dean of the University of Pennsylvania, persuaded the White House to separate Jews from the rest. The army, UNRRA, and JDC were delegated to look after them. And fortunately, General Patton, no great sympathizer of the Jewish plight, was replaced as commanding officer.

While the military provided basic sustenance for DP camps in Germany, Austria, and Italy, the surviving Jews in Romania, Poland, Hungary, and Czechoslovakia were mostly derelict and hungry. Some of them returned to their home countries. Others wanted to immigrate to anywhere, but only Palestine was ready to accept them, and then only 1,200 visas were given each year.

It has been estimated by Bauer that, in the immediate postwar period, JDC was providing relief for one out of every two Jews surviving in Europe. American Jewish philanthropy contributed $102 million in 1946—in today's dollars, well more than $1 billion. By 1947, JDC had a staff of 2,000 people in the camps and was supplying 300,000 meals each day. Another 400,000 Jews outside depended on JDC aid. Tens of thousands of tons of supplies were shipped to Europe. An army of doctors, nurses, teachers, and social workers was recruited and mobilized.

Schwartz decided that there was no alternative but to bypass the British blockade and worked closely with Aliya Bet forces in the Bricha, the illegal movement of Jews out of Eastern Europe. Many expeditions were intercepted by the British and diverted to Cyprus. And in Cyprus, JDC established programs to prepare for their arrival in Israel and the coming war of independence.

To meet the enormous challenge of the survivors, including the DP population, Schwartz recruited a large number of local personnel to create Jewish communal infrastructures covering all of war-torn Europe and, later, North Africa. And when Israel was established, Schwartz established care services for immigrants with special needs, and provided nascent Israel with technical services for a fledgling government struggling to meet the needs of the influx of Jews from many lands.

And at the same time, JDC was involved in the planning and the financing of Operation Magic Carpet on the Wings of Eagles, which airlifted Yemeni Jews to Israel.

I never met Joe Schwartz. But I know many of his colleagues. Some of them are here today—some still work for the JDC. I am told that he was soft-spoken, deliberate, and decisive. He gave impassioned speeches stateside to recruit support.

He had charm and humor. His charisma came from his vision, deep dedication, effectiveness, and determination. He was persuasive, practical, and effective. He carried with him the constant burden of his huge responsibilities.

JDC Legacy of Joe Schwartz

Joe Schwartz was a driven man in his service to the Jewish people. He left behind a legacy which prevails to this day in JDC's organizational culture—integrity, nonpartisanship, encouraging Jewish community building, Jewish empowerment, self-direction, independence, and a love for the State of Israel.

His legacy carries on. His example has molded his successors at the helm of the Joint.

For 54 years since the Holocaust, the Joint has continued the work in meeting its terrible consequences, by rebuilding the communities of Western Europe and by providing aid for those survivors who returned home behind the iron curtain. Today the Joint provides relief for 200,000 impoverished victims of Nazi persecution. In our daily work since 1945, we come face-to-face with the consequences of the Shoah in the faces of the Jewish poor across East Europe and the former Soviet Union, most of whom are victims and survivors.

We still help to build the Jewish state. We help small communities across the globe to sustain a viable Jewish life. We rescue Jews in distress.

We are helping East European Jewry to emerge from the double trauma of the Shoah and of Communism.

We now face our greatest postwar challenge—the restoration of Jewish life in the former Soviet Union so that we bring back to us, culturally and organizationally, this last great reserve of the Jewish people after decades in the wilderness.

It's what Joe would have done if he were still with us. It is part of the legacy he left behind for the entire Jewish world.

LIFE IN THE DP CAMPS: THE SPECIAL ROLE OF THE JDC

Ted Feder

Missions and VIP Coordinator, The American Jewish Joint Distribution Committee; Deputy Director, JDC Program, American Zone of Germany

Good afternoon. President Kolker, Michael, Ted Comet, friends, and those of you who are still with us from the Sh'erit ha-Pletah. I was told by Ted Comet I had eight minutes and, of course, I protested. However, after listening to the brilliant presentation by Michael, I knew why Comet said to keep it to eight minutes, because there isn't a great deal I can say about the JDC that hasn't been said by Michael Schneider. But, nevertheless, I'll try to bring a different aspect of the JDC work in the DP programs in Germany and Austria, when I was an eyewitness as well as a representative of JDC.

I'll give you an overview of what Munich, Germany, was like. I'll talk about the Jewish Central Committee. I'll talk about the security blanket, which was established by JDC and the American Jewish community in order to protect the DPs. And, then, I'll tell you about our program. And, I'll have the temerity as well to give you information specifically on the budget—the budget that I dug out of our archives—for the period after World War II.

Mohlstrasse, that's a name that rings. The street lay in northeast Munich, a former "upper-class" section. Despite the cobblestones in the streets, it was a "high-class" area. The offices of the Jewish Agency, the Bricha, HIAS, and of course, the JDC was there. The Central Jewish Committee was on Siebertstrasse 3 and 4, right across the street from JDC. The U.S. Army ran our own "officers' mess." Above all it contained the headquarters of the Jewish community of Munich. Its leader was Mr. Schwimmer. He called himself a *ba'al hagola*. That's Yiddish for the horse-and-wagon driver. He was essential in bringing supplies to Palestine and to Israel. There was Jewish rhythm in this part of Munich. Hundreds of Jewish people walked up and down the half dozen blocks of Mohlstrasse coming to one of the Jewish organizations, or going to the committee where business was going on which didn't involve us.

And, above all, there was the Central Committee. Its full name was the Central Committee of Liberated Jews in the U.S. Zone of Germany. A committee that, when we arrived in August of 1945, was working on its second meeting, to be held in Berchtesgarten in December of 1945. In other words, we came in when the committee had already functioned for months. One man was responsible for its formation: Chaplain Klausner of the U.S. Army Chaplains Corps. I'm sorry that he is not here today.

The committee was made up of some very important leaders, people with whom, if it hadn't been that they were on the committee and we were on different sides of issues, we would have enjoyed to be friends. But we did get along.

A number of them eventually went to Israel. There were David Treger and Pesach Piekatch, Dr. Boris Pliskin, who became the head of JDC medical department; Dr. Avraham Blumovicz, who was a top officer in the medical corps of the Israeli army; and Leon Retter, who later was Golda Meir's assistant.

If there had been no committee, we would have had to build one, and we probably couldn't have done as well as the political parties of Palestine did in raising this committee. But, they were there. We worked with them, we worked closely with them. If we had to bring in staff to do the work of the committee and its counterparts in all of the DP camps, it would have been a disaster, because we couldn't have found that kind of professional know-how in the United States.

But what is important is that the JDC, the Central Committee, and others brought to the attention of President Truman that the army wasn't carrying out the policy of giving some priority to Jews as Holocaust victims. Jews were mixed with antisemitic groups of Poles, Baltics, and Ukrainians. Truman appointed Earl Harrison to conduct a thorough investigation, with the result that Jews were moved into separate camps and suddenly there was a little Palestine.

I'm serious. These were camps of Jews, run by Jews. The administration was Jewish, the workers were Jewish, the garbage collectors were Jewish, and it was part of a security blanket which was helpful to the rebirth as we saw it take place. It was a rebirth with over 5,000 children born in the DP camps of Germany from 1946–49.

The other element that was very important was that it was decided to establish an advisor's office on Jewish affairs to the commanding general of the American army. There we had some great American Jews who staffed that office. Bill Haber, for example, one of the important people in our government during the war in organizing and getting staff into factories. There was Judge Leventhal of Philadelphia. There were Phil Bernstein, Harry Greenstein, and, above all were the Jewish chaplains, Herb Friedman and all of his cohorts. Yes, it was a rebirth with over 5,000 children born in the DP camps of Germany, from 1947–49.

And, this security blanket worked. Whenever there was a U.S. constabulary raid on a Jewish camp, they called the chaplain. In the U.S. zone, the advisor on Jewish affairs would dispatch an observer. This security given to our people, I think, marked a very important element in the total eventual development in the camps. Our people were happy to be "protected."

I want to give you some idea of the magnitude of our postwar program. It wasn't only in the DP camps; it was the million Jews who were living outside of the DP camps, in Eastern Europe and Western Europe. The Jewish communities of these countries were almost totally destroyed by the Nazis and the Communists from 1939 until Communism fell.

First Germany and Austria: The DP camps there had over 250,000 Jewish DPs. In 1947 it was a $6 million budget. In 1948 it was a $17 million budget. And, when everybody talks about the programs in the DP camps, whether it is in the British zone or whether it's in the U.S. zone, whatever those programs cost, it came out of this money. There was no other funding in Germany and no other major Jewish organization funding the DP program. There was a bit through the religious organizations, but not the kind of money that would allow for the expansion of programs such as we established.

In Hungary, the budget for 1948 alone was $10 million. The total 1948 budget for all of Europe's Jewish DP program was $96 million. Those resources were available to the victims of the Holocaust living in communities.

Let me take just a few moments to go through very quickly some parts of the program and what was involved, and also showing the total number of staff. For example, in 1946, there were 44 employees. Thirty-eight were from out of the country, and six locally. In 1947 it was reversed. We had 86 foreign service staff with 200 local staff. And in 1948, we had 452 local staff and 108 foreign service staff. What did this mean? Please remember that UNRRA and the military covered housing, care, and maintenance, etc., and basically cared for all DPs in camps. JDC programs were supplementary because UNRRA had limited funds and set minimum standards for feeding and administration.

What I'm trying to say is that not only were there all of these Jews in the camps who were getting our food and our packages, some cigarettes in it as well. You needed that. But, more importantly, one must see the atmosphere that prevailed in the camp at that time. There was a little immigration to Palestine in 1946 and 1947, with little movement to other countries. The Jews certainly weren't happy in the DP camps, despite the security blanket, despite JDC programs beginning in 1946. Although the people were willing to work, they were not willing to work for Germans. We set up work projects. We put 3,000 people to work making clothing, carpentry, and all the jobs necessary to run the camps.

I already talked about the self-administration, and then there was ORT. Interestingly enough, the people in the camps, even before we got there, were setting up training projects. And when we came in, we took over, and when ORT came in, we turned the training program over for ORT to run.

There were also religious needs. We brought in tens of thousands of *machzorim* and *talitot*. The majority of the Jewish DPs were not religious, but they were certainly fighting that we give the biggest budget possible for religious needs.

Last but not least was resettlement. HIAS was there. But the situation was so massive with the tens of thousands of people who wanted to immigrate—whether it was to Palestine or to other countries—that we had to set up a JDC immigration project.

We were accused of being late in Germany. That's true. It wasn't our fault. You know, an army is built to fight. It is not built to deal with civilians. The army didn't like civilians; they wanted no part of civilians. As early as July of 1944, the American army asked the UN to set up UNRRA because they knew that the 10 or 11 million refugees would require housing, medical help, food, clothing, and amenities. The army had won a war and was not interested in caring for millions of refugees. We eventually were allowed to enter Germany with UNRRA in July 1945.

There were problems in the camp, especially with children. We set up three nutrition centers where over 3,000 children were sent in order to help them put on weight. Of course, the army was involved in the medical care, but that didn't mean that it did not need help. We brought surgeons into the TB hospitals. All told, there were over 216 medical institutions that were staffed by JDC. There were also summer camps.

I'll just say one thing about education because that was truly remarkable in the DP camps. There were 116 schools, 700 teachers, and 8,000 students, and we brought 50 teachers from Palestine—all financed by the JDC.

I want to end on a personal note. I think among us, there were four JDC staff members who did the ultimate. They looked and found amongst the DPs their mates. I was one of them. I made certain that my wife finally got her diploma from the medical school she was attending and then we got married. And my knowledge of what was taking place amongst the DPs was enhanced by her knowledge of how she was treated by the JDC.

Life in the DP Camps: The Special Role of the JDC

Isaac Norich

Holocaust survivor; Feldafing DP camp; The American Jewish Joint Distribution Committee official in Foehrenwald and Munich Office

My name is Isaac Norich. For those who know me from Lodz, Poland, or know me from the Feldafing and Foehrenwald DP camps in Germany, I am Itche Norich. It's the same spelling but sounds different in English. I came to the DP camp Feldafing on August 13, 1945, from a hospital in Geretszied.

I applied for a job and worked in the UNRRA camp administration from September 1945. In my capacity as vice president of the Camp Committee in charge of different departments of the administration, I came in contact with representatives of the JDC when they established the central office in Munich.

I worked very well with the UNRRA officers, but when JDC came into the camp it was something new. We had Jewish people and they were representatives of the Jews in America. They brought what we call a *Yiddishe Neshume*.

The Joint had the means to help with services which supplemented the social work for the UNRRA administration. Mr. Feder mentioned the care for children. When I came into camp Feldafing there was only one baby in a camp of 4,500 population. The child was born to a young Jewish woman from Lithuania who came to concentration camp Dachau. She gave birth in a working camp of Dachau and the Germans let the child survive and she came with the child into camp Feldafing. Whoever arrived at Feldafing at that time went to Block 1-B to look at the miracle.

The Joint brought to the displaced persons help in providing financial assistance, additional food, and cigarettes to those who worked in the camp. There were about 1,500 people and the Joint provided for the general population.

But, the most important thing was the care the Joint provided for the sick people and for the children and pregnant women. In the material you received at registration there is in one booklet a picture (taken in a hospital) of a woman who gave birth to triplets. The triplets were a boy, a girl, and a boy. I was at that *Brith Milah* for the two boys. To my knowledge it was the only set of triplets born into DP camps during 1945–1956.

Because of the help from the Joint it was possible to employ more people in the DP camp, to help the camp population. They stayed in the camp waiting for the possibility of emigration. The majority of the people wanted to go to Palestine and would not accept repatriation to Poland or other countries under Communist occupation. The Jews were exempt from repatriation against their will, and Jewish DP camps were established. We thought that it would be a short period, but it took until 1948, when the U.S. Congress passed the law that exempted the displaced persons from the regular quota restrictions. That is when mass emigration from the camps started.

That was when the DP camp population started dwindling. There were some people who couldn't emigrate because no country would accept them. They included the sick people in hospitals, those afflicted with tuberculosis or other diseases. It was decided to retain two camps for those people. The two camps were called hard-core camps. The camps were Feldafing and Foehrenwald. I was in charge of Feldafing. Later it was decided to close camp Feldafing and retain the only Jewish camp in Foehrenwald.

I was called to the IRO headquarters in Munich and offered the management of camp Foehrenwald. I accepted the appointment. My title was deputy field supervisor, and I was in charge of the administration. I took over the camp on April 1, 1951. On December 1, 1951, this last Jewish DP camp, Foehrenwald was handed over to the German administration.

I could have had the job of assistant to the German camp administration, but didn't care for it.

I had established an excellent cooperation as camp administrator with the then Joint director for the camp, Mr. Jerry Kolieb. It was no surprise that I was offered the job as his assistant. In December of 1951, I became a member of the Joint, finally. But the Joint was in the process of closing down its operations in Germany. The Foehrenwald office was moved to the headquarters in Munich where I worked until February 1956, while still living in the camp.

In February 1956, I resigned from my job in the Joint knowing that the office in Munich would soon be closed. I accepted a job as manager of a company (Jewish ownership) that manufactured stockings where I worked until the day of my departure for the U.S., March 6, 1957.

When my appeal for admission to the U.S. was approved, I didn't hesitate and left the good job and the beautiful apartment with the new furniture in a new house and new section in Munich. I am happy that I came here where my two children, Sam and Anita, then nine and four years old, received an excellent education, and I myself didn't do bad.

The last Jewish camp in Germany, Foehrenwald, was closed in February 1957.

CLOSING REMARKS

Ted Comet

Honorary Associate Executive Vice President, The American Jewish Joint Distribution Committee; student volunteer, JDC program to rehabilitate war orphans in France

I want to congratulate the United States Holocaust Memorial Museum for extending its parameters beyond 1945 and into the post-Holocaust period. This has major psychological and spiritual consequences, enabling us to move from the exclusive images of death in the concentration camps to the inspiring images of life reborn in the DP camps. Our motto must be not only "Never Again" to the Holocaust but also "Forever Again" to rebirth, renewal, and reconstruction.

I also want to commend this conference's Second Generation planning committee. It was a deeply rewarding experience working together with such committed, gifted, and articulate young people, led by Romana Primus, Sam Norich, and Menachem Rosensaft. A major concern of veterans like myself is whether there will be a successor generation to pursue the vision. This conference gives us much hope.

In 1946, as an impressionable young student serving as a JDC volunteer in France, I was overwhelmed by two opposing emotions: the extent of the horror of the destruction; and on the positive side, the resilience of the survivors and their capacity to respond to love, care, and concerned handling. Through JDC, I saw how it was possible to make a difference, to bring healing and solace. I wanted to be part of this JDC culture of dedication and service; of integrity and nonpartisanship; of the desire not to dictate but to foster local independence and control, even when that proved very difficult. (I'm familiar with the many stories of battling over control.) These principles have remained cardinal JDC values to this very day.

What does it mean for JDC to be "the overseas arm of North American Jewry"? The worldwide importance of JDC is having the readiness to react swiftly and effectively in the areas of rescue, relief, and reconstruction—and to be able to count on the support of the American Jewish community. That support is still extraordinary, but the awareness of Jewish needs overseas is declining and we all have a responsibility to heighten the recognition that we are a global people, responsible for one another. For we are few in number—two-hundredths of one percent of the world's population—and we need each other not only for solace, but also for global strength.

Rescue takes many forms: among those rescued by JDC during the war in Sarajevo were a group of elderly Jews whom JDC set up in a village, providing them with a place to live and a sheltered workshop. One day, a box arrived at JDC headquarters, filled with yarmulkes knitted by the group, with a letter that read: "Dear Joint, this is our way of saying thank you for saving us twice: first, by bringing us out of Sarajevo, you saved our lives; and now by giving us a place to live and work to do, you are saving our dignity."

Two other forms of rescue are taking place at this very time in the former Soviet Union: rescue from hunger through JDC's care and feeding of 175,000 needy elderly; and spiritual rescue by connecting Jews to their heritage and to the Jewish people.

I want to close on a personal note, by sharing with you a work of art that for me captures the life reborn theme of this conference. My wife, a survivor, psychotherapist, and artist, wove a series of large tapestries depicting her Holocaust experience. The concluding tapestry was woven on the occasion of our son's Bar Mitzvah. What was her message? At the top of this six-foot-high weaving are the Ten Commandments. Instead of the usual smooth-shaped tablets, these are jagged-edged, symbolizing their being wrenched out of the rock of Sinai: If you take your Jewishness seriously, it makes demands.

The Hebrew letters are not static, locked into the tablets, but fall out and add up to the priestly benediction: "May the Lord Bless You and Keep You." This blessing cascades over our son, who is represented at the base of the tapestry by a thick purple yarmulke, the double profile of his face bowing his head as he receives the blessing, and wearing a tallit shaped like wings, to bear him up to Sinai. Her message as a survivor to her son: You stood at Sinai. Since Sinai is located in a desert, and the desert is a metaphor for a hostile world, it is precisely when most challenged that our Jewish tradition commands that we affirm life.

This gathering is more than a conference. It is a declaration that in spite of the Holocaust, we are and will remain an eternal people. Your presence here is an affirmation that truly: *"Am Yisrael khai."*

SECOND GENERATION PERSPECTIVES ON THE DP YEARS

INTRODUCTORY REMARKS

Felicia Figlarz Anchor

Vice President, National Council of Jewish Women; Second Generation Advisory Group, United States Holocaust Memorial Council

Good evening. It is a pleasure and honor to be chairperson of this evening's program. Last night, Miles Lerman spoke eloquently about the passage of time. Each of us, seated in this ballroom, understands the urgency of his remarks. Time as well as the ability and willingness to remember are our foes.

Our parents and loved ones hold the unenviable position of eyewitness to the Shoah. Of course, we understand that we can never know or see what they experienced. Still, each one of us is here because we have our heart, soul, and *"kishkes"* embedded and intertwined in the most horrific event ever perpetrated against humankind and our families. As we cherish and learn from our parents, we face the sad reality that they will not be with us forever.

And so, the Second and Third Generations continue to undertake the fulfillment and responsibility of Zahor—to remember—transmitted as part of what we have been taught as our legacy and accepted as our obligation.

For many of us, this conference has enhanced our understanding of life and death before, during, and after the Shoah. We have learned more about our parents' lives and decisions and our own lives as well.

I was born in Bergen-Belsen to two young Polish survivors: Yitzhak and Genia Figlarz. We came to America in 1949 to small-town life in Toledo, Ohio. Unlike others—who grew up wrapped in the intensity and concentrated life of a large survivor community—my experience as a child of survivors was significantly different.

We had a core of two other families who became our extended family in a community that did not care to hear or know about our particular voice.

I mention my circumstances because as you will learn from this evening's speakers, each of us has taken our legacy and interpreted it through a means and message that provide a meaningful voice for ourselves and for others to see, hear, learn, and understand how the legacy of the Holocaust and DP era impacts our lives and the life plan we have chosen.

Miles Lerman elaborated on the richness of our Second Generation diversity, the impressive credentials we have attained, and the accomplishments we have contributed to our communities. Tonight's speakers represent a cross-section of the means by which our message is delivered.

In the past, Isaac Newton set forth a scientific theory that every action has a reaction.

Tonight, the Second Generation, children of Holocaust survivors, continues to add to the memory, recognition, and significance of the Sh'erit ha-Pletah by providing their particular responses to this historic legacy through the work of their hands and heart.

CHOOSING LIFE:
OUR PARENTS, OURSELVES

Samuel Norich

General Manager, Forward Association

I was born in Feldafing, Germany, in 1947. We left for the States, for New York, in 1957, and ten years later, in the summer of 1967, I went back for a visit. I got a grant from my college to spend the summer doing research on political ideology in the Jewish DP camps in a number of archives in Israel, Germany, and at the Wiener Library in London. At least, that was the excuse for my trip. The reason was that, even though I was already 20, this was an adolescent odyssey for me. I went to find myself.

As it turned out, I found much more of myself in Israel, where I had never been before, than in Germany, where many memories connected me—and connect me to this day—to friends I grew up with and to places I remember.

I decided I would have to go back to Israel for a longer stay, and I did, two years later, when I spent the 1969–1970 academic year, my second year of grad school, at the Hebrew University, taking courses with several of the great teachers of that great university. One was a seminar with Yehuda Bauer on the Sh'erit ha-Pletah. That course confirmed in me what has remained a fascination with the history and culture of the place and time in which I was born. I didn't become a scholar of it; but I remain a student of it.

I must tell you that for me, the central mystery of my parents' lives was, and remains, not what happened to them in the years from 1940 to 1945, but what they managed to do in the years just after 1945. My father, *tsu lange yor,* never spoke about the war years. My mother, *z"l,*[1] never ceased to speak about the war, and I think—though she gave birth to and brought up two children, and made a warm home for Anita and me and our father for another four decades—I think she never quite recovered from the anguish of losing her mother Khane, her sister Gitl and her sister's baby Taybl, and my mother's little brother Moyshe, in Auschwitz. I think I feared that if I were to approach the events of those years too closely—even if vicariously—I would be hurt, maimed.

The mystery of my parents' and other survivors' lives after liberation was, simply, where did they find the strength to choose life? What did they think they were doing? That is, how did they understand themselves at that time? What, precisely, was the psychological or the cultural well from whence they drew their strength?

The fact that most of our parents, most of the time, did find the strength to choose life may blind us to the possibility that they could have chosen otherwise. I remember the impression made on me by my first reading, in the late 1960s, of Bruno Bettelheim on psychological trauma in the concentration camps, and especially his description of the extreme passivity to which some inmates succumbed. Such people were called "muselman," and Bettelheim describes their extreme personality change as follows:

---

[1]*Hebrew abbreviation for "May her memory be for a blessing."—Editor's note*

. . . [T]hey were people so deprived of affect, self-esteem, and every form of stimulation, so totally exhausted, both physically and emotionally, that they had given the environment total power over them . . . all conscious awareness of stimuli coming from the outside was blocked out, and with it all response to anything but inner stimuli. [They became] objects, but with this they gave up being persons . . . they behaved as if they were not thinking, not feeling, unable to act or respond, moved only by things outside themselves.

Why didn't most of our parents, most of the time, become zombies of this sort, not during the concentration camps, and not after? And the fact is that they didn't. On the contrary, as you heard from Professor Bauer last night, they demonstrated a degree of initiative, inventiveness, determination—*gevureh*—which played the key role in lowering the curtain on the British Empire in *Eretz Yisrael*. They couldn't have done what they did without the eventual help and direction of the Jewish Agency's *shlichim*, of the Joint, and the Jewish chaplains of the American and British armies. But they began to organize themselves before the Jewish Brigade arrived in late June 1945, and before the Joint came on the scene in August of that year. The Bricha organization and the central and camp committees in the American and British zones remained their show. To be sure, not everyone was an Abba Kovner, a Yossel Rosensaft, a Samuel Gringauz, a Zalman Grinberg, a Treger, a Shalit,[2] but there were quite a few of them, and there were so many others who put their shoulders to the wheel, who were willing, in the later idiom of my generation, to put their bodies on the line.

There must have been hundreds who worked on the DP newspapers, which Professor Bauer mentioned only in passing. Despite the difficulty of obtaining printing presses and Hebrew type, the first newspapers[3] appeared in Landsberg, *Landsberger Lager Cajtung*, beginning on October 8, 1945, and Munich, *Undzer Weg*, published weekly beginning October 22, 1945. These were joined in the winter of 1945–46 by others: *A Heim* in Leipheim, *Oyf der Fray* in Stuttgart, *Undzer Hoffnung* in Eschwege, *Undzer Wort* in Bamberg, *Undzer Leben* in Berlin, *Undzer Mut* in Zeilsheim, *Der Neuer Moment* in Regensburg, *Dos Fraje Wort* in Feldafing, *Bamidbar* in Foehrenwald, *D.P. Express* in Munich, and *Der Morgen* in Bad Reichenhall.

Where did the feverish social and cultural activism of our parents during those days come from? And what explains the unmatched birthrate of the Jewish DP camps in late 1946 through 1948?

For me, the clue to that mystery is to be found in the name they gave themselves: Sh'erit ha-Pletah. That term has a certain currency in Jewish tradition. Sh'erit ha-Pletah means "saving remnant." Not "saved remnant"; that would have been a redundancy. Not even "surviving remnant" as you'll find in the historical overview the Museum prepared and included in our portfolios for this conference. They saw themselves as the remnant that saves, that redeems, the family and the community as a whole, the community from which they came. That is why the first book-length history of the displaced persons, Leo W. Schwarz's 1953 work, was titled, *The Redeemers*. And when Herbert Agar published a history of the DPs and the Joint seven years later, he called it *The Saving Remnant*. In the title page of that volume, Agar quotes a sentence from Chaim Weizmann, written in 1933: "If, before I die, there are a half million Jews in Palestine, I shall be content,

[2] *Abba Kovner, who later became one of the foremost Israeli poets, was a Jewish partisan commander in the Lithuanian-Belorussian forests, and a leader of the Bricha. Josef (Yossel) Rosensaft was the leader of the Jewish DPs in the British zone of Germany. Samuel Gringauz, Zalman Grinberg, David Treger, and Levi Shalit were leaders of the Jewish DPs in the American zone.—Editor's note*

[3] *Samuel Norich's reference is to DP camp newspapers published in the American zone of Germany. The first issue of* Undzer Shtimme (Our Voice) *appeared in the Bergen-Belsen DP camp in the British zone on July 12, 1945.—Editor's note*

because I know that this 'Saving Remnant' will survive." The earliest reference to this concept that I'm aware of in Jewish texts occurs in Genesis, chapter 45, verse 7: "*Vayishlakheni elokim lifneykhem lashum lakhem sherit ba'aretz u'le'hakhayot lakhem lifleyta gedolah.*" It occurs when Joseph reveals himself to his brothers, who now fear that the second to the pharaoh in Egypt will exact retribution on them for what they did to him. But Joseph tells them no, that it was in fact God's plan to save them and their family: "And God sent me before you to give you a remnant on the earth, and to save you alive for a great deliverance."

They didn't call themselves survivors, though they knew the term—in Yiddish it is "*Lebn-geblibene.*" Later, when we arrived in America, Americans and American Jews called us "refugees" at first. Still later, when we entered the public consciousness of America, it was as "survivors" and "children of survivors." That term may be fine for external consumption—*klapey khutz*—but for understanding ourselves and the sources of our parents' motivation, Sh'erit ha-Pletah tells us more. Perhaps we can even get America to use the term "saving remnant."[4]

Far from the Holocaust having created the State of Israel, it was the instinctive need of the survivors to save Vilna—to save something of the destroyed families and the destroyed Jewish communities from which they had come—that animated them and other Jews who created the Jewish state.

I'd like to close with one more personal recollection. I remember, in 1987, during the *shloshim* after my mother, standing in a *minyan* at the Teaneck Jewish Center, when a feeling came over me that it was now up to me to give her life, that the genetic and biological relationship between us—that she had given me life—was now reversed. I know I'm not the only one to have had that feeling while mourning the death of a parent. I don't know whether it's common among children of the Sh'erit ha-Pletah, whether it is in fact a feeling known to every mother's child. But of one thing I am certain: that our parents felt exactly that feeling in 1945 and 1946. And here we are.

[4]*The term* lifleyta *is used earlier in Genesis 32:9, describing Jacob's return to his native land after spending 14 years at the home of his father-in-law, Laban. Concerned about a possible attack from his brother, Esau, Jacob divided his family and possessions into two separate camps, so that if Esau were to attack one of the camps, "the camp which is left shall escape," in Hebrew, ". . . ha-makhaneh ha-nish'ar* lifleyta.*"*

The one time that the full term "Sh'erit ha-Pletah" is used in the Bible is in Chronicles 4:43, where the descendants of Judah are recorded as having destroyed "the remnant of the Amalekites that had survived," that is, in Hebrew, ". . . et sh'erit ha'pletah la-amalek. . . ."

In a footnote at page 18 in the 1953 book, The Redeemers: A Saga of the Years 1945–1952, *cited above by Sam Norich, Leo W. Schwarz actually discusses the biblical origin of the term "Sh'erit ha-Pletah," and its use by Jewish Holocaust survivors to describe themselves following their liberation: "As there is no exact equivalent of this expression in English, and its use among the liberated people was constant, there has been no alternative but to introduce it into English. The phrase Sheerit Hapletah is Biblical in origin, being used in the Book of Chronicles to describe the remnant that survived the Assyrian conquest [sic]. At the period in the above page [that is, May 1945] it was used to denote the Surviving Remnant of the Destruction during the Second World War; but as time went on, it came to be used with ideas and shades of meaning that are only partly suggested in the Saving Remnant."*

She'erit Ha'Pletah in Celle, a July 1945 publication listing 2,134 Jewish survivors in a DP camp near Bergen-Belsen in the British zone by name, previous nationality, date of birth, and town of origin, was one of the earliest times that the term was used in print. (See Isaac Levy, Witness to Evil: Bergen-Belsen, 1945 *[London, 1995], 54.) Thus, certainly at first, "Sh'erit ha-Pletah" was primarily a descriptive term to denote those who had survived the Holocaust, that is, the "surviving (or saved) remnant," of European Jewry.—Editor's note*

THE CHALLENGE WE FACE TODAY

The Honorable Sam Gejdenson

Member of Congress (Democrat—Connecticut)

Good evening. I was born in a displaced persons' camp in Eschwege, Germany. My parents were displaced Jewish Holocaust survivors. I'd like to begin today by telling you a bit about my own history and where I come from. Like many of you, my parents are from Eastern Europe. My father was born in a small village called Parfianiavo, located in what was then Poland, and what is now Belarus. My mother comes from Vilna. She never lets him forget that he came from a *shtetl,* a *dorf,* while she grew up in Vilna—the height of Jewish civilization at that time—*Yerushalayim D'Lita,* the Jerusalem of Lithuania.

This past June, I traveled to each of my parents' birthplaces. I saw Vilna, the place from which my mother, like so many others, fled during World War II to escape from the Nazis, and Parfianiavo, home to 400 Jews, including my grandparents, who saw their last day in 1941, when they were marched to their deaths by German troops. In Parfianiavo, I met the Catholic woman who saved my father's life. My father and his brother were taken in by Mrs. Stankevich, a Catholic woman, who gave them shelter in her family's barn. I will never forget the story she told me, as she sat on her bed, an elderly woman of 94 years. It was Christmas night, during the height of World War II. Her son, who was working in a business occupied and run by the Nazis, came home for Christmas that night. She saw him and she started wailing. "What's wrong?" he asked. In tears, she responded, "We have eight children and not enough food. I'm hiding two Jews in the barn, and now that I've told you, you'll get drunk and tell your friends. Your friends will tell the Nazis and they will come and kill the Jews." "No, mother," he replied. "If I get drunk and tell my friends, the Nazis will kill our entire family and maybe even the whole village."

And that was the truth. This woman risked everything—her life, her home, her children— to do the right thing. Her courage just astounds me.

My family came to the United States on October 13, 1949, on the USS *General Stewart.* We began a new life in America, in Eastern Connecticut. As a young kid, listening to the story of this Catholic woman, I used to ask myself, "If faced with similar circumstances, would I have the courage to act so selflessly?" As a young person, it was fairly easy. Now, as a husband, and the father of four children, the trial is more complex.

Our generation is unique, in the sense that while we experience a lot of angst, anger, hurt, pain, frustration, and fears, we really have no way of knowing the kind of suffering our parents went through. The Holocaust was not on our watch. We weren't tested by this occurrence. And sometimes, I think we forget what a challenge it really was, not just to Jews, but to non-Jews as well.

We face different tests today. As I look around this room, I recognize a lot of the faces here—of people deeply involved in the Jewish community, in Jewish issues. But we've got to do more than that. Think about it for a moment. What if we'd gone back to Mrs. Stankevich and said, "Why didn't you save the two Gejdenson boys when they came to your barn that cold winter night?" And she said, "Oh you know, I was worried about them, but I had to take care of my *own* family. I had to worry about *our own* well-being. Our village was in trouble, occupied by the Nazis. I cared, but I couldn't do anything about other people."

Those of us who bear the legacy of suffering cannot accept that answer. We have to lead the fight no matter where it is. And we are tested in strange ways each and every day. Where are the Jewish voices when Bob Jones University demonizes Catholics? Where were we when others tried to denigrate Hispanic Americans by pursuing English-only education? Where are we when gay rights come under attack? Where is the indignation we felt when the world was silent to our own suffering?

This year in Congress, the foreign aid bill originally contained no money for the Wye peace process, no money for Africa, and no money for Latin America. As the senior Democratic member of the House International Relations Committee, I got the Jews together in the House—about 20-some of us—and we unanimously decided to oppose the foreign aid bill. Not an easy thing to do. Especially when you consider a lot of that money is going to Israel. A few days later, the money for the peace process was restored. But there was still nothing in there for Africa or for Latin America. We stood firm. This time, I brought in others: Sandy Berger, the White House national security adviser, and Jack Lew, the head of the Office of Management and Budget. Close to a majority of Jews in the House voted against the bill. As a result, we were able to get the funds for Africa and Latin America as well.

As Jews I believe we have an obligation. We bear a unique legacy that obligates us to fight for others in need.

It is a little frightening sometimes. I was sitting in the White House on the eve of the war in Kosovo. To me, it was a simple decision. Do we allow Mr. Milosevic to continue his campaign of ethnic cleansing or do we intervene? Suddenly, one senator gets up and says, Mr. President, I'd be with you, but they haven't killed enough people yet. The numbers aren't that big. It reminded me of my father's story—of the Jews of Parfianiavo. One day, the Germans went into the ghetto; they took out the Jews, about 400, and they put them in a little area. They gunned them down and buried them. It wasn't 10,000; it wasn't 6 million; it wasn't a large number. It had been done probably dozens of times before. This wasn't an astounding act. But it was one act of many. And it was only at the end of the war that somebody with a calculator figured out we hit an all-time record.

I was proud to see that the Jewish members of Congress, a number of them Democrats, were the first ones to stand up. There was no perfect answer here. But allowing Milosevic to go through Kosovo and kill people because they were of Albanian ancestry, or Muslims instead of Christians, is something we simply cannot abide by. And with American leadership, we stopped Milosevic. But there are plenty of places we haven't acted. They killed a million and a half Cambodians. Nobody batted an eye. In Rwanda, they killed close to 800,000 people in 90 days. There's murder going on in much of Africa—West Africa and East Africa.

It's not that the world doesn't care about these people. But it's hard to get the world to focus. If I told you that you could save people right here and now, with little or no cost to you, most of you would probably do it. Now, if I said that might entail putting your kids in harm's way, it's an entirely different equation.

Each and every one of us here stands as a legacy of hope, courage, and determination. I challenge you to lead the fight to ensure that none of these hatreds flourish unabated. It's not an easy job. And it's not just a job for the federation or for Jewish organizations. Reach out to Black and Hispanic members of your community before there's an incident. Don't wait for leaders to solve this problem. It's up to you. You are more powerful than the elected leaders or the religious leaders. At the end of the day, it's the people who make the difference.

I remember a rally on the Mall to fight for the rights of the Soviet Jewry. Close to a quarter of a million people came out: Jews, non-Jews, regular people. There were about a hundred big shots on this podium at the front of the Mall, elbowing their way forward to make sure that CNN and ABC and CBS would get a good shot of them for their own constituencies. I happened to be at the back banister, not because I don't need publicity as an elected official, but because I had my two little kids with me and it is hard to elbow people when you are with kids who are only knee-high.

And suddenly, it dawned on me. If there had been no podium, no raised platform for the big shots, 250,000 people would still have been there, and the networks and the live coverage would still have continued. If a hundred heads of organizations, presidents, congressmen, senators, heads of synagogues, and rabbis showed up on the Mall, nobody would care. It would be a blip on the TV screen, a little protest today in Washington from people who do it professionally. But this was real; it was significant. This was real people making a real difference.

I'm not a biblical scholar, but the interesting thing to me about the character of Moses is that he was part of the "establishment." He wasn't a slave. He ate with the pharaoh. He was in the country clubs, in the boardrooms. But he joined the revolution to fight for people who were being abused.

For those of us who have attained some power in society, who are no longer on the outside looking in, we ought not take that status as some form of long-term protection. German Jews were in Germany long before the Holocaust. They were heroes of World War I and the military. To the rest of us, they appeared so assimilated that it was hard to recognize our brethren until after the war. Jews may not be the first targeted, but we are seldom the last.

The challenges we face today are much more subtle. Gone are the yellow armbands, the numbered tattoos. In their place are more subtle questions, like aid for parochial schools or the battle over school prayer. How many of us have said, "Well, maybe aid for parochial school wouldn't be so bad? After all, some of these are even Jewish schools. What's the harm done in saying a prayer at the beginning of class?" Yet, we fail to realize that the separation between church and state has been critical to making this country great. We neglect to consider the alternatives, places like Bosnia or Kosovo, where religion continues to drive a wedge between people.

We would like to think that we are safe here, that nothing is going to happen to us. But we had better guarantee that it does not happen here. Jefferson said it best. "Eternal vigilance is the price of liberty," he said. Take our life and renewal and use it to fight for freedom. Thank you very much.

THE DP EXPERIENCE

INTRODUCTORY REMARKS

Romana Strochlitz Primus

This morning we will hear about the DP years from several different perspectives. First, Sam Bloch will give an overview of the Jewish DP experience. He is the president of the World Federation of Bergen-Belsen Survivors Assosications, and senior vice president of the American Gathering of Jewish Holocaust Survivors. He was also the youngest member of the Jewish Committee in the Bergen-Belsen DP camp.

Sam will be followed by Rabbi Herbert Friedman, who brings the perspective of the military chaplain to this conference. Rabbi Friedman is now the executive director of the Wexner Heritage Foundation. During the DP era he was military assistant to the advisor on Jewish affairs in the American zone of Germany.

Following Rabbi Friedman, to wrap up the session, we will hear a brief discussion of relevant historical issues from Professor Henry Friedlander, a Holocaust survivor who is professor of history in the Department of Jewish Studies of Brooklyn College, City University of New York.

A HOLOCAUST SURVIVOR'S PERSPECTIVE

Sam E. Bloch

President, World Federation of Bergen-Belsen Survivors Associations; Holocaust survivor; member, Jewish Committee, Bergen-Belsen DP camp

This is an extraordinary program that mirrors fully the aftermath of the Holocaust and our rebirth and rehabilitation in the DP camps. Before anything else, let me express our most heartwarming thanks to our young friends of the Second Generation for their initiative and thoughtfulness in organizing this comprehensive program of remembrance.

As to the subject itself, one might ask: What significance can there be for the roughly five years we, the survivors, spent in displaced persons camps in Germany and Austria, compared with our long history of exile and dispersion, throughout the world? Five years versus 2,000 years of exile! We cannot find any comparison just as we cannot compare our tragedy, the slaughter of a third of our people, with any other wave of pogroms and massacres that our people faced in the Diaspora. I do not want to dwell here on our tragedy. By now, the facts are well known to all: the barbarism of the German Nazis and their helpers, the humiliation and dehumanization of the victims, the shooting and the gassing, the robbery of our possessions, the fire which had engulfed us, and the indifference of the world around us. The purpose of our meeting is to bring back memories of rebirth of the survivors, the epic story of rehabilitation and the return to life.

Take Bergen-Belsen, for instance, the largest DP camp, where I spent nearly five years after the liberation, serving in many capacities as an elected member of the camp's Jewish Committee. Bergen-Belsen became a unique symbol not only of the horrors of the Holocaust but of the great miracle of rebirth. Of course, the infamy of the Nazi concentration camp with its mass graves will remain attached to its name till the end of time. There was, however, another Belsen, one that was the very opposite of our suffering and destruction. This was the post-1945 Bergen-Belsen, which proved that the flames that had consumed Jewish flesh and bones were powerless to kill the sources of our dreams for life and regeneration. This applies not only to the Belsen DP camp, but to all other DP camps throughout Germany and Austria, where about 200,000 survivors found their first temporary shelter-home to begin life again. Looking back to those years, they are sometimes beyond comprehension by the human mind for those who were not there, who may have heard or read about the aftermath of the war in some books or descriptive articles.

When freedom dawned over Belsen and the other places in the valleys of death, it seemed to awaken among the survivors, just out of the ashes, all the dormant springs of Jewish creativity. The survivors emerged from the death camps with a strong will to rebuild their lives, with boundless determination and dedication, as rapidly as possible. Belsen, Foehrenwald, Landsberg, Zeilsheim, Feldafing, Linz, and so many other small or larger DP camps, became vibrant centers of rehabilitation, reconstruction, and rebirth, manifested by both individuals and organized groups. Life broke through the harsh German and Austrian soil to assert its superiority to death and destruction. The reawakening, the physical, emotional, and spiritual revival of the survivors, is the greatest miracle of those years. And so was the extensive dynamic cultural activity which turned people, who only yesterday were almost lifeless heaps of bones, into creative Jewish communities, with blessed vitality and dynamism. Despite the bygone years, the life in the DP camps is still vivid in our memory.

We came from many lands, diverse cultures and traditions, and varying ways of life, even speaking different languages. But despite all this, we were motivated by a strong feeling of our common fate, our common past, our common sufferings, and our common hope for the future. This feeling forged among us a brotherly unity of common dreams and aspirations. What a mixture of people it was. The traditionalist Polish Jew and his Hungarian brother and sister, remnants of German and Czech Jewry, splinters of Lithuania and Greek brothers. We all closed ranks and stayed together in mighty unity.

We remember too well how we had to fight for recognition of our Jewish identity as "Jews," especially in the British zone. The British military authorities, for their own political reasons, classified us as displaced persons of our respective earlier national origins of the countries from which we came. We insisted on a pure and simple identification as Jews and Jews only, without reference to the countries of our origin to which we refused to return. This was a powerful manifestation of Jewish pride, and finally, we prevailed. And so, we had to remain in the DP camp for several years—homeless.

Of material goods we possessed nothing, and yet we were not helpless. We knew that we had to stand on our own feet from the start, without minimizing the help of overseas Jewish organizations. As a result, life in the DP camps was a reality of our common action and unified Jewish behavior. The DP camps witnessed the beginning of Jewish self-administration in the fullest sense. In this respect the historical achievement of the Sh'erit ha-Pletah, will remain unique and permanent—the determination to transform the collapse of European Jewry into the beginning of national redemption; to give the national striving for revenge the character of a folk renaissance; to act as an awakener of national Jewish consciousness throughout the world; to transform the painful respect the Jew feels for our martyrdom into an imperative for Jewish independence.

For the Jewish survivors in the DP camps it was not necessary to be exposed to Zionist propaganda in order to embrace the cause of a Jewish free homeland. Our national consciousness and Zionist sentiments had been with us since our childhood, in our destroyed homes—a legacy of previous generations. But in the DP camps, especially in view of our own homelessness, this sentiment acquired a deeper meaning and motivation.

A few words about the political activities vis-à-vis the outside world. In June 1945, President Truman's special emissary, Earl G. Harrison, came to Belsen where he met with leaders of the Jewish DPs. His task was to find the ways and means to help the survivors, which resulted in President Truman's historic demand for the British to allow 100,000 Jewish survivors to immigrate to Palestine.

In November 1945, David Ben Gurion came to Belsen, proclaiming a message of hope to the survivors. "Don't despair," he said, and pointing to his hair, he added, "I can assure you that these white hairs will live to see the free sovereign Jewish state which will provide for all of you a final home."

In January 1946, the Anglo-American Committee of Inquiry on Palestine came to Belsen to take evidence, and in the spring of 1947 the UN Special Committee on Palestine arrived in Belsen. In both cases they heard the loud and clear voice of the survivors: There is only one place on the globe for us—Eretz Israel. It so happened that at the time of the second of these visits, a transport of several hundred *olim* departed to Palestine. The committee witnessed their departure and the mighty *Hatikva* of the onlookers, which moved them more than any other statement.

All these events were part of the struggle for the Jewish homeland. Belsen and all the other DP camps played a pivotal role in the political struggle for Jewish statehood, which was fully recognized by leaders of world Jewry and the State of Israel.

Long before the proclamation of the State of Israel, the Sh'erit ha-Pletah established their own miniature states within the DP camps. Battling against the occupying power, as I mentioned earlier, the Jews attained recognition as a unique independent entity. The DP camps became seeds of a Jewish state in the making. Thanks to national concentration in the camps, some 200,000 surviving Jews were ingathered, economically sustained, culturally organized, and humanly rehabilitated. Tens of thousands of new families were established resulting in an unsurpassed birthrate. In Bergen-Belsen alone, more than 2,000 babies were born after the liberation.

The Jewish DPs yearned for a warm hand of friendship, for outside people to accept them as they were, ill or healthy, strong or weak. Overseas organizations came to the DP camps to render assistance. We expected from them complete identification with us, based on national Jewish brotherhood, not only pity. The overseas organizations, the JDC, the British Relief Units, HIAS, ORT, the Jewish Agency, the World Jewish Congress and, above all, the soldiers of the Jewish Brigade stretched out to us their warm reassuring hands. Yes, they appeared ready to understand our burden of pain and our aspirations.

The readiness of the *Yishuv* in Eretz Israel to help us at any price and take us out of Germany forged a strong bond between us. They helped us in so many ways, helping to reawaken in us our self-respect and the consciousness of equality.

The flight and rescue operations, known as the Bricha movement, the epic story of Aliya Bet, the so-called illegal aliya of the survivors trying to break the British blockade of the shores of then Palestine, will forever remain a chapter of superhuman heroism. The *Exodus* affair in September 1947 went into history as a symbol of the inevitable spirit of bravery and determination and yearning for a new homeland. The DP camp of Bergen-Belsen played a very special role in these events, especially after the *maapilim* were forcefully brought back to Germany, and brought to the Pappendorf and Amstau internment camps close to the Belsen DP camp. The final stage of this historic drama was played out at Belsen.

Permit me to relate to you a dramatic, until now, unpublicized episode which involves the *Exodus* in Hamburg. When the British deported the *maapilim* back to Germany, thousands of survivors assembled in Belsen in a stormy demonstration against this evil act. From Belsen we proceeded to Hamburg to the docks at the harbor, precisely at the time the *maapilim* were unloaded from the British military vessels. The tension was high as the mass of our people pressed closer to the shoreline, closer to the naval vessels, screaming to make our voices heard by the *maapilim* as they were forced into trucks. We were surrounded by British troops, commanded by a colonel of the military police.

As the mass of people almost stormed the gates at the docks, the colonel threatened to shoot. At that tense moment, Josef Rosensaft, the chairman of the Central Jewish Committee in the British zone, and all of us heading the demonstration, unbuttoned our shirts, exposing our bare chests, exclaiming: "Shoot! We witnessed such acts from the German murderers, shame on you. You are our liberators!" The colonel, probably moved by our behavior, ordered the guards to lower their arms, at which time the mass opened up with a mighty *Hatikva*. Believe it or not, he saluted with his right hand. And there was no violence, which could have easily ended in bloodshed.

Later on, we shared with the deported *maapilim* our food in brotherly solidarity and helped them gradually to disappear by moving them illegally in small groups to Belsen. This was the last stage of the historic drama, played out at Belsen, before they finally came to Palestine.

Another dramatic story is that of a successful operation of clandestine arms shipments from Bergen-Belsen for the Haganah in Palestine in the years preceding the proclamation of the State of Israel. Also, there was the training of volunteers for the Haganah disguised as members of the Jewish camp police, which possessed arms legally in Belsen, and the radio broadcasts at 6 p.m. of the news from Palestine. Time does not permit us to describe in detail all these activities of which we are so proud.

Ours is not only the legacy of our tragic past and heroic return to life. There is more to it. The question is: What will remain of the cultural heritage of our parents and grandparents? After all, we the survivors are the last generation of a glorious history. Our younger generations, together with us, are the bridge between yesterday and tomorrow. I refer particularly to the creative, spiritual, and cultural history of European Jewry of which we are the surviving remnants. What will we leave behind to nourish the Jewish historical process of the future? What will we bring forth upon the Jewish world of our children from the world of yesterday which is no more? The Shoah and our experiences, of each and everyone of us, brought forth a profound indelible influence upon the Jewish community—in general, on its self-perception and outlook.

Having emerged from the ashes of the kingdom of death, our concern was not only to begin life again, but how to transmit to our children and to the world around us, the innermost meaning of Jewish existence, the prerequisite understanding of the unique process of Jewish history. All our cultural and educational activities in the DP camps were part and parcel of this effort. Yes, we carried in the DP camps the torch of our cultural heritage and values, which was demonstrated daily in our life and actions. The Jewish spirit of our destroyed homes and knowledge succeeded to secure the traditional Jewish continuity. Exhausted as we were, we nevertheless managed to rejuvenate ourselves, practice and promote self-reliance and self-assurance. There was in all of us a wonderful creative drive. All these stirring trends rekindled in all of us the Jewish soul of our parents, with many ideas of collective renewal. Yes, we succeeded to produce from our own internal spiritual sources the needed dynamics to join the march of Jewish national renewal. We remained faithful to the cultural and spiritual foundations of the world of yesteryear, in is fullest dimensions, which was reflected in every aspect of life in the DP camp.

Memory requires that we remember not only death, but also life—the flourishing Jewish communities of Eastern and Central Europe. The many monuments, memorials, commemorations of the Shoah, essential as they are, almost all of them, in most cases, are dominated by the account of the manner in which Jews were murdered and Jewish communities destroyed. The manner in which they existed, flourished prior to the destruction is quite often overlooked and overshadowed. Our martyrs, we see them abused, dehumanized, beaten, shot, gassed, and burned, but not enough is shown of their outstanding achievements, creativity, private and public, individual and collective. Our young people, whom we try to expose to the horrors of the Holocaust, are not enough exposed to the richness of the Jewish world that was—to the great academies of learning, the schools, Hassidic courts, the extraordinary Yiddish and Hebrew literature, to the Jewish contributions to music, art, and culture. So, we must remember not only whom we lost, but what we lost. We must give our children and grandchildren a sense of spiritual purpose, remembrance, and a living connection and identification with Jewish values and traditions. After all, the link for each generation to the next is the cement that binds us as a people. One future will be shaped by our Jewishness, by acting together and not alone.

It is difficult in one limited presentation to depict in more detail all aspects of life in the DP camps. It will remain forever a most glorious chapter in the history of the Holocaust—a unique example of organized Jewish political, cultural, and social activity, the scene of a successful struggle for Jewish and human rights. Throughout this conference, I hope that you will be able to sense the daily life, the joys, and sorrows of the survivors, the cultural activities, the kindergartens and schools, weddings and births of new babies, the yeshivot, the medical facilities, the sports clubs, the theatrical groups, the orchestras, the kibbutzim, the demonstrations, the festivals and memorial meetings, the celebrations, Zionist activities, the publications, the newspapers, exhibitions, and so forth—all the manifestations of human life and dynamic existence. All this is also depicted in the relevant exhibition at the United States Holocaust Memorial Museum. A very special comprehensive exhibition on the Bergen-Belsen DP camp is also on display in the B'nai B'rith Klutznick National Jewish Museum here in Washington. I want to give special recognition to Jean Bloch Rosensaft for her invaluable help as curator of the Belsen exhibition.

In conclusion, the memory of the Shoah and of our experiences during the DP era, as I said earlier, created a lasting bond of friendship, solidarity, and unity among the survivors, along with their dedication to remembrance, of which we are so proud. To quote from the last issues of one of the DP newspapers on the eve of the closing of the camp and the departure of the survivors to Israel, America, and other lands:

> Years will pass, people will fade, leaders will vanish, groups will disintegrate. New people, leaders, groups will arrive. But over land and sea, through the years and generations, through chaos and rebirth, the achievements of the Sh'erit ha-Pletah will shine forever. Because it gathered the remnants of a decimated Jewry, hewed out a path for the State of Israel, and handed down the torch of Jewish civilization to people everywhere.

A Military Chaplain's Perspective

Rabbi Herbert A. Friedman

Executive Director, Wexner Heritage Foundation; Military Assistant to the Advisor on Jewish Affairs, U.S. Military Authorities in Germany and Austria

Yes, it will be a different perspective. Sam Bloch gave us a beautiful, emotional, comprehensive, Jewish, nationalistic view of all the right factors. And yet that's not the whole story and the people who arranged this conference showed wisdom in asking for you to hear the complete background.

I was a military chaplain, a captain in the 9th Infantry Division of the Third Army commanded by General Patton. We ended the war at Wasserburg-am-Inn, which was almost opposite Salzburg, Austria, and not far from Hitler's house in Berchtesgaden. When the war ended I started to take trucks from the quartermaster and the transportation depot to comb the area south of Munich in which there were several large DP camps—Foehrenwald, Feldafing, St. Ottilien, and others. That area is full of lakes and dark forests, and in those woods there were units of *Edelweiss,* an extremist fanatical Nazi youth organization. Even though the war was over, they continued to try to terrorize the small numbers of survivors who came out from the underground munitions factories where they had been working as slave laborers in German armaments factories to keep the German military machine going. Thousands died, thousands more emerged and came to the surface. I started to go through the woods, picking them up. They were not just Jews. We could only put 50 to 60 people on a truck, a six-wheel GMC. And if you collect 60 people you have to look for a place where you can find a building that has got two walls or one wall and a roof. Germany was laid flat at the end of the war, you know that, and if you have 60 people and they have just come out of the hell of several years and they are miraculously alive, you then begin with the very basic things: Where can I place them? I then go and bring blankets, I then go and bring DDT powder, I have to fight the lice— the lice eat human blood, etc., etc., etc.

It was during those tumultuous days, truckload after truckload, and finding a wrecked barn, finding a small German city hall in a little village, throwing everybody out, all you did was come into this little Rathaus, hit your Colt 45 with a hard bang on the table, and say, "This house is *Beschlagnamt.*" (This house is hereby requisitioned.) By whose authority? Nobody's except the Colt, the American uniform, and the ragged survivors out on the truck. You want that house evacuated and you want all the German workers out and you want the house clean and you want it in 24 hours and the Germans understand that. And so that's how the Jewish DP camps gradually came to be.

There was no order, there was no super body giving instructions, it was all hit and miss. The war ended in May and by September we had already collected some thousands of people. Suddenly I got a telephone call. I was in a little village called Bad Tölz down near the Alps near Garmisch Partenkirchen and the lady on the phone said that she wanted to meet me, and she offered me the name and room number of her hotel. So why not? She was in Paris. And so some days later I was at the Royal Monceau Hotel on Avenue Foch and she answered my knock at the door and left me standing in the corridor, did not invite me in. Asked me if I would work for them. I said, "Who is them?" And she said, "Haganah, Aliya Bet, Bricha." You know I'm a rational person and I'm accustomed to thinking things through, pro and con. I try to get facts on both sides of an issue in order to try to decide what to do. Well, all of that falls apart in this atmosphere of tension, nervousness, the fate of thousands of people to be decided. And so your gut has to tell you, not your intellect. I said yes.

She then walked across the room, I could see she had the door open and out of another door at the end, a short fellow with white hair whom Sam described so properly, walked out. She did not introduce him, he walked up to me, she said, "Friedman says he'll work for us." He said, "Thank you." Turned around, walked out. I never saw him again for a year. I said, "Who was he?" She said, "His name is David Ben Gurion." I said, "Who is he?" And she said, "He's the chairman of the Haganah. He is hiding from the British here in this hotel and if you remember Edgar Allan Poe's story about the purloined letter, if you want to hide something, hide it right under the other person's nose." When Ben Gurion was hiding together with Moshe Sneh from the British, who had arrested everybody in Palestine connected with the Jewish Agency, where did they go? They went to British army headquarters in the Royal Monceau Hotel, with the British flag flying outside the hotel. And these two guys are running the Haganah operation right under the British nose, it was brilliant, it was gorgeous. She then invited me from the corridor into the room, sat me down, gave me a cup of coffee, and I asked, "What do I do now?" She said, "Number one, get yourself transferred to Berlin. Number two, we will send you men from the brigade, the Palestine brigade." Bivouacked in Belgium there were thousands of Jewish trained soldiers who had fought with the British up the Italian Peninsula, they were good soldiers, they were well armed, they were experienced, and the British did not want them to go back to Palestine at that point. So the British kept them in bivouac in Belgium. What were they doing? They were picking up cigarette butts; they were painting stones, whitewashing them. You know what you do in a camp when you have nothing else to do? Well you don't know. But what you do in a camp when you have nothing else to do, you try to keep the house clean.

"I will send you," said she, "all the drivers, gunners, and mechanics you need, and you will do the following: In Berlin you will get yourself situated, then you will let me know, then I will send you all these men. You steal enough trucks and enough gas tickets to last you for a year and you will go every day at 6 p.m. in the evening from Berlin up to Stettin." How many people in this room came out of Stettin into Berlin? Okay, well I brought you and I'm delighted.

From Berlin up to Stettin on the Polish border up near the Baltic Sea was 150 kilometers. It was six hours of driving through the Russian zone of Germany, more difficult. The border was Russian on one side, Polish on the other side, six trucks, 50 people on the truck, 300 people. Load the trucks, cover it up with a tarpaulin, that whole thing has to take a half an hour. Pay the bribe on both sides, the bribe was one carton of cigarettes per Jew and the carton of cigarettes on the black market was $150; 300 people times $150 is $45,000 a night every night, every night, every night. We brought 90,000 people down through that route in 1946. It was a schlep to get the money, to get the cigarettes. I was the only Jewish chaplain in Berlin, that's an incidental fact, but it gave me a resource. British, French, Russian, and American armies, four Allied troops, were there, headquartered in Berlin. In all four armies there were 2,000 Jewish soldiers. The first seder we had in Berlin after liberation was held in Schöneberg Rathaus, the very building from whose balcony President Kennedy later made his famous speech, *"Ich bin ein Berliner."* He didn't know that Berliner was a slang word for a jelly donut. He thought he was saying, "I am a Berlin citizen." He wanted to express friendship between America and the new Germany. So that's always been a great inner story.

Two thousand troops at a Passover seder after liberation, Jewish troops. I got cigarettes from all of them. I got cigarettes from my father in Connecticut. I had the army postal officials on my doorstep in Berlin every single day looking at these huge mail sacks full of cigarettes. And finally, finally when we had one port opening in Europe at Antwerp, the Joint, the blessed Joint Distribution Committee, brought shiploads in and I then began to get freight car loads full of cigarettes, and then the flow was going smoothly.

Now I was in uniform. I'm an American army captain chaplain and I have military duties, of which I didn't do very many. And I was very busy with this operation. Now I tell you this as the background story of how the DP community assembled itself. In the beginning, the minute that the war was over, the Jews were intermingled, they were not separate. There were 10 million slave laborers on German soil when the war ended—French, British, Dutch, from every country, Romania, Bulgaria, and as far east as Tajikistan and Azerbaijan, way beyond the Ural Mountains, deep in Russia. All of these people whom the Germans had captured as prisoners and who were working as slave laborers, millions dying, but also millions living. All had to be repatriated back to their home countries.

At the beginning under General Patton who was a pragmatic, nonemotional, tough soldier, he made no distinction and he said, "I don't want to bother with any of them. I'm an army man, I don't know how to deal with civilians." He had an argument with General Eisenhower on that subject. General Eisenhower said, "You are right, the army does not know how to deal with civilians but the thing you have to understand is that Jewish civilians are different from other civilians and we have to separate out the Jews from the others. The Jews cannot go into the same camp with people—Lithuanians, Poles, other people—who were cooperating with the Nazis and who were persecuting Jews. So you have to separate them." And that's how separate Jewish camps began to come into existence, about three months after the war ended. There was a big fight later on between Patton and Eisenhower because Patton was setting those Jewish camps up with sentries around them, with the gates locked, requiring passes in and out, and word of that got back to Eisenhower and he didn't like it and he called Patton in and said, "George, why don't you be nice to these people." And Patton said, "Why the hell should I be?" And Eisenhower said, "Well among other reasons because I'm ordering you to do so." Finished. Later, Eisenhower removed Patton as commander of the Third Army.

The Jewish camps were set up. A huge influx of Polish refugees into Germany took place after the pogrom in Kielce, on the 4th of July 1946. Forty-two Jews were killed and laid out like firewood, like logs around the central fountain in town. Rabbi Phillip Bernstein and I were there a week later, at General McNarney's request. We reported to him that 150,000 Jews would be flooding in. That's when the flood started. Our figures at army headquarters at the end of 1946 were 250,000 people in 64 camps in the American zones of Germany and Austria. In 1947 the *Exodus* ship of Bricha loaded in Port-de-Bouc near Marseille and sailed from Sète, on the other side of Marseille. I helped bring 5,000 people to that ship. That required a convoy from the American zone of Germany, down across France into French territory, of 100 trucks with 5,000 people. You can imagine how many side runners we had and how many armored cars we had at fore and aft. We got 4,400 onto the ship and off she went. She wound up of course back in Sam Bloch's territory, in Bergen-Belsen. He told you the end of the story.

So now what we have is a growth of camps, each place grew up by itself and slowly but surely internal organization developed inside the camps, creating schools and orchestras and a police force on bicycles and everything that a community needs. Then a national organization was formed called the Central Committee of Liberated Jews and a big fight took place about the preposition. Liberated Jews *of* Germany or Liberated Jews *in* Germany. You understand what the difference is. And the fight was finally resolved. We do not call ourselves *of* Germany, we do not intend to stay here, etc., etc. We are *in* but we are not *of*, we want out, we want Palestine. And they were unanimous. The Central Committee of Liberated Jews in Germany was the governing body, it was sort of a DP national cabinet. There were about 13 or 15 members, I don't remember all of them, just some. I'm getting old, I'm going to be 82 years old and you lose track of some names after a while. And then we did the thing which really locked it in.

General McNarney, the successor to General Eisenhower, agreed with our request to grant a charter of recognition to the Central Committee, which gave that committee official status. When the next seder came, I took a convoy of trucks down to army headquarters in Mannheim, brought back matzoth from America, wine from Algeria, etc., etc., all under the Central Committee of Liberated Jews. They were an official body and designated to care for the welfare and the health of the people in the camps. McNarney signed the charter of recognition in a great ceremony at U.S. Army headquarters, which was in the IG Farben building in Frankfurt. Frankfurt was bombed flat, while the IG Farben building didn't have a window broken. That had been predesignated as future U.S. Army headquarters, and that's where the general's staff sat. And our office was right next door to General McNarney's office.

Now let me tell you how the army operated. Eisenhower said at the beginning, as I told you, he didn't know how to handle, and he didn't want to handle civilian affairs. But he did co-opt the only Jewish chaplain who was there at the time, a major by the name of Judah Nadich who later became the rabbi of Park Avenue Synagogue in New York, and some of you may know that synagogue. He is still alive, he also is now 80-something. Eisenhower asked Nadich to be his advisor on what to do with these Jews. When Eisenhower went back home, demobilized, so did Nadich. Then a new office was created by the War Department in the United States at the request of the army that an official advisor on Jewish affairs be assigned to the commanding general in Europe. Such a person should be designated and shipped over and be situated physically next door to the commanding general's office. One caveat—the non-Jewish civilians in the War Department knew perfectly well that one of the outstanding characteristics of the Jewish people is they don't agree with each other. They argue, they fight, they have committee meetings, they have endless conferences on process before something can be decided. The army doesn't work that way. The army says you guys in America get all of your Jewish organizations together, get everybody to agree on one man, we don't want to hear how you do it, send us one man. We will give him the simulated rank of a two-star general. He's a civilian, not in uniform, but he is a two-star general, which gives him all the perks. He gets a car and a driver, he gets a military man in uniform as his deputy. He gets two cases of whiskey a month, he gets a house to live in of the rank of a German general and we lived in a house in Bad Homburg, a suburb of Frankfurt where the former owner, a German general was in jail. His wife and two daughters asked if they could live in the house with us in the attic.

The man appointed as advisor on Jewish affairs, Rabbi Phillip Bernstein, pulled me out of Berlin and brought me down to Frankfurt to be his deputy.

Most of the army top brass didn't know anything about Jewish psychology; they didn't know anything about Jewish yearnings, about Palestine, about Jewish values. They don't know how these people were living in the camps. The brass needed help in terms of background. The background knowledge took place in Bernstein's house. I lived with him in that house in Bad Homburg and watched him do his masterful work. With the assistance of lots of cigars and the two cases of whiskey, he taught them Jewish history, past and present, as well as Jewish mentality. About once every ten days, three four-star generals, two-star generals, one-star general would sit for several hours asking questions and getting answers. Then a bunch of full colonels. Generals and colonels are the people who make the army's decisions. Army decisions are made from the top and if you get acquiescence to something at the top, then you have got it and the order goes all the way down the line and everybody obeys the order. That's it. And so Bernstein and I performed our indoctrination of about 30 of the top American officers about how the Jews have to be handled and why and what the Holocaust was all about. They are all bright, you're talking about very bright men. Most of them went through West Point and if any of you know the West Point curriculum, it's hard, it's tough, and it does not just contain technical subjects. There are courses in philosophy, there are courses in religion, it's a very high academic standard. Many who didn't go to West Point came out of other universities with master's degrees. So when you are talking about 30 or 40 top officers of the army, you are talking about people who can understand the subtleties and the intricacies of the behavior of this very ancient Jewish people. They were fascinated. We made the connection between Judaism and Christianity for them and they warmed up and they were sympathetic and friendly. It was the most important thing that the advisor did. The first advisor was a judge from New York by the name of Simon Rifkind from a very important law firm and he came over and spent a few months doing it. Then the champion came over, a rabbi by the name of Phillip Bernstein. And the army knew him and they loved him because he was the man in charge of vetting rabbis to be sworn in as army chaplains and his choices the army accepted and they knew that he understood the army. So when the Jewish organizations in America appointed him and he came over, General McNarney was delighted. Now our office really began to function on important issues. Something like that should have happened in the British zone, but it didn't. Nobody bothered to indoctrinate the top military staff of the British army.

After Bernstein finished his tour (about one and a half years), let me tell you the names of the other men who came as advisors. They deserve to be mentioned. You might not recognize them, no reason why you should, but their names should be in the record. There came a judge from Philadelphia by the name of Louis Leventhal, he was there from August 1947 to January of 1948, then there was Dr. William Haber, who was a professor of economics at the University of Michigan, and served from January of 1948 to January of 1949. After that was Harry Greenstein, the executive director of the Jewish Federation in Baltimore. He remained there from February 1949 to October 1949. And the final acting advisor was a Major Abraham Hyman who was there from October 1949 to 1951 when Foehrenwald was closed as the last camp. Previously, he was the top lawyer in the army and joined Rabbi Bernstein's office. He stayed with each successor advisor, and finally became the last advisor himself. He was a wonderful person.

Now I know that there is a big argument about whether Foehrenwald was closed in 1951 or 1957. And I don't want to take you into that argument, it's totally irrelevant. Whichever you choose to believe is okay by me. There are reasons for both dates. General McNarney had gone now and the new commanding general was a man named Lucius Clay, a truly brilliant person. And the greatest brilliance he performed was to save me from a court martial because I had stolen a lot of things, broken a lot of rules. There's no time to go into all those stories. Finally, he said to me, "Okay Friedman, you have done enough, go home."

I'd like to tell you something about the attitude of these top army men toward the DPs. I referred to the Eisenhower/Patton thing so there is no point in my repeating that. Remember the quote: "If for no other reason, George, you be nice to those people because I'm ordering you to do so." Now Eisenhower was never known particularly as a great friend of the Jews or as a great enemy of the Jews. But he went to one concentration camp, Ohrdruf, and that shocked him. He had his assistant with him, General Walter Beddell-Smith, that name might be known to some people. And ever afterward he was a different man. Eisenhower's sympathetic attitude permeated the ranks. Eisenhower took Patton with him and they attended a Yom Kippur service in 1945 in the DP camp Feldafing. He asked to be taken to some place where he would sense the emotions of the people. And so he attended a Yom Kippur service, October 1945. It was the last thing he did before going back to America.

Later on in Berlin I took General Clay to a *yizkor* service in Schlachtensee in 1946. He cried. General McNarney had attended a Hanukkah party in 1946 in camp Lindenfels, where there were 300 Jewish orphans. He got out on the floor and he danced with them and he sang songs with them. I mean this was a four-star commanding general. And afterwards he said, "It was refreshing, I felt good."

The last thing I want to refer to is General Keyes, who became the Third Army general following Patton. And that has to do with an episode that occurred in a camp called Babenhausen. Just think for a minute of some of the things I have told you before. You have an organization called the Haganah, the Aliya Bet, the Bricha, all those names are the same thing. They were a small handful, no more than about 100 or 150 Palestinian kids, young men, working on the European continent like shepherds, shepherding hundreds of thousands of people from the east, as far east out as I said beyond the Ural Mountains in Russia, moving the refugees west across Europe. Where are they headed? They are headed for the American zone of Germany. Why there? Germany of all places is a refuge? Yes, because it's the American zone of Germany and the American flag is there and the American army is feeding 2,000 calories a day and the Joint is supplementing—God bless the Joint—supplementing 1,000 calories a day so the people are being fed 3,000 calories and they are coming back to life and getting medical attention. The Jewish Agency from Palestine is sending over all kinds of personnel. They were working inside the camps, they were not working with the Aliya Bet. There were doctors, nurses, schoolteachers, children's special education, social workers, everything you could think of that was needed for a normal society. All this was coming from the Jewish Agency in Palestine; it was a strong, powerful organization at that time. It was so for a half a century. It's now struggling with its own sense of identity of what it should do and what it should be. That's a whole other story.

The flight, the illegal immigration, took the northern route coming into the American sector of Berlin by truck. The southern route was by train. From Silesia in Poland, via Nachod across the border into Czechoslovakia, down to Bratislava on the Hungarian border, west to Vienna, Vienna into Munich. The southern route was feeding into Munich, the northern route was feeding into Berlin.

One day a trainload of about 1,200 people who had been schlepping on the train, for days—tired, nervous, stopped at Babenhausen. Every camp in Germany was set up by the United States Army. The army picked the place. The first camp I had anything to do with, Schlachtensee in Berlin, used to be a German army camp where they kept Russian prisoners of war. So what was a prison camp became a DP camp.

Well, the train pulled in on the track in front of this camp and the DPs won't get off the train. Why? Barbed wire all around the camp, watchtowers standing up at places around the perimeter, dirty straw pallets out in view, and the people on the train said this is another concentration camp, where are you taking us? Strike, nobody got off the train.

General Clay ordered me to get down there and straighten this thing out, that's what you are supposed to do. You're my advisor, the army has got a problem, fix it. So there we go and the first thing we did was set up some microphones on the side of the tracks, opened up all the cars—they were the same German freight cars that the people were very familiar with. They were the same cars that went to Auschwitz, Treblinka, and all the other camps. So that was a not very happy beginning. But there was no other transportation, what are you going to do. We started talking to people over the loud speakers, talking Yiddish. My Yiddish was not really very good. I learned *Hochdeutsch* at Yale University and had to transfer that into Yiddish. It took me a year. But after that my Yiddish got to be pretty good. Talk to them in Polish, talk to them in Romanian, talk to them in Russian, we had all kinds of people translating for us into languages the DPs could understand.

What had happened very simply was the army had been opening up so many camps so fast that somebody overlooked something, somebody forgot to tear down the barbed wire and failed to tear down the watchtowers and the people's first image of the place was absolutely correct. They refused to enter it. Right away the army brought in a whole gang of soldiers, tore everything down, tried to clean it up, and slowly but surely a few people got off. But then I tried one trick that didn't work. I got the chief chaplain of the Third Army, a full colonel, a Catholic priest, to agree to come and he started talking on the microphone to them, pleading with them and they could see that he was sincere and they could see that he meant it, but they didn't react very well. So there was only one shot left. And that was to call the commanding general himself, three-star General Keyes, Patton's successor, and darned if he didn't say, "I'll be right over, give me a couple of hours." And he came over and I would like to read to you what General Keyes said to them.

> I know this place is far from ideal but it's the best housing we can give you right now. You left your homes because you feared for your life. Here in Germany with us you can drop this fear. We are in the midst of setting up new and better camps. As soon as a better place is available I will see that you are moved there. [And he kept that promise within about three months.] If you do not accept what we offer you, you will give us no choice but to send you back to Poland. This is something you do not want, nor do we. If you make difficulties for us, you will be hurting not only yourselves but also the innocent people at the borders who are waiting and pressing to come in after you. I plead with you to accept our hospitality, you will not regret it.

And he got in his jeep and he started to drive. Now the barbed wire is gone so there is no gate, there is nothing, he started to drive away from the tracks into the camp area and the people began to get off the trains, jumping off the long line of freight cars, jumping off, jumping off, and pretty soon there you had General Keyes in his jeep leading a whole column of Jewish DPs into the camp in Babenhausen.

The end of the story comes a couple of months later. This was October. Ben Gurion called and asked for permission to come into Germany to visit a DP camp. We got him a permit. He said, "Don't send me to an easy place," and I said, "I'm going to take you to Babenhausen." He didn't know where it was. But when he came and I took him into Babenhausen he stood up on the platform in front of the thousands and said very simply, "I have no British certificates for Palestine in my pocket for you. I know you want to come as much as we want you to come. Hang on, hang on, just live with hope and live with the assurance that you have a lot of us working for your future." And then he turned to me and said sing *Hatikva*—hope. Well I have a monotone and I can't sing. Abe Hyman was standing over here, our legal deputy, and his musical ability was worse than mine and Ben Gurion . . . well, you couldn't get a song out of that man's mouth. So some of the people started to sing and gradually the whole people started to sing. Then we all joined in and from that point on the Babenhausen saga spread through all 64 camps in Germany and Austria and we all lived happily ever after.

Historical Issues

Henry Friedlander

Professor of History, Department of Judaic Studies, Brooklyn College; Holocaust survivor

I am not on the program for this general assembly, and you are no doubt wondering what I am doing here. I am just a pinch hitter for the opening speaker who has unfortunately been delayed. I was thus asked on very short notice to present a brief conclusion to this session. So please don't expect me to say anything very profound. You have just listened to two riveting accounts of personal experiences during the DP period, and anything I might say is obviously going to be anticlimactic. I shall not attempt to talk about my personal experiences as a displaced person, but instead talk about how historians might view the DP experience. As I realize that many find the facts historians teach as somewhat tedious, I shall confine myself to three issues historians consider important about the DP period.

First, there is the question of continuity. Remember, history does not move backwards or sideways, but always forward in one direction. In Germany, the population has named the time slot of May 1945 the "hour zero" *(Stunde Null)*. They consider the Nazi years as a break in continuity, with May 1945 a new beginning. In other words, the 12 years of Nazi rule were not part of the continuity of German history. In colloquial language: The Nazis arrived in January 1933 from somewhere—maybe Mars—and disappeared again in May 1945. This "zero hour" works for the Germans.

I do not think this construct of a "zero hour" works for Jews. I see no benefit for the Jewish survivors in a similar break of continuity. Although the survivors dwell on the years before the catastrophic events we now call the Holocaust, they also realize that the years between 1938 *(Kristallnacht)* and 1945 (liberation) cannot be erased, and that they form the essential link between their earlier life and the future. And historians agree that you cannot understand the DP years without considering the Holocaust years.

Please permit me a brief digression. The period between 1938 and 1945 encompasses seven years. Those years were so packed with tragic events that to all of us they appear much longer than the number seven would imply. But it was only seven years. Let me put it another way: It was one year shorter than the life of the Clinton administration. A sobering thought.

Second, when we look at the DP years, we find that different groups of survivors had different experiences. There were also the liberated non-Jews. I am not talking about the non-Jewish displaced persons who, for example, fled the Baltic lands because they had collaborated or because they feared the Soviets. I am talking about non-Jewish concentration camp prisoners. Jews made up less than half of those liberated from the Nazi camps. The majority were non-Jewish camp prisoners from all over Europe: Germans, Austrians, Dutch, Belgian, French, Poles, Russians, and others. Most of them were rapidly repatriated to their homes and families. Their experiences were thus different. Jews (and Gypsies) no longer had homes or families and thus could not return to them.

But even among Jews there were national differences. Jews deported from the countries of the West—France, Belgium, Holland, Italy—were repatriated to their home cities. Primo Levi has provided for us the best description of such a repatriation in his second memoir's account of his return to Italy. Some Jews even returned to countries under Soviet rule, for example, Hungary and Czechoslovakia. We thus need to know more about the dispersion of liberated Jews during the DP years.

Third, we need to know more about the end of the DP experience, that is, about emigration and adjustment to a new life outside the continent of Europe. That story has not been explored. For Israel, we have a recent book by Tom Segev, which explores some of the issues about adjustment to a new life. We have nothing comparable for the United States. Of course, we have memoirs and accounts about success stories, but, after all, not every displaced person adjusted successfully. We should study what happened to the survivors after they landed in the New World. We should investigate how the Jewish organizations treated the DPs then commonly called "greenhorns." That is a story that ought to be told. It is a story buried in the files of the Jewish federations. No one wants to spend money to make these records available, and the subject is not sufficiently jazzy to attract research money. Still, these records are vast enough for countless doctoral dissertations in Jewish studies and other disciplines.

Finally, I would like to suggest that we stop looking at the postwar DP experience as a different, new subject. It is part of the Holocaust years, which should thus stretch to include the period from 1938 to 1950. Those 12 years—equal in time to the Reagan and Bush administration years—form one continuing event, one interconnected experience. Thank you.

REMEMBRANCE

MY FATHER: A MODEL FOR EMPOWERMENT

Menachem Z. Rosensaft

Good afternoon. I am the son of Josef and Hadassah Rosensaft, and I am pleased to welcome you to this afternoon's plenary session.

Three days after the liberation of Bergen-Belsen, some 200 of the healthier Jewish survivors of that camp elected Josef Rosensaft, a 34-year-old Polish Jew who had survived months of torture and solitary confinement in the notorious Block 11 at Auschwitz, to head the DP camp's first Jewish committee. Its purposes, my father recalled 12 years later, were ambitious: "We concentrated on four main tasks: the physical rehabilitation of the survivors; the search for relatives, if any; the political fight for our rights; spiritual rehabilitation."[1]

Writing in 1953, Leo W. Schwarz observed that during April and May 1945, my father had become recognized as the undisputed leader of the Jewish DPs of Belsen, "leaving nothing undone to assist his people. When the British Military were selecting a limited number of the sick for convalescence in Sweden, he interceded for members of families who were again being separated. With an unfailing nose for German and Hungarian collaborationists, he hunted down dozens who had concealed themselves among the liberated. He spurred British soldiers to collect clothing for the thousands being discharged from the temporary hospital, in the former Panzer Training School. He possessed an uncanny ability to locate danger spots and to hammer at the highest authorities for action."[2]

In September 1945, the First Congress of Liberated Jews met at Belsen and elected the Central Jewish Committee for the British Zone of Germany, representing both the Jewish DPs from Eastern Europe and the newly reconstituted German-Jewish communities of cities such as Hamburg, Cologne, Bremen, Duesseldorf, and Hanover, with my father as its chairman and Norbert Wollheim, an Auschwitz survivor originally from Berlin, as vice chairman. My father headed both the Central Committee and the Belsen Jewish Committee until the DP camp was closed during the summer of 1950.

My father's first serious confrontation with the British military authorities occurred in late May of 1945. In an effort to reduce the Jewish population of Belsen, the British decided to transfer several thousand Jewish survivors to Lingen and Diepholz, two camps for stateless DPs located near the German-Dutch border. When the first transport of 1,117 Jews reached Lingen, they discovered that conditions there were far worse than in Belsen. My father prevented a second transport from leaving Belsen, and told "his" DPs who were already in Lingen to disregard the British military orders and return "home," as it were. The British authorities, outraged by his defiance, put him on trial before a military tribunal, which eventually acquitted him.

---

[1] *Josef Rosensaft, "Our Belsen," in* Belsen *(Tel Aviv, 1957), 27.*

[2] *Leo W. Schwarz,* The Redeemers: A Saga of the Years 1945–1952 *(New York, 1953), 32–33.*

Other crises followed. The British, like the Americans for that matter, initially wanted to classify the survivors by their nationalities of origin. The Belsen leadership demanded that they be formally recognized as Jewish DPs. Unhappy with the notoriety associated with Bergen-Belsen as one of the most infamous Nazi concentration camps, the British decided to change the DP camp's name to Hohne. Equally aware of the publicity value and symbolism inherent in the "Bergen-Belsen" name, my father and his colleagues simply ignored the new designation. Official communications sent by the authorities to my father at "Hohne" were responded to on stationery that gave "Bergen-Belsen" as the Central Committee's address.

When the military authorities refused to give permission for the First Congress of Jewish DPs to take place in Belsen, my father convened it anyway, sending formal invitations to prominent Jewish leaders from England. In December 1945, when he was invited by the JDC to address the first postwar conference of the United Jewish Appeal in Atlantic City, he was notified by the military authorities that he was free to leave the British zone, but that if he did so, he would lose his DP status, would be forced to give up the chairmanship of the Central Committee, and would not be allowed to come back. He traveled to the United States anyway, spent several weeks there telling American audiences about the condition of the Jewish survivors in Europe, and returned to Belsen without official permission in January 1946 to resume his leadership role.

He repeatedly and publicly criticized the British government's anti-Zionist policies. Testifying before the Anglo-American Committee of Inquiry on Palestine in early 1946, he told its members that if the survivors would not be allowed to go to Palestine, "We shall go back to Belsen, Dachau, Buchenwald, and Auschwitz, and you will bear the moral responsibility for it."[3] In 1946, when the British sought to prevent thousands of additional Polish Jewish refugees from entering the British zone, my father and his committee openly defied the military government by giving them sanctuary in Belsen.

In her excellent *Belsen: The Liberation of a Concentration Camp*, historian Jo Reilly cites official British Foreign Office documents in which my father is referred to as an "extreme Zionist," a "dangerous troublemaker," and "clearly the chief nigger in the woodpile." "The difficulties our authorities have had in dealing with Jewish DPs in the British zone," one senior British official complained, "are directly attributable to him."[4] Already in August 1945, Maurice Eigen, the JDC director in Belsen, reported that "Rosensaft, a veritable Jewish Lincoln, is a national leader but is always incurring the wrath of the Army officials here. He is always threatened with arrest. Rosensaft had been a labor organizer in Poland and has a tremendous following here. He thinks nothing of flaunting military regulations repeatedly and has made my task of interpreting the committee to the military an exceedingly difficult one."[5]

In the spring of 1947, Menachem Begin, the leader of the militant Irgun Zvai Leumi—the underground Zionist paramilitary group engaged in a violent armed struggle against the British in Palestine—sent an emissary to my father in Belsen with an urgent, desperate request. Several young Irgun members had been apprehended by the British military in the act of placing explosives on railroad tracks near the German city of Hanover, not far from Belsen. Their intended target was a train filled with British soldiers. The four were tried and sentenced to death by a military court in Hanover. My father was their last hope.

[3] S.J. Goldsmith, "Yossel Rosensaft: The Art of Survival," in Twenty 20th Century Jews (New York, 1962), 90.

[4] Joanne Reilly, Belsen: The Liberation of a Concentration Camp (London and New York, 1998), 100 & 105.

[5] Henry Friedlander, "Darkness and Dawn in 1945: The Nazis, the Allies, and the Survivors," in 1945: The Year of Liberation (United States Holocaust Memorial Museum, Washington, D.C., 1995), 27.

My father flew to London where he met with senior government officials, including the anti-Zionist foreign minister, Ernest Bevin. "Do you believe the convicted men to be innocent?" Bevin asked. "No," my father replied. "Do you think that they did not receive a fair trial?" "No." "Do you have any doubt that if they had been successful, they would have killed British soldiers who had nothing whatsoever to do with Palestine?" "No." "Can you offer any mitigating circumstances?" Again, the answer was, "No." "In that case," Bevin asked, "on what basis are you asking for clemency on their behalf?" My father replied, "We will not allow you, less than two years after the end of the war, to give the Germans the satisfaction of seeing Jewish boys executed in Germany. If you want to carry out the sentence, bring them to London and execute them here."

My father had come armed with the knowledge that applicable British law precluded the authorities from transferring the Irgun men out of Germany for execution elsewhere. He never learned whether Bevin ever considered or explored such an option. Shortly after their meeting, however, the death sentences were commuted.

The DP years were also not without humor. On one occasion in February 1948, when the British raided Belsen in search of black market merchandise, they found only a handful of illegal cigarettes and one unauthorized cow. According to Samuel J. Dallob, the Belsen JDC director at the time, my father commented that the British authorities' confiscation of the cow was perfectly proper since it did not have a DP card.[6]

And then there was the incident of the three converts. My father made it a point to walk through the Belsen hospital frequently. He would speak with the patients, offer them encouragement, make them smile. One day in the summer or early fall of 1945, he came across three heavyset men lying by themselves in a closed-off corner. Their bulk alone was unusual at a time when most survivors were still emerging from a state of emaciation. His Yiddish greeting evoked grunts. Walking away, he asked one of the doctors who they were. "Oh," was the reply, "these are Rabbi Helfgott's patients," referring to the head of the Belsen rabbinate. It turned out that the three were Germans with either a Jewish parent or grandparent who had undergone conversion to Judaism in order to become eligible for DP rations. The good rabbi had apparently also promised each of them an orange. They were now recovering from the circumcision ritual, which had been performed at the hospital. Intrigued and amused, my father went back to talk to them. "Tell the rabbi," one of them said, "he won't get us to do this again."

I have spoken at some length about my father, but I could just as easily have talked about my mother. Immediately upon the liberation of Bergen-Belsen, Brigadier H.L. Glyn-Hughes, the deputy director of medical services of the British Army of the Rhine, appointed my mother, then Dr. Hadassah Bimko, to organize and head a group of doctors and nurses among the survivors to help care for the camp's thousands of inmates who were suffering from typhus, tuberculosis, dysentery, extreme malnutrition, and countless other virulent diseases. A dentist from Poland who had studied medicine at the University of Nancy, she had lost her parents, first husband, five-and-a-half-year-old son, and sister in the gas chambers of Auschwitz-Birkenau, and had spent 15 months in Birkenau before being transferred to Bergen-Belsen in November 1944.

For weeks on end, my mother and her team of 28 doctors and 620 other female and male volunteers, only a few of whom were trained nurses, worked round the clock with the military doctors to try to save as many of the critically ill survivors as possible. Despite their desperate

[6]*See Joanne Reilly,* Belsen: The Liberation of a Concentration Camp *(London and New York, 1998), 112; and Yehuda Bauer,* Out of the Ashes: The Impact of American Jews on Post-Holocaust European Jewry *(Oxford and New York, 1989), 270.*

efforts, the Holocaust claimed 13,944 additional victims during the two months after the liberation. And those who lived had to face a grim reality. "For the greatest part of the liberated Jews of Bergen-Belsen," my mother later recalled, "there was no ecstasy, no joy at our liberation. We had lost our families, our homes. We had no place to go to, nobody to hug. Nobody was waiting for us anywhere. We had been liberated from death and from the fear of death, but we were not free from the fear of life."[7]

My mother went on to be the head of the health department of the Central Jewish Committee in the British Zone. She was also one of the principal witnesses for the prosecution at the first trial of Nazi war criminals. In September 1945, she testified at a military tribunal in Lueneburg against those commandants, doctors, and guards of Auschwitz and Bergen-Belsen who had been arrested by the British at Bergen-Belsen.

Twenty-six years ago, in a classic lecture entitled "Against Despair," Elie Wiesel, in a different context, recalled a wonderful Hassidic tale: "Somewhere," said Rebbe Nahman of Bratzlav, "there lives a man who asks a question to which there is no answer; a generation later, in another place, there lives a man who asks another question to which there is no answer either—and he doesn't know, he cannot know, that his question is actually an answer to the first."[8]

Our conference this weekend may provide the beginning of the answer, or, at least, of an answer, to a question that has hovered in a peculiar twilight for decades. Most people, including most Jews, think of Holocaust survivors as skeletal figures in striped uniforms staring aimlessly into the distance on the day of their liberation. And then they fast-forward 40 or 50 years to somber commemorations at which gray- and white-haired men and women mourn their dead by lighting candles and reciting memorial prayers. But what happened to the victims when they ceased to be victims?

Various prominent historians have chronicled the Holocaust primarily if not exclusively from the perspective of the perpetrators, basing themselves almost entirely on German sources while ignoring both the memoirs and the memories of the survivors. This has enabled some of them to characterize the victims of the Holocaust as two-dimensional figures whose sole purpose on earth was to be marched into the gas chambers. Most recently, Peter Novick, a retired professor of history at the University of Chicago, has gone so far as to dismiss the survivors' memoirs in general as "not a very useful historical source." As far as he is concerned, the survivors' memories serve only for "evoking the Holocaust experience," rather than as reliable testimonies.[9] Indeed, many of these self-anointed authorities on the Holocaust appear to resent the survivors for knowing more about the experience than they will ever learn or understand.

That is one major reason why the DP period has been largely glossed over if not completely ignored by many who polemicize about the Holocaust. Any discussion of the DP camps requires a focus on the survivors not as faceless objects but as protagonists. The common depiction of European Jewry, including the survivors, as passive victims requires the history of the Holocaust to end in the spring of 1945. Expanding the historiography of the Holocaust to include the DP period forces historians to give the survivors names, faces, and voices. And the Jewish DPs' successful defiance of the Allied military authorities over issues of principle—their

---

[7] *"Holocaust Survivor Hadassah Rosensaft Describes the Day She Was Liberated from a Nazi Extermination Camp," in* In Our Own Words: Extraordinary Speeches of the American Century, *eds. Senator Robert Torricelli and Andrew Carroll (New York, Tokyo, and London, 1999), 159–60.*

[8] *Elie Wiesel, "Against Despair," in* A Jew Today *(New York, 1978), 158.*

[9] *Peter Novick,* The Holocaust in American Life *(Boston and New York, 1999), 275.*

creation of schools, newspapers, religious institutions, and theater companies in the DP camps, their determination to create new families and reclaim the lives that had been torn from them—shatter the convenient stereotypes that have become commonplace.

Those of us whose parents spent months or years in the DP camps see the Holocaust as a whole through a prism that sets our parents' suffering in the context of their postwar accomplishments. And we understand that the resolve and resilience they demonstrated in the DP camps is the same physical and spiritual strength that had enabled them to survive with their values and their humanity intact.

My parents met several weeks after their liberation and fell in love. Both were prominent leaders of the survivors, and they were soon known to be a couple. But they did not marry immediately. It was too soon, their wounds were still too open, too raw. As my mother told the story, one evening shortly after they had met, my father took her back to her room and stayed. In the late spring and summer of 1945, when survivors told my father that they wanted to get married, he counseled them to wait: "Why don't you live together for a while to see whether you really have enough in common to build a future together, to create a new family, or whether you are just looking for human companionship, for some warmth to ease your loneliness."

The following summer, on August 18, 1946, my parents were married. I was born on May 1, 1948, in the Glyn-Hughes Hospital of the Belsen DP camp. Romana Strochlitz Primus, the chairperson of this conference, was born in the same hospital. So was Felicia Figlarz Anchor, another of the conference organizers. Rositta Ehrlich Kenigsberg, who chairs the United States Holocaust Memorial Council's Second Generation Advisory Group, was born in the Bindermichel DP camp in Austria. Eva Fogelman and Ritalynne Brechner, two other members of the conference steering committee, were born, respectively, in a DP camp in Kassel and in Stuttgart, Germany. My wife, Jean Bloch Rosensaft, is the exhibitions chairperson for the conference and co-curator together with her father, Sam Bloch, of *Rebirth after the Holocaust,* the exhibition on the Bergen-Belsen DP camp presently on view at the B'nai B'rith Klutznick National Jewish Museum. Her parents met and married in Belsen, and her father was the youngest member of the DP camp's Jewish Committee. Sam Norich, who helped shape the conference program, was born in the Feldafing DP camp. This conference is very personal to all of us. It is our tribute to our parents, and to our past.

INTRODUCTION OF ELIE WIESEL

Menachem Z. Rosensaft

While each of our parents' life-stories is distinct, there are influences that are common to most if not all of us. Beyond question, the one person who has had the greatest impact on the Second Generation as a whole is Professor Elie Wiesel. His autobiographical *Night* enabled us to relate to our parents' experiences through the eyes and heart of one who experienced the Holocaust as a teenager. His novels allowed us to identify with fictional characters who asked the very questions that were haunting us. And his commitment to human rights, his readiness to apply the lessons of the Holocaust to contemporary issues while at all times emphasizing its Jewish particularity, have enabled us to synthesize past and present.

A survivor of Auschwitz and Buchenwald, he spent the immediate postwar years not in a DP camp in Germany, but in France in schools run by the OSE, the *Oeuvre de Secours aux Enfants,* the Children's Rescue Society. His writings, culminating in the recently published second volume of his memoirs, *And the Sea Is Never Full,* constitute one of the most far-reaching, comprehensive bodies of work ever produced by a single individual. He has educated us not only about the Holocaust but about humankind's responsibility in the face of genocide. His teachings cover the world of Hassidism, the Bible, and the Talmud. His *The Jews of Silence* called international attention to the plight of Soviet Jewry long before it became a priority of the organized Jewish community. His appeal to President Reagan not to go to the German military cemetery at Bitburg is one of the classic speeches of the twentieth century.

In 1986 he received the Nobel Peace Prize. He has also been awarded the Presidential Medal of Freedom, the United States Congressional Gold Medal, and the French Legion of Honor. He is the Andrew W. Mellon Professor in the Humanities and University Professor at Boston University. He is the founding chairman of the United States Holocaust Memorial Council. But for us, the sons and daughters of Holocaust survivors, he fulfills a special role. He has been and continues to be simultaneously our teacher and our older brother. On a personal level, I have had the privilege of being his student and his friend for more than 35 years. In 1972, when Professor Wiesel began to teach at New York's City College, I was his first teaching assistant. He delivered the eulogy at my father's funeral. In 1981 he asked me to chair the United States Holocaust Memorial Council's first Second Generation Advisory Committee. He has been a constant source of inspiration and guidance. It is now my great personal pleasure and privilege to introduce the keynote speaker of our conference, my friend and mentor, Professor Elie Wiesel.

Keynote Address

Elie Wiesel

Founding Chairman, United States Holocaust Memorial Council; Nobel Peace Prize Laureate

I have always believed that no one has the capacity for gratitude as deeply inserted in his or her life and conscience as the survivors.

For us, every day is an act of grace, every gesture, an offering. And so, almost according to a Talmudic injunction, we should begin with words of gratitude.

Naturally, first of all, to Menachem, Romana, and Rositta, and all their friends on the organizing committee, who prepared this extraordinary conference.

They have done so with talent, they have done so with passion, they have done so with a sense of devotion, which brings honors to them, and to their parents.

We also must acknowledge, I do so with pleasure, the leadership of the Council and the Museum. Miles, Ruth, and Sara, who have given all the help, all the commitment on their part, to this project, and to so many others.

And to all of you for being here. I believe there is no place in the world where so many stories are accumulated under one roof. Every one of you has a story, every story deserves to be told.

And every life is for all of us a miracle, if we accept that there were miracles in those times. Now, this is of course, about life reborn, about the experience of the DPs.

DP is one of the words invented by and for the twentieth century, whose vocabulary has been both enriched and perverted by what is best and worst in the human being.

A conference devoted to its meaning, to its implications is important, singularly important, for it brought together parents and children, in a common quest for remembering events that inflicted despair to a world which discovered the absolute power of evil, whereas the power of goodness remained limited.

In truth, the story of what was called in Yiddish, or in Hebrew, the Sh'erit ha-Pletah, is as fascinating, and even mysterious, as that of those who perished.

Both categories are part of the same extraordinary tale. And it is enough to listen to survivors as you all have, and I have this morning, especially at the meeting of Belsen survivors; it's enough to hear them tell of their experiences to realize that for them, the tragedy of the Holocaust did not end with the end of the war.

For many years, I was myself a kind of displaced person, but not technically so, because I had no personal experience of life in a DP camp, as you heard from Menachem.

Together with 400 Jewish children, adolescents, we came from Buchenwald straight to France. Later, I did visit my sister in a DP camp. She was there, and twice I came to see her. What I have seen there, I tried to describe in several of my books.

Now, first of all, I was struck by the lively, dynamic, almost joyous atmosphere I found there. And whatever happened there, apparently as I know now, has happened everywhere.

On the ruins of their past, on the ruins of the hope and ecstasy from before, people built new homes, in spite of that infinite nostalgia for lost families, vanished communities.

They had the courage to begin again. Marriages were celebrated, circumcisions arranged, schools established, projects formulated, dreams glorified.

And new and ancient hopes invented. Now how did these men and women, who had seen the absurdity of what we call culture, education—how did they get, where did they get the courage, the imagination, the need, to believe in them? And how come that these people were, or at least looked, happy?

Were they really happy? How did they manage to overcome the despair that they must have carried in themselves through ghettos, hiding places, and death camps?

Now, there is today a kind of international organization, to which I belong, that deals with tortured people, with victims of torture. All over the world, they have therapy groups that deal with victims of torture.

And what we have learned from these lessons is that a tortured person remains tortured. Now, this is probably true of all of us.

A person who went through those experiences hasn't really changed. For we know now that there are wounds that don't heal. There are wounds that time doesn't heal.

There are wounds that faith, even religious faith, doesn't heal. But if so, how did you, parents, grandparents, manage to behave with so much humanity in spite of the pain that remained in you, and that you carried?

Now, on one hand, one may say that this is actually part of the Jewish tradition. For 2,000 years, there wasn't a land in the world where Jews at one time had not suffered.

For 2,000 years, there wasn't a land, a country, where persecution didn't exist against our people. And yet, I read the books of martyrology of the Middle Ages, or during the Crusades. Three of them are, *Yeven Metzula, Shevet Yehuda,* and *Emek ha-Bakha.*[1]

When you read those horrible, terrifying stories, what strikes you is that soon after the story ends, meaning soon after the enemy left, some Jews somehow managed to emerge from their hiding places, and right away, they rebuilt a community.

Right away, they opened schools. They consecrated grounds for cemeteries. And I ask always, why did they do that? Why didn't they convene a tribunal, and say to God, Master of the universe, You don't want us? Have it Your way. You want another people? Go ahead. You don't like us anymore? Okay, You have somebody better, take them. How come that they continued life as it was? The judges judged, the rabbis taught, the children studied Torah.

Is this what we have learned, then, and therefore we have done it in these camps, simply we continued our tradition as if, not as if nothing happened, but simply as if that was the norm, the law that governed our history?

I must tell you that although I was not in a DP camp, I discovered the DP experience in the mid-sixties when Yossel Rosensaft, Menachem's father, came to see me. I accompanied him to Belsen.

I learned so much about Belsen. And from Belsen I learned all the other things about all the other camps. But I had more contact with their children.

---

[1] *Hebrew literary chronicles of the persecution and martyrdom of Jewish communities, written in the sixteenth and seventeenth centuries, considered to be significant sources of Jewish historiography.—Editor's note*

When I began teaching, Menachem was my teaching assistant. Suddenly, I think, both of us discovered that most of our students were children of survivors.

At the beginning we didn't understand why. We were not teaching primarily the Holocaust; we taught it in the beginning, because very few others did.

We taught Hassidism, Midrash, Rabbi Nahman; what did they want to learn from us? Then we understood that they came to me because they couldn't speak to their parents. At that time, their parents didn't want to speak. Why burden their children? Also, who wanted to hear them? Then the parents came to school. So I became a kind of surrogate son, a surrogate father.

And one day, this is a story which some of you may know, it is about one of my most heartbreaking moments that I had as a teacher.

We had a very, very brilliant student. He was then a hippie, with long hair, but he was the best student we had in class.

I usually see every one of my students alone. Then this one came in. He closed the door. I was waiting for him to begin talking. But he broke into tears.

After a very long time, he said, "My father was married before the war. His children and his wife were killed. My mother was married before the war. Her children, her husband were killed. They married in a DP camp, and I am their son. But I know that whenever they look at me, they don't see me." He sobbed, he sobbed, and he sobbed.

So, here we are, here you are. Some of you with your children and grandchildren. And nobody here, believe me, wants you or your children to sob. Your children are the hope, the consolation, which is yours and mine.

Our children, your children now, write, speak, want to be involved, want to help us to tell the story which we so poorly told.

There are at least two young writers here in this audience, I think you heard them. One is Thane Rosenbaum, and the other one is Melvin Bukiet.

When I read their books, I cannot tell you the pride and the pain that I feel as a reader. I imagine their pain, and their pain has become an expression of art.

And so we thank them for being who they are.

Now, there is also anger. When I think of the DP period, I feel anger. Not at DPs, now; I feel anger at the world that allowed the DP experience to continue so long after the war.

What was it that prevented the free world and our own Jewish world, from helping the DPs earlier? I remember your father, Menachem, I remember Yossel telling me that there was a typhus, or typhoid epidemic in Belsen. Then he asked me, "How many Jewish physicians left their practice and came to help us? Not one." Then he asked, "We had synagogues for the High Holy Days; how many rabbis came to conduct services with us? From America, London? Not one." What happened to our people, then? What happened to the Jewish heart, what happened to Jewish solidarity?

As for the non-Jewish world, I have seen it in Kassel, the humiliations that future immigrants had to be subjected to when they went for visas, to any consul.

They were so humbled, shamed, treated with indifference. Why? They deserved something better.

During the war, during my being *over there,* I never thought I would live through the war. Believe me, I didn't know. I was weak, bashful; I was a coward, I wouldn't take any initiative.

But still, if I had thought of the liberation, I would have been convinced that when the nightmare would be lifted, every one of us would be carried on the shoulders of people, saying, "Come, we open our doors, we open our hearts, we open everything for you! Because you have paid your dues, you deserve it!"

Let me give you an example. We saw in recent years that when hostages come back to America, the way they are received. With trumpets and orchestras, the president receives them. And ticker tape parades in New York. How many occasions such as this took place then? For whom? I'll go further. How many Jewish communities, let's say until, 10, 20 years ago, simply felt it necessary to have an annual dinner for DPs?

How about one in ten years, a dinner honoring the survivors there? How is it possible that until 1979, when President Carter first created his Commission on the Holocaust, there wasn't a single survivor occupying a position of leadership in the American Jewish community?

May I tell you a secret? One of the reasons why I accepted President Carter's nomination to become the chairman is because I thought of the survivors.

I felt that because of Washington, the White House, I will do at least whatever I can, in a small way, to honor them—that thanks to the President's Commission, they will receive the dignity which is theirs. And so at that time, there wasn't a committee which I created without a survivor being its chairman.

Sometimes it created many problems for me, I had so many committees—so many I didn't know what to do with them!

But nevertheless, from the administrative point of view, it was a disaster, but humanly, I felt I had to do it.

Today, today the Holocaust became a fashionable endeavor. Is it good? I don't know. I confess to you, I don't know. Maybe it was better then, when so few of us tried to knock at the gates of humanity, but we were so few, and therefore, there was something pure about it.

Now, in every school they study something, in every college there are programs. And in Israel, too, there are some extraordinary, extraordinary programs. One is under the leadership of Professor Dina Porat, who heads the Institute of Anti-Semitism at Tel Aviv University.

There are others that bring honor to the subject, but here, and in France, and in Europe, Hollywood discovered it, Broadway discovered it.

What is missing, really, is a kind of humility. When you deal with that subject, there must be something that makes us humble, something that makes us realize what we don't know.

We will never know. And forgive me for repeating, but it's a kind of mantra: only those who were there know. Others won't know. What we can do simply is bring them closer to the gates, give them as much information as possible, and historians do that.

But between information and knowledge, there is an abyss. And between knowledge and sensitivity, there's another abyss.

This is really what I think this conference is all about: one generation giving to the other what is so needed. A sense of humility, at the same time, a sense of gratitude.

Now let me go back in conclusion to my first words about DPs. "Displaced persons" means what? People who were displaced geographically from their homes, and found themselves in Auschwitz, or in Treblinka. But it's not only a geographical notion; it's also a philosophical notion. One can be displaced not only in space, but also in time.

I think your parents, young people, are displaced, not only geographically. They are displaced in time. Somehow we live in two time zones.

Something is there still. We still remember, and we want to remember better and better.

And we want you to remember. And we want you to write. I repeat now what Dubnow[2] said to his companions when they went to their death: Write, write, write!

And I'm saying it to you now, to us. Please write. This is the last chance. Thirty years from now, who will still be here? Then, with every one of us, something of Truth, with a capital T, will die with him or her. That is why some of us are trying to establish a special publishing house, just to publish memoirs, diaries, prayers of survivors.

So please, do that. For, to be displaced in time, too, is something which is so traditionally Jewish. The Romans and the Babylonians destroyed a temple 2,500 years ago, then 2,000 years ago, and yet we live in that time. We remember the destruction of the Temple. On Tisha be'Av we fast. At Passover, we remember the Exodus from Egypt. Because we live now and we live then. And this is what makes our life so rich, so intense.

And so, my good friends, as you came here to tell each other stories, go on telling some more, more, and more.

Thank you.

---

[2] *The renowned Russian Jewish historian and political theorist, Simon Dubnow (1860–1941) is considered to be the pioneer of modern Jewish historiography. In December 1941, he perished in the Riga ghetto.—Editor's note*

COPING WITH THE PSYCHOLOGICAL AFTERMATH OF EXTREME TRAUMA

Eva Fogelman

Psychologist; Second Generation Advisory Group, United States Holocaust Memorial Council

Victor Frankl, a psychiatrist liberated in the camps, wrote of the morning when the white flag was hoisted above the camp: "Suspense was followed by total relaxation. But no one went 'mad with joy.'"

Frankl reports that the prisoners dragged themselves out of the camp and limped into their surroundings for the first time with the eyes of free men. "'Freedom'—we repeated to ourselves, and yet we could not grasp it. We had said this word so often during all the years we dreamed about it, that it had lost its meaning."

That night they spoke to each other about their feelings. It turned out that they had literally lost the ability to feel pleased and had to relearn it slowly.

Elie Wiesel, liberated from Buchenwald, echoes Victor Frankl "We did not 'feel' the victory. There were no joyous embraces, no shouts of songs to mark our happiness, for that word was meaningless to us. . . . Some of us organized a minyan and said Kaddish. That Kaddish, at once a glorification of God's name and a protest against his creation, . . . It was a thanksgiving for having spared us, but it was also an outcry: 'Why do you not spare so many others?'"

Primo Levi, liberated in Auschwitz, writes of that day: "Liberty. The breach in the barbed wire gave us a concrete image of it. To anyone who stopped to think, it signified no more Germans, no more selections, no work, no blows, no roll-calls, and perhaps, later, the return."

And Levi continues with what is now familiar to us, "But we had to make an effort to convince ourselves of it, and no one had time to enjoy the thought. All around lay destruction and death."

As soon as the concentration camps were liberated, people judged the survivors, and asked if they were too damaged to resume normal life. Golda Meir clandestinely asked Bergen-Belsen survivor Hadassah Rosensaft how many of the survivors were normal. Dr. Rosensaft said, "We are all crazy because we are so normal."

David Ben Gurion, then the head of the Zionist executive of the *Yishuv*, sent envoys to assess the survivors' condition.[1] One envoy from Palestine described the camps as "cemeteries."[2] Others said: "These are torn and broken shadows of men, plagued by lice and boils and eye diseases."[3]

An opinion shared by the envoys was that "those who remained alive lived because they were egoists and looked out for themselves first."[4] Even Ben Gurion agreed that "among the survivors of concentration camps, were those who, had they not been what they were—harsh, evil, and egotistical people—would not have survived, and all they endured rooted out every good part of their souls."[5]

The press reported: "The few that remain to us in Europe are not necessarily Judaism's best. The nation's jewels were destroyed first, and many of the survivors are suspected of low morality."[6]

While envoys were warning that if 5,000 Jews from the Sh'erit ha-Pletah were to immigrate to Palestine they would turn the country into "one big madhouse," psychiatrists who evaluated the Holocaust survivors reported differently. They were amazed to find that survivors were eager to work and did not present severe psychopathology.[7] Ben Gurion also encountered many displaced persons who kept saying to him that they wanted to come to Palestine to work.

At first psychiatrists, like others, were skeptical. In February 1946, the first meeting of Jewish physicians took place in the American zone in Landsberg after a group of doctors, among them psychiatrists, evaluated the well-being of the DPs. Psychiatrists thought they would be overwhelmed by the job. Instead, they were asked for jobs, which meant that social workers had to be recruited instead of doctors.

Dr. Herman Pineas, a Jewish neurologist and psychiatrist who survived the war disguised as a non-Jew in Germany, spoke at the conference. He concluded that when survivors would be moved to decent surroundings they certainly would be able to be productive again and would be able to restore peace to their souls.

Ralph Segalman, the director of the Joint Distribution Committee Vienna office, summarized his work with the DPs in the June 1946 issue of the *Jewish Social Service Quarterly* by saying: "Never before in the history of social work has it been necessary to plan for so large a group of disturbed people." In other words, if a survivor took an extra potato, he was a hoarder because he did not get over starving in the camps; if a child kicked a soccer ball too hard, they labeled him violent. If a Jew became involved in the black market, he was immoral. Negative labels abounded.

A psychiatrist came to Dr. Rosensaft in the Bergen-Belsen DP camp and said he found his first patient. She wanted to know what he saw. The psychiatrist said: "I saw a woman in her barrack looking into a broken mirror and combing her almost bald head with a broken comb."

---

[1] *The following reports are discussed in Tom Segev,* The Seventh Million: The Israelis and the Holocaust *(New York: Hill and Wang, 1993).*

[2] *Yosef Bankover at the Histadrut Executive Committee, September 5, 1945, LA.*

[3] *Eliahu Dobkin at the Mapai Central Committee, April 29, 1946, LPA, 23/46; at the Histadrut Executive Committee, September 5, 1945, LA JAE, April 30, 1946, Central Zionist Archives.*

[4] *David Shaltiel at the Mapai Central Committee, September 11, 1945, LPA, 24/25.*

[5] *David Ben Gurion at the Mapai Central Committee, July 22–23, 1949.*

[6] *Arieh Gelblum, "Fundamental Problems of Immigration Absorption,"* Haaretz *(September 28, 1945): 3.*

[7] *Dr. Herman Pineas's report found in the archives at the Leo Baeck Institute, New York.*

Dr. Rosensaft (then Dr. Bimko) suggested, "Why don't you offer her an unbroken mirror and comb, and if she refuses to exchange them, then you have yourself a patient."

The DPs were an enigma to mental health professionals as they are to us more than a jubilee later. Today we wonder where the survivors got the inspiration to continue especially in the deplorable conditions in the DP camps themselves.

Paul Friedman, a psychoanalyst who had the opportunity to study the DPs in Europe, Cyprus, and Palestine under the auspices of the JDC, wrote: "One cannot live for years in a world in which one man kills another for a cigarette, in which cannibalism is a reality, and then revert instantly on liberation to the man one was before." In view of all this, it is truly amazing to him that the DPs in Europe were capable of any social expression at all.

It is impossible to understand the DP as he is now, whether he was an inmate of the camps or not, if one does not understand clearly the enormous dislocation the Nazi terror wrought.

We need to understand how people subjected to prolonged barbaric brutality are able to learn to live and love again, and to integrate a fragmented self into a whole person.

To explain how individuals cope with massive psychic trauma, one cannot reduce the process to a few common characteristics. Not all the displaced persons were the same. Emotional states are multidimensionally determined, and are dependent on internal and external factors. There was no stability around Shoah survivors. In addition, there are different clusters of survivors according to age and duration of persecution, the mode of survival, and the extent of loss. Furthermore, the quality of life and opportunities in the DP camps or "the outside" impeded or enhanced rehabilitation and integration into society.

The early researchers understood these differences. Nonetheless they agreed that one common denominator, to a greater or lesser degree, existed for all DPs, adults and children alike: emotional numbness or shallowness. The French psychiatrist E. Minkowski thought they all exhibited this state of "affective anesthesia." The condition developed as a defense against daily dangers and anxieties that they suffered during the war.

Victor Frankl explains this as "depersonalization." This emotional anesthetization is further explained by the internationally acclaimed psychoanalyst Henry Krystal, who has conducted psychiatric evaluations with thousands of Holocaust survivors and was himself liberated. Krystal explains these emotional states as anhedonia and alexathymia—the inability to enjoy oneself and to know what one is feeling, which describes what Wiesel, Frankl, and Levi were explaining of their liberation.

Aside from this emotional state, survivors underwent a psychological process during the initial phase following liberation, which started with rediscovering and establishing their own identity.

What was the identity of the DPs? How does one make the transition from being oppressed to being a free person, when you are surrounded by well-meaning and often not so well-meaning antisemites? (Classic examples are General Patton and the British.)

In each survivor's recovery there comes a moment of realization—the creation of a new identity or loss of an old one. Elie Wiesel poignantly describes his arrival at a splendid chateau in Ecouis, France, with other children from Buchenwald. Representatives of the OSE, a children's social service agency, gave them *tefillin,* religious books, and pencils and paper.

Said Wiesel, "We held our fist *Minha* (afternoon) service, and we all said Kaddish together. Though we knew it well enough, that collective Kaddish reminded us that we were all orphans."

Many inmates had a sustaining fantasy in the camp, in hiding, or on the run—the fantasy of being reunited with loved ones. How does one restore oneself when the sustaining fantasy does not come true? Finding out that no one has survived eradicated the mental courage that sustained camp inmates. Can you imagine not knowing who you are, what your real name is, or when you were born? Who was left in your family?

We are often defined by our roles in our family, our sexual identity, religious identity, professional identity, national identity. Living without closure and without an identity impedes adaptation to the real world.

For example, if you were a young girl in the camps, you had no figure, you did not menstruate, and you probably convinced yourself that your reproductive system no longer worked. So who were you? How did you become a woman?

Imagine being a young man in the early twenties. Before the war, you were expected to get a trade or attend school so you could have a profession and support a family. You are now too old to go to school, and you have not practiced a trade for as long as six years. Who are you? Who would marry you?

You were a mother whose child was taken from your arms never to be seen again. You gave your child to an orphanage and upon your return no one knows the whereabouts of your baby. You have lost your identity as a mother. You ask yourself, "How can I bring any more children into the world if I could not protect my child?"

Consider a survivor's Jewish identity. You are a child who feels loyal to Mary and Jesus because they rescued you from a certain death in the convent. You are now living among Jews who think you are "crazy" for crossing yourself and saying "Hail Mary." You are angry with the Jewish God who took away your mother and father. How do you begin to develop a positive Jewish identity when being Jewish was a death sentence? What Jewish values do you embrace as a free person?

Not only was the survivors' Jewish identity disrupted, but their whole self was detached from their core identity. Survivors needed to bridge this gap by reconnecting to their core identity. The core identity had to be strengthened via integration of fragmented components. A fragmented self occurs in a person who experienced a massive trauma that prevents the process of normal emotional development. Such a traumatized person cannot fully proceed in his or her emotional development. Regression to an earlier level of functioning may also occur.

Imagine being an active community person, husband, and father, and that after liberation you are hospitalized with typhus, and you barely know your name. This unimaginable dissolution of the self requires various positive transitional experiences to reestablish itself.

For children whose life was disrupted for six years, and whose pre-Holocaust memories are vague or nonexistent, it is almost insurmountable to reconnect to an amorphous previous self. To be in a physical body of a preadolescent or adolescent or young adult and to be emotionally developed only to a previous developmental stage complicates the integration of the self.

The DPs had to reconnect themselves to their pre-Holocaust selves and reintegrate this with their most recent horrific past and thereby ready themselves to rejoin the human race. They had to get well physically, they had to train themselves in new jobs, they had to learn new languages, to learn to interact with others, and to trust. Without transitional objects, people, places, values from the past, the rupture is more onerous to reconnect.

That is why when survivors are interviewed or they write their memoirs it is so important to include the histories of their prewar families and lives. Often it is these family histories that inspired the survivors and drove them to choose life.

Living with other European Jews in the DP camps was an important vehicle in reconnecting to the pre-Holocaust life and one's identity in that destroyed world. The DP camps were also an environment that enabled group mourning, socialization, and identity formation.

The internal drive for integration of the self was a motivating force for daily living as a displaced person. For some, the first step was to go back to their hometowns or cities. They longed to be connected with the place, familiar objects, and people. But in many instances Jewish Holocaust survivors were not welcome, so they searched out people with whom they could share common values, religious and political views.

Displaced persons experienced emotional voids due to losses. Some filled the void by helping others. Youngsters busied themselves with learning and playing. Some adults tried to make a living or prepared to "make aliya." A large percentage of single men and women of marriagable age filled the void by getting married.

All of the above were coping mechanisms that facilitated a movement toward a life-affirming force and moving away from a death force. Today, the behavior of Holocaust survivors is scrutinized, and stereotypes are passed off as fact. The high rate of marriages and births in the DP camps has been criticized by psychotherapists as "marriages of despair."[8] Some of those people also criticize the survivors at the time as being too obsessed with sex or not being sexual enough. True, at times, a quick marriage to alleviate the pain led to inappropriate relationships for life. But that could also have been influenced by social conditioning, and was certainly not true in many cases, as survivors themselves will tell you.

Today psychotherapists are making assumptions without factual underpinnings. No systematic study has ever been conducted to research the success or failure of these early marriages or the sexualization of survivors. It is reasonable to say that those survivors or their children who seek out mental health professionals have problems, but these are statistically few in numbers. Considering that today one out of every two marriages ends in divorce, who is to say that the statistics are higher among the survivors, or that survivor marriages were any worse? Few of them ever divorced.

Another major issue is repressed anger, distrust, and hatred that the DPs must have felt during the years of persecution. The psychiatrists thought they would erupt uncontrollably. While there were incidents of rage and sexual acting out, these behaviors were very limited.

Frankl explained that the sudden release from mental pressure can cause damage to the moral and spiritual health of the survivor. He observed that during this initial phase people with natures of a more primitive kind could not escape the influences of the brutality which surrounded them in camp life. Now free, they thought they could use their freedom licentiously and ruthlessly.

---

[8]*Yael Danieli, "The Heterogeneity of Postwar Adaptation in Families of Holocaust Survivors," in* The Psychological Perspectives of the Holocaust and of Its Aftermath, *ed. Randolph L. Braham (Boulder, Colorado, 1988) 109–28.*

The DP camps helped restore the dignity of the survivors as human beings. The DP camp served as a self-help community. It was a holding environment in which people felt they could communicate with others who understood them. They empowered themselves by "doing," by building schools, by training themselves, and generally by coming back into a world of politics, religion and "normalcy." By electing their own leaders, they stopped feeling helpless and became members of the world community.

But they were like broken vessels, the fragmented selves that had to put themselves together. They did so by creating Jewish communities that replicated the ones they had lost. They taught their children to celebrate the holidays, Jewish songs, Jewish values. They created something they were proud of, and that pride was the glue that held the pieces together. But even the finest craftsmen who repair broken vases cannot always hide the cracks.

When the Israelites crossed the Red Sea, there was a distinct demarcation between slavery and freedom—their identity changed from *avadim,* slaves, to *b'nai chorin,* sons of freedom. When Jews were liberated from concentration camps, from ghettos, from hiding, from living as non-Jews, from fighting, they followed the biblical precedent. They built families.

The Book of Exodus is about community building and nation building. The survivors took this task very seriously. The Israelites in the desert had 40 years to make the transition before reaching the Promised Land. Most of the saving remnant of the Holocaust integrated themselves in only six years into communities in free countries around the world, in Communist countries, and most successfully in Palestine.

In the end what remains is that the survivors are very much the people they were before the war. The central core of their personalities survived with them, and their Jewish values, whatever form they took, often assisted and sustained them, and still do. The mourning that began the day of liberation continues to this day.

Some survivors are still in shock and denial. Others are still feeling the emotional void and are depressed or enraged, or are full of survivor guilt or helpless, or are ashamed at what they did or did not do. And yet, most survivors have channeled the rage, guilt, helplessness, shame, and grief to affirm life.

The Second Generation are the symbol of the survivors' creative endeavor and an affirmation of life.

Liberation jolted the indifferent bystanders into facing their inaction. Instead of truly repenting, they judged the liberated victims, in some cases treating them like pariahs. Thus, the identity of displaced persons was not only shaped by their years of persecution, but also by the reaction they faced as they tried to integrate into their old societies or new environments. At times the pain of not being accepted by fellow Jews in America or Palestine exacerbated the existing scars more than the physical pain they endured under the Nazis. Shattered identities had a chance to be restored in the DP camps as a result of young adults marrying and creating new families, and experiencing an enriching group experience. These integrated identities, however, were shattered again when displaced persons were rejected in their new environments. Needless to say, fragmented identities of the parent generation were transmitted to the next generation.

In order to feel the liberation more than the oppression, a survivor and his or her offspring need to feel part of a community that embraces them, with all their scars and with all their strengths, a community in which the survivor and his family feel a sense of belonging because we are all part of the same human family.

This was the "human" reality. Let me close with an observation. A few days after liberation Victor Frankl walked through the country past flowering meadows, for miles and miles, toward the market town near the camp. He had but one sentence in his head: "I called to the Lord from my narrow prison and he answered me in the freedom of space." Frankl felt that on that day his life started: "Step for step I progressed, until again I became a human being."

L'CHAIM—TO LIFE!

DEDICATION

Rositta Ehrlich Kenigsberg

L'Chaim—To Life! *was an evening performance of material drawn from the DP era and dedicated by the Second Generation to their parents, the survivors of the Holocaust. The performance was made possible by an array of gifted and acclaimed artists who generously donated their time and talent in honor of the survivors. The artists included The Robyn Helzner Trio: Ms. Helzner, Mike Stein, and Dov Whiteman; Herman and Susan Taube; Adrienne Cooper; Zalmen Mlotek; and the Frieda Enoch ensemble: Ms. Enoch, Vladimir Gamarnik, Daniel Roses, Michael Singer, Mira Yemini-Small, and Bart Weissman, with guest performer Michael Creadon. At the conclusion of the performances, the evening's chairperson, Rositta Ehrlich Kenigsberg, placed the entire program in the context of the* Life Reborn *conference and the DP era.*

For my father—the sole survivor of his family—May 5, 1945, finally meant the answer to his prayers. It meant freedom. It meant life. It meant hope. It meant gratitude. It meant relief. It meant a new beginning, a rebirth from tragedy to triumph.

Yet, there was no greater disappointment for our parents after the joy of liberation than to find themselves displaced and dispossessed and in camps once again. As the late and beloved Hadassah Rosensaft stated, "We had no place to go to, nobody to hug. Nobody was waiting for us anywhere." However, despite the desperate and harsh conditions such as those reported by Special Envoy Earl Harrison to President Harry S. Truman, the DP camps throughout Germany and Austria became a symbol of the survivors' indomitable spirit, their remarkable resilience, and their ability to rebuild and overcome their shattered lives. With limitless determination, they re-created life, once again raising families—defying and challenging the notion that they were defeated, because that would have meant an unbridled victory for the Nazis and a condemnation of the future of Jewish life and Jewish continuity.

How could you, our parents, have possibly been capable of such courage, such energy, such incredible physical and spiritual resilience, after all you had experienced? Where did you find the strength and the courage?

Our parents chose life, not death. Remembrance, not vengeance. Hope, not despair. Love, not hate.

For us, our parents have always been our mentors, our sages, and our protectors, who

> From destruction gave us creation,
> From despair gave us hope,
> From hate gave us love,
> From evil gave us goodness,
> From memories gave us lessons,
> And from the ashes, gave us roots.

Tonight's words, melodies, poetry, and songs are dedicated to you, our parents, in tribute to your life reborn, by the new generation of *Yiddishe kinder*, the generation that has inherited the memory and will guard your legacy. This evening—*L'Chaim—To Life!*—epitomizes the essence of renewal and the return to life.

The subject of the lives of our parents, the survivors, in the period following the Holocaust from 1945 to 1951 has been relatively underrepresented in Holocaust education and scholarship. It is of critical importance for a full understanding of Holocaust history, and is exemplary of the inextinguishable resilience of the human spirit.

Tonight's remarkable performances capture, reveal, emphasize, and underscore the most profound, compelling, poignant, and significant truth that the legacy of the Holocaust is not just about death and despair. It is also about life and life reborn, and the miracle of survival—the triumph over the tragedy. It is a testament of our parents', the survivors', spiritual strength, heroic defiance, and somber dignity. In the days ahead, the story of the DP era and life reborn will continue to be told because, as my father has always said, "As long as there is someone to tell the story, there is life. And as long as there is someone to listen, there is hope."

As we celebrate our parents', the survivors', wondrous commitment to life and life reborn, we call upon an individual whose very name is synonymous with two words, "together" and "gathering." He and his loving wife, Vladka, are the recipients of many honors for their tremendous lifelong commitment to remembrance. It is a profound privilege to introduce the president of the American Gathering of Jewish Holocaust Survivors and chairman of the Days of Remembrance Committee of the United States Holocaust Memorial Council, our beloved Ben Meed.

RESPONSE

Benjamin Meed

President, American Gathering of Jewish Holocaust Survivors; Chairperson, Days of Remembrance Committee, United States Holocaust Memorial Council

More than 50 years ago, when we gathered in displaced persons camps throughout Europe, many survivors wondered whether there would again be a place for us in this world. In those days, we did not imagine and could not dream that one day there would be an event like the *Life Reborn* conference, where survivors in a new millennium would come together to tell and retell their stories, to sing and to dance, and to remember that which was lost and created anew.

Today, the Shoah is commemorated all over the world. But that was not the case at the end of the war. Those of us who through some miracle had managed to survive found ourselves with nothing. Abandoned, alone, with no place to go, we were literally displaced persons. Those who returned to their homes in their former communities found nothing—only hatred. The streets were familiar, but there was no trace of their earlier lives—no families, no homes, no businesses, no one to look to for support. So we looked to one another as we began rebuilding Jewish communal life. That reaffirmation of life began in the DP camps.

We married and brought children into the world. We developed schools and institutions. And, in spite of our experience, we taught our children the values of love and peace and hope, transmitting to them the moral values with which we had been raised, and which sustained us throughout those years immediately after the war.

Although we were isolated and our opportunities were limited, our energy and ambition knew no bounds. From the DP camps, survivors moved to establish lasting homes in all parts of the world. We became artists and musicians, industrialists and philanthropists. Today we can speak of the remarkable achievements of you, our children, and your children as well.

We need you, our children and grandchildren, more than ever before. Despite our achievements, we are greatly concerned about who will tell the story when survivors are no longer alive. You are the last generations to hear firsthand the testimony of the survivors, the living witnesses to the kingdom of *Night*. You have also heard our stories of rebirth. Today you are the affirmation of life and our hopes for the future. As we pass from the scene, the preservation of our memory must become a partnership among your children, who inherit the legacy of the Holocaust; educators and scholars, who research and study the Holocaust; and those who lead institutions dedicated to preserving and transmitting Holocaust memory.

More than 20 years have passed since those of you called the Second Generation, our younger colleagues, accepted this legacy in Jerusalem. Since then, the American Gathering of Jewish Holocaust Survivors has continued to bring us all together for three reasons: Holocaust education for all, documentation of the Holocaust for future generations, and commemoration of its victims, so that they are never to be forgotten. You, our children, along with your children, are charged with carrying on this sacred heritage. Your efforts to educate generations to come will ensure that our life work will not end with us. We know you will keep the legacy alive.

DP Camp Ziegenhain

Susan Strauss Taube

In the darkness of the night
In languish we lay on hard, cold berths,
All of us are tired,
The stench here is choking,
As if someone stabbed us with a dagger,
Our lips are burning
And our eyelashes are covered
With blurred, dark shadows.

My mind is disturbed,
I keep thinking of what this war-tremor did to us . . .
A deep pain is aching my heart,
Everything looks dark,
Shadows hover on the wall over me.
I am rudely awakened and recognize
In the depth of the night
The images of my mother and my little sister.
My heart is so heavy with pain,
Tears rolling down on my cheeks,
I shiver over all my body,
Even though the hot air in the barrack is unbearable.
I wonder, "how did my mother die?
Where is she buried?
What happened with my little sister in Stutthoff?"
I hear them calling me every night. . . .

My mother's voice is full of rage:

A whole people perished. God, Why?

Do not forgive! Do not forget us!

The spilled blood of innocent martyrs.

In the darkness, I lay on a straw mattress

And keep thinking of the other DP's

Sleeping around me,

Young faces turned gray, the whole world is closed for them . . .

Finally, at dawn, I fell asleep,

I dreamt that we escaped from the DP camp,

That we crossed borders

And arrived in America,

Away from the cursed European soil.

Still, we carried with us images of our murdered Families.

The memories of Six Million innocent Jewish martyrs and heroes . . .

Ziegenhain, Hesse, American Zone of Germany
August 1946

ALLIED POLICY TOWARD THE DPS

INTRODUCTORY REMARKS

Dina Porat
Professor of Jewish History, Tel Aviv University

G ood morning. This session is the beginning, lamentably, of the last day of this exceptional conference. Before introducing today's topic and speakers to you, it is appropriate to mention that today is Martin Luther King Jr. Day, and that while we are commemorating our own troubled history, it is appropriate to remember other communities, the struggles they have been through and are going through, and our efforts to work and cooperate with other communities.

This morning's topic is "Allied Policy toward the DPs." Certainly, this is a topic that has been mentioned frequently during our conference, but not formally and certainly not in the manner that our distinguished speakers are going to do. Each of them will deal with a distinct aspect of Allied policy toward the DPs, a policy which in many ways determined their political fate. Our first speaker will speak about the American policy toward the DPs; the second about the British; and the third about Soviet policy, including what we know about it today, and how it could have affected former policies had we known then what we know today about the Soviet policy.

Our first speaker, Professor Leonard Dinnerstein, heads the Department of Judaic Studies at the University of Arizona. His publications include *The Leo Frank Case, America and the Survivors of the Holocaust,* and *Anti-Semitism in America.*

Our second speaker, Dr. Jo Reilly, is education and outreach officer at the Wiener Library in London, and lecturer in history at Southampton University. She is the author of *Belsen: The Liberation of a Concentration Camp,* and coeditor of *Belsen in History and Memory.*

Our third speaker, Professor David Engel, is Skirball Professor of Modern Jewish History at New York University. His publications include *Between Liberation and Flight: Holocaust Survivors in Poland and the Struggle for Leadership* (in Hebrew); *Facing a Holocaust: The Polish Government-in-Exile and the Jews, 1943–1945;* and *In the Shadow of Auschwitz: The Polish Government-in-Exile and the Jews, 1939–1942.*

AMERICAN POLICY

Leonard Dinnerstein

Director of Judaic Studies, University of Arizona

I'm supposed to be talking about American policy toward the displaced persons. America had both a policy and no policy at all.

Now before I go into the talk, if you have a pencil, if you have a paper—and you know that I am a teacher, so I teach—you should write down the dates April 12, May 8, August 6, August 9, August 14, September 2, and December 22, 1945. These are crucial dates not only in American history, but in world history and especially for the displaced persons.

The first date, April 12, 1945, Franklin Roosevelt died. Harry Truman becomes president and he did not know which way is up. From January 20 until April 12, Roosevelt had met with Truman twice. He certainly didn't tell him anything that was going on and Truman had to be briefed later on about the development of an atomic bomb.

May 8 is Victory in Europe Day, V-E Day. Actually, the war was probably over by April 30, May 1, May 2, but May 8 was the new president's birthday, so they proclaimed V-E Day on the new president's birthday.

August 6, the first atomic bomb is dropped. August 9, the second atomic bomb is dropped. August 14, the Japanese sue for peace, and September 2 is V-J Day, when the peace treaty is signed. It is during this period that we have the chaos starting with the displaced persons. Plans had been made for handling what was anticipated to be displaced persons after the war. But once the war ended, it seems that the plans that had been made for UNRRA and for SHAEF, the Supreme Headquarters Allied Expeditionary Forces, were not appropriate for the kinds of problems that developed.

The assumption was that practically all of the displaced persons would be sent home. And in fact, in the spring and summer of 1945, 65,000 people were sent home every single day. However, there remained about a million, 900,000, or so. Statistics are just impossible. Every day the statistics changed. One has to question the accuracy of the statistics. Of the approximately one million displaced persons—I'll use that figure—about 50,000 to 100,000 were Jewish.

Now I know that Henry Friedlander said yesterday that the top figure for Jewish DPs was 200,000, but I never saw that particular statistic. I saw the range being from 50,000 to 100,000.

Very quickly, word got back to Washington that the people who survived the war were being kept in camps behind barbed wire. They were given less food every day than the prisoners of war were given and they were being treated worse than the prisoners of war.

Some people in Congress heard this, and started making a fuss. Secretary of the Treasury Henry Morgenthau went to President Truman and said, "Why don't we set up a displaced persons board, something like the War Refugee Board?" Truman rejected that idea. Truman was concentrating on other things.

So Morgenthau went to the acting secretary of state, Joseph Grew, and said to him, "I think we'd better investigate conditions of the displaced persons." And Grew responded, "Yes, that's a good idea," and he appoints a commission and he appointed Earl Harrison, former commissioner of immigration and law professor at the University of Pennsylvania, to lead this investigation. When the preparations were completed, Grew went to Truman and said, "Look, I'm appointing this commission. It'll have much more stature if you appoint the commission." Truman said okay, so it became the Truman appointment of the Harrison Commission.

Earlier I gave you this whole slew of dates. Harrison reported by the beginning of August that conditions were absolutely dreadful in the displaced persons camps. Among his comments are, "we appear to be treating the Jews as the Nazis treated them, except that we do not exterminate them." That's pretty powerful.

Practically all of the Harrison Report is summarized in the *New York Times* of Sunday, September 30, 1945, beginning on the front page. Who was paying attention, however? The war is over. Brothers, fathers, husbands, sons, they were coming back home. The Japanese had already surrendered; the Germans had surrendered in May. There was euphoria in the country. The focus was on how we readjust to peacetime. Besides, how many people read the *Times* and how many people cared about Europe's displaced persons?

For example, let me take this group of people in the room. A few years ago, how many of you protested what was going on in Bosnia? The Serbs were killing the Croats, the Croats were killing the Muslims, the Muslims were killing other people, the Serbs killed everybody. We had a lot of news about it, it was on television. How many of you were marching, protesting, writing to your congressmen, "We can't allow this to happen?" Oh, you said, "That's too bad," turned the page in the newspaper and you read about what was on the next page.

I know the Jews are incensed today that nobody paid attention to them or to the Holocaust during World War II. The truth is that from the American government's point of view, and from the British government's point of view, it was not in anybody's best interests to halt the slaughter.

Now let me just go back briefly because you need some background for this. Antisemitism reached a peak in the United States some time between 1944 and 1946, depending upon which poll you favor. We are pinpointing it right there. Antisemitism during World War II was rampant. Ten senators elected in 1942 were known antisemites. You never heard of most of them, like Henrik Shipstead of Minnesota, Reynolds of North Carolina, and so forth.

Roosevelt made one crucial error in his presidency and he learned from it. He always had his wet finger to the wind. He made a mistake in the Supreme Court fight when he tried to pack the court in 1937. He never went ahead of public opinion thereafter. You know, there has been a lot of criticism of Roosevelt for not doing this, not doing that, and comment about how he could have done more to help Europe's Jews. Some of you may remember that when President Clinton entered the White House, within the first week, he tried to integrate homosexuals in the army. How successful was he? Some of you may pay attention. Because President Clinton wants something, does that mean it happens?

Roosevelt spoke to the vice president, the Speaker of the House, and the majority leader of the Senate in 1942, and said, "Can we get an immigration bill passed?" They said, "You're out of your mind, no way is that possible." In 1943 he tried again. He wanted Congress to give him emergency authority to deal with the movement of peoples and goods into and out of the country. The House of Representatives was incensed at such a proposal. They would not give the president more authority than he already had.

Now most of you who pay attention to politics know President Clinton has been more successful when he is solely in control than when he needs the cooperation of Congress. Roosevelt was not about to sacrifice everything for the Jewish DPs and he said, which is quite accurate, "The best way to help the people in the concentration camps is to end the war quickly." He died just before the war ends, Truman came in, and as I have said, Truman didn't know which way was up, so he had a lot of learning to do. And the people in the concentration camps who have now gone into DP camps were not high on his agenda.

However, when the Harrison Report came back in July 1945, Truman wrote a letter to Eisenhower, the commander in chief of the American armed forces and said, "This will not do." And it was at this point that Truman appointed an advisor to the army who would advise the military about how to deal with the Jewish displaced persons, then conditions for DPs improved.

Now for those who were in the camps, the DP camps, again, the statistics are bizarre. On any given day, there could have been 300 to 500 different displaced persons camps. Some were former concentration camps, some were prisoner-of-war barracks, some were beautiful hotels in the Austrian Alps. People lived under all kinds of different conditions. But what generally seemed to be true was that in southern Germany, where Patton was in command, the displaced persons were treated much more harshly than in northern Germany and, in fact, Harrison made this comment in his report.

The Harrison Report suggested that 100,000 Jews be allowed to go to Palestine and that the United States should also do something about bringing these people to America. Truman focused on the 100,000 Jews who should have gone to Palestine. He wrote to Prime Minister Clement Attlee and advised him to accept that recommendation. Truman made no comment about changing American immigration policy because, as Samuel Dickstein, the chairman of the House Immigration Committee said in 1945, that if he "were to hold hearings, they would cut immigration figures, rather than raise immigration figures."

In 1944 and 1945, three patriotic organizations, the Daughters of the American Revolution, the American Legion, and Veterans of Foreign Wars, called for a total ban on all immigration to the United States for the next five to ten years, even though Jews comprised, at most, 20 percent of the DPs and probably 10 percent at that time. In the United States, the word "refugee" was synonymous with the word "Jew."

Also, most Jews in the United States wanted a Jewish state in Palestine. The Zionists were working very, very hard to get a Jewish state in Palestine. Seventy percent of the Senate supported a Jewish state in Palestine. Nobody called for immigration expansion. In the fall of 1945, I think it was Jacob Blaustein and Irving Engel of the American Jewish Committee—which, as many of you know, considered itself non-Zionist—who went and said to Truman, "Look, within the immigration quota laws, why don't you give preference to the displaced persons?"

The immigration laws were quite restrictive. If you were born in Germany, you had no difficulty coming into the United States. If you were born in Poland, forget it. If you were born in Russia, forget it. Your name went on a list and maybe in 20 or more years, your name might be reached.

But on December 22, 1945, Truman issued an executive order giving preference within the quotas to displaced persons. In the meantime, Clement Attlee, the prime minister of Great Britain, had contacted Truman and asked, "Why don't we appoint a committee to see if the Jews can go to Palestine, if there's room for them?" As a result the Anglo-American Committee of Inquiry on Palestine—which I'm not going to talk about this morning—came into being.

From about the beginning of January 1946 until April they investigated. They then recommended that 100,000 Jews be admitted to Palestine. Although it was a unanimous recommendation, some of the British members felt uneasy about it. They also recommended that the United States open its doors as well for the displaced persons.

The United States ignored the part about America taking the immigrants. On the other hand, Prime Minister Attlee said, "We'll be glad to admit the 100,000 Jews to Palestine if the United States helps finance it and agrees to the Haganah being disbanded." As Attlee well knew, the United States could never agree to having the Haganah disbanded.

So we get to the summer of 1946. The American Jewish Committee and the American Council for Judaism, which were non-Zionist and anti-Zionist, respectively, went to Truman and again requested him to seek legislation admitting more displaced persons into the United States. Truman agreed, proposed legislation to Congress in 1947, but never made it a priority item.

In the fall of 1946, the American Jewish Committee and the American Council for Judaism established the Citizens Committee on Displaced Persons. Naturally, they found a Gentile to head it, and put many Gentile names on the letterhead so that the organization would not appear Jewish. The campaign called for the admission of 400,000 displaced persons to the U.S. Once the campaign began it emphasized that 80 percent of all DPs were Christian. The Protestants started taking an interest in displaced persons.

On April 1, 1947, a congressman from Illinois—William Stratton—introduced a bill to take 400,000 displaced persons into the United States and Congress dawdled. Again, you have to remember there were many antisemites in the country and in the Congress. In 1948, after the establishment of Israel, the Displaced Persons Act, the first of them, was passed and it gave preference to the *Volksdeutsche,* those Germans who had been collaborators with the Nazis got preference in coming into the United States.

And, here's where December 22 comes in. To be eligible for admission into the U.S., the DPs had to have been registered in the western zones of Germany by December 22, 1945. Something like 150,000 Jewish DPs came out of Russia in 1946, hundreds of thousands came in the summer of '46. All of these people were not covered by the law. But the *Volksdeutsche,* they did not have to come into the western areas of Europe until July 1, 1948. The legislation also gave preference to agricultural workers and farmers, occupations that only 2 percent of the Jews had had.

President Truman, however, undermined the intentions of the Congress by appointing a Displaced Persons Commission, which was favorable toward the immigrants. The commission interpreted the law broadly and expanded the meaning of agricultural activities to include anyone who had any business dealings with agriculture.

BRITISH POLICY

Jo Reilly

Education and Outreach Officer, Wiener Library; Lecturer in History, Southampton University

Traditionally, historians writing on the Jewish DPs in Europe and the period before the establishment of the Israeli state, have tended to concentrate on the American zone of Germany and the reactions and responses to the DPs from all levels of American authority.[1] The concentration on the American zone is understandable given that, as from 1946, the greatest number of Jews in Germany resided in this area. The result, however, has been the neglect of the significant Jewish community in Belsen, the largest in the British zone numbering well over 10,000 people from the second half of 1945, but also the hub of a thriving society and a concerted political campaign to open Palestine to Jewish settlement.[2] Against this background, the role of the British in the lives of the DPs has only been considered at a governmental level, that is, in respect of the British government policy on Palestine. Again, this has led to the neglect of an examination of the policies of the British authorities on the ground in the British zone of Germany, and the way in which they responded to the situation of the Jewish DPs.

It is often assumed that all of the British policies toward Jewish displaced persons (DPs) were directly linked to its policy on Palestine. Thus the rather simplistic argument runs: The British government held the Palestine Mandate; they did not want to see an Israeli state, choosing rather the appeasement of Arab opinion to protect British interests in the Middle East—all action concerning Jewish DPs in Europe reflected this attitude. Naturally, one would not attempt to suggest that the issue of Palestine did not become important in the expression of British attitudes toward the Jewish DPs, but this brief presentation seeks to demonstrate that an examination of military government policy on the ground in the British zone reveals a more complicated attitude based on local factors and different rationale.[3] Initially, the British regarded the two questions—the situation of the Jewish displaced persons and the Palestine question—as quite separate issues. The refusal to link the two problems became unworkable and absurd as the months went by and events unfolded in Europe and in Palestine.

The policy toward Jewish displaced persons agreed upon between the British and Americans before the end of the war was simple enough. It was thought undesirable (or illiberal) to echo the Nazi theory that the Jews were a separate race. They were a religious group and in common with other such groups they should be classed according to their nationality.[4] This viewpoint can be better understood if we bear in mind that in general in the British consciousness there was little understanding of the level and nature of the Nazi persecution of the Jews. It was acknowledged that the Jews had suffered in the concentration camps but then so had other groups. The idea of special treatment was a notion unacceptable to British liberal

---

[1] *For example, A.L. Sacher,* The Redemption of the Unwanted: From the Liberation of the Nazi Death Camps to the Founding of Israel *(New York, 1983); Y. Bauer,* American Jewry and the Holocaust: The American Joint Distribution Committee, 1939–1945 *(Wayne State University Press, 1993); L. Dinnerstein,* America and the Survivors of the Holocaust *(Columbia University Press, 1982); A. Grobman,* Rekindling the Flame: American Jewish Chaplains and the Survivors of European Jewry, 1944–1948 *(Wayne State University Press, 1993).*

[2] *For the social and political life established in* Belsen, *see J. Reilly,* Belsen: The Liberation of a Concentration Camp *(London: Routledge, 1998), chs. 3 & 5; H. Leivick, etal,* Belsen *(Tel Aviv: Irgun Sheerit Hapeita Mehaezor Habriti, 1957); S.E. Bloch, ed.,* Holocaust and Rebirth: Bergen-Belsen 1945–1965 *(New York: Bergen-Belsen Memorial Press, 1965).*

[3] *For a longer treatment of these issues, see Reilly,* Belsen, *ch. 3.*

[4] *Public Record Office (PRO) Foreign Office (FO) 1030/300: Letter, Dewing (CCG) to WO, August 18, 1945.*

monoculturalism.[5] What is more, segregating the Jews would seem in accordance with theories propounded by the Nazis and sit uncomfortably with the policy of de-Nazification. And finally, such a policy was thought to be detrimental to the interests and security of the Jews themselves—it was felt that any policy which appeared to favor the Jews over other DPs would only lead to disruption and racial persecution in the camps. In any case, military government did not make provision for special cases. Jewish DPs were DPs nonetheless, and the army, as a huge bureaucratic organization, was concerned simply with getting the assembly centers to run as smoothly as possible. They did not see any need to complicate matters further in what was already an administrative and logistical nightmare.

In effect, the policy sanctioned further Jewish suffering. Very often German Jews and other prewar nationals from Axis countries, although many were camp survivors, were, nevertheless, classified as enemy nationals and thus denied privileged rations. It was expected that ex-internee German Jews would return home to be cared for by German civilian authorities, with little thought given to the implication of that policy. Furthermore, those who remained in the camps sometimes found themselves among former guards or tormentors, antisemites, and collaborators. The Jewish Committee in Belsen from the beginning set out to oppose the policy that left the Jews suffering from "the curse of national anonymity."[6]

In the words of the chief of the Political Division of the Control Council in the British Zone: "In short we cannot accept the theory that the Jews are a separate race—and as it was one of the principal tenets of the Nazi creed it is rather odd that they should now be trying to put it across."[7] It is clear that the claim of the Jewish DPs for a distinctive handling of their situation in Germany was not based on a claim that they were a separate race, but on the fact that because designated as a race, they had suffered particular persecution. The latter was a fundamental reality in the lives of the Jewish DPs. For the majority, there could be no returning to prewar norms. And no amount of British liberal conviction would change the situation.

The pressure for change in Allied policy came from many quarters in Britain and America over the summer of 1945, not least from the Jewish Agency, Anglo-Jewish leaders, and the World Jewish Congress, who drew attention to what they called the "callous and shameful neglect and indifference" with which Jewish DPs were treated.[8] The British did not welcome such interference and intervention, and when the American government-appointed Earl G. Harrison recommended a fundamental change in policy following a widespread review of DP camps and assembly centers in Europe, the British government was dismayed.[9]

The Harrison Report could not have expressed the political views of the Jewish leaders more persuasively. His main recommendation was that the United States government should press for the issue of a significant number of immigration certificates for Palestine. Whereas Washington was shocked enough at the condemnatory nature of the report to segregate Jewish DPs in the American zone, increase their rations to twice that of the German civilians, agree to improve the facilities for recreation, and appoint a Jewish liaison officer who would serve to advise the army on problems specifically relating to the Jewish DPs, the British were implacable and particularly unimpressed with the call for immigration certificates.[10]

[5] For an explanation of this idea, see T. Kushner, The Holocaust and the Liberal Imagination (Oxford: Blackwell, 1995).

[6] Leivick, Belsen, 35.

[7] PRO FO 1049/81/177: Steel to Britten, July 24, 1945.

[8] See Jewish Chronicle, June 15 and July 20; Jewish Standard, June 29; New York Times, July 21, 1945.

[9] See Dinnerstein, America, ch. 2, for the ramifications of the report. Report cited in full pp. 291–305.

[10] See Y. Bauer, Out of Ashes: The Impact of the American Jews on Post-Holocaust European Jewry (Oxford: Pergamon Press, 1989), 47–51; PRO FO 1030.300: Directorate Civil Affairs, WO to Chief of Staff, CCG, August 11, 1945.

"Mr Harrison's report is not in accordance with the facts, at any rate as far as the British zone is concerned" was the haughty conclusion of a report by the military authorities justifying the status quo.[11] At governmental level the reaction was equally negative. The Foreign Office requested that the decision to segregate Jews in the American zone be reversed to avoid the embarrassment a divergence in policy would bring. To accept the policy advocated by Harrison, the Foreign Office stressed:

> . . . is to imply in effect that there is no sure future in Europe for persons of Jewish race. This is surely a counsel of despair which it would be quite wrong to admit at a time when conditions throughout Europe are still chaotic and when effect of antisemitic policy sedulously fostered by Nazis has not yet been undone: indeed it would go far by implication to admit that Nazis were right in holding that there was no place for Jews in Europe.

> . . . at a time when there is a crying need for all possible displaced persons, Jews no less than Gentiles, to return home . . . to build up their native lands where they all have their own part to play, . . . our task surely is to create conditions in which they will themselves feel it natural and right to go home rather than to admit at this stage that such conditions are impossible to create.[12]

In government circles there was a genuine sympathy for what the victims of the Nazi regime had endured. Those kinds of conditions would not have existed in a democracy, and the thinking was that if the DPs gave the Allies time, democracy would be restored in Europe and life for the victims would return to normal. What was missing from the British analysis of the situation in Germany was an understanding of the deep feeling of the Jewish DPs concerning their own future.

At an international political level, the writing was on the wall as far as Britain's mandate in Palestine was concerned. Economically exhausted following the war, Britain was now dependent on the United States for its own reconstruction and its strategic cooperation in containing Soviet encroachment into Europe and the Middle East.[13] Truman's intervention narrowed significantly Britain's freedom of decision making on the issue. Truman repeated in writing to Attlee the request that restrictions on Jewish entry to Palestine be lifted and 100,000 certificates be issued to the refugees in Europe. The Americans saw clearly the link between the Palestine question and the Jewish DP problem in Europe. One offered the solution to the other (with the added gain that the U.S. Senate would not have to warrant an increase in immigration quotas). The British continued to prefer to consider them as separate issues.

Bevin was increasingly keen that Britain should not shoulder the burden of Palestine alone. It was on his suggestion the cabinet agreed to invite the USA to join Britain in setting up an Anglo-American Commission of Inquiry to examine the position of the Jewish DPs in Europe and how the situation could be relieved. He felt sure that once the American contingent of the commission was made to understand the complexity of the question, they would no longer be prepared to welcome uncritically the naive solution presented by the Zionists. How wrong he was.[14]

[11]*PRO FO 1049/195/107: CCG to WO, September 6, 1945.*

[12]*PRO FO 1049/81/177: Telegram, FO to Washington, October 5, 1945.*

[13]*See A. Sela, "Britain and the Palestine Question, 1945–48: The Dialectic of Regional and International Constraints," in* Demise of the British Empire in the Middle East. Britain's Response to Nationalist Movements, 1943–55, *M.J. Cohen and M. Kolinsky (London: Frank Cass, 1998).*

[14]*Hansard, 415, cols. 1927–35, November 13, 1945: Statement by Bevin announcing the Anglo-American Committee of Inquiry; Alan Bullock,* Ernest Bevin: Foreign Secretary 1945–1951 *(Oxford University Press, 1985). See R. Crossman,* Palestine Mission. A Personal Record *(London: Hamish Hamilton, 1947).*

Eventually the British yielded to American persuasion and a report emerged which endorsed Truman's original entreaty that 100,000 Jews be admitted into Palestine. Needless to say, the British government was disappointed at the result. Moreover, in June the Jewish armed struggle against the British Mandate was renewed, accompanied by intensified efforts at illegal immigration, settlement activity, and propaganda. Soon these efforts and their impact on Anglo-American relations began to influence British public opinion, Parliament, and even the cabinet, reinforcing the view that Britain should rid itself of the "thankless" duty in Palestine by returning the mandate to the UN and withdrawing altogether.

The different American and British worldview was mirrored in policy on the ground. Rabbi Herbert Friedman, former military assistant to the advisor on Jewish affairs in the American zone, talked earlier of the sympathy he and his colleagues received from the American military in helping the Jewish DPs and implied the strategy might have been enlisted in the British zone.[15] The situation in the two zones, however, was incomparable. Jewish representatives simply did not have the same authority and were mistrusted by the British. The authorities did eventually also appoint a Jewish advisor, a Colonel Solomon, but his hands were largely tied in an official capacity when he was seen to be supporting the line of the Jewish Central Committee.[16] And although members of the Jewish Brigade did help in the illegal movement of DPs, it was arguably more difficult for regular British soldiers to be as sympathetic when their countrymen were being killed at the same time in Palestine.

On the ground too there was a great deal of mistrust concerning the activities of the Central Jewish Committee, and in particular the power of Josef Rosensaft as a provocateur. In the period following Bevin's statement, relations became particularly strained. British authorities sought to restrict his movements as the president of the Central Jewish Committee. While he was on a trip to America, the Foreign Office cabled the British Embassy in Washington:

> . . . please report anything you may hear regarding his political activities. He is an extreme Zionist inimical to (Social Democratic) Jewry and has done his best to blacken British treatment of the Jewish displaced persons in Germany.[17]

According to British reports "a horrifying state of affairs" prevailed in Belsen whereby the British no longer had any control.[18] British paranoia had no end. Against the background of the escalating Cold War, one captain convinced himself Rosensaft was a Russian Communist. The damning proof? That he had once been sighted taking the Communist salute of the clenched fist at a demonstration.[19]

As Zionism became more of a perceived threat to the status quo in the British zone, so then British policy became more cautious. Careful distinctions were made between Jewish organizations on a political basis. Thus, representations from non-Zionist groups tended to be more welcome, and greeted less suspiciously, than those from overtly Zionist bodies. For example, in September

[15] *Rabbi H. Friedman, Morning Plenary Session, "A Military Chaplain's Perspective," Life Reborn, Jewish Displaced Persons, 1945–1951 Conference, Sunday, January 16, 2000.*

[16] *PRO FO 371/55705/410: Parliamentary question, Hynd to Orbach, March 18, 1946. See Reilly, Belsen, 107–108; PRO FO 1049/626: Steel to Dan, personal and confidential, October 8, 1946.*

[17] *PRO FO 1049/81/177: Telegram, FO to Washington, December 18, 1945. (Parentheses in original.)*

[18] *See PRO FO 1049/417: Comment by Pink to King (secret), August 31, 1946.*

[19] *Hebrew University, Institute of Contemporary History, Oral History Department: Interview with L.E. Levinthal; on the same theme see, Sacher, Redemption, 186–87.*

1945, the World Union for Progressive Judaism addressed a letter to Bevin requesting that a rabbi, a German refugee living in Palestine, be permitted to return to Frankfurt so that he might aid the revival of religious life in Germany. In the chaos of postwar Europe, the standard reply to such an application was that no facilities for private travel to Germany were available. In this illustrative, interesting case, however, it was felt that an exception should be made:

> The WU is a sensible and moderate body, whose objectives do not conflict with the policy of His Majesty's Government. . . . For this reason we should like to give the Union any facilities that we reasonably can, more particularly as we wish to discourage the view that Jews would be unable to establish themselves in Europe after the present period of emergency. There is reason to believe that the Zionists in Palestine are exerting pressure on this ground to prevent Jews from applying for permission to return to Europe.[20]

A further major strain on relations between the British on the one hand and the Americans and the DPs on the other was the issue of infiltrees from Eastern Europe. British policy in dealing with the new influx into Germany was repressive.[21] Refugees were refused entry to the zone and those who got through were denied DP facilities and the means to continue their journey. Many did get through. British policy then in dealing with the Polish infiltrees was not terribly effective, not only because of the defiance of the DPs and the Jewish organizations, but also because the policy was followed in isolation. By far the greatest number of Jews fleeing from Eastern Europe headed for the American zone. The Americans recognized the plight of these people and, unlike the British, offered them rations and accommodation. UNRRA policy too, was to provide the new influx of people with full DP status and privileges. Any firm British action against the infiltrees only served to direct more refugees into the American zone, which gave more direct access to southern European seaports, and so to Palestine.

In June, the British announced there would be no further registration of new DPs after July 1, 1946, in the British zone.[22] In addition, orders were issued that food and transport should only be supplied to the authorized DP population, and that steps should be taken to confiscate all illegally procured stocks of food.[23] Yet the Polish Jews continued to pour into the zone, and into the Belsen camp, confident that they would be provided for. In August of that year, 1,064 people were thought to have arrived in Belsen in just one week. The British orders were ignored by the Jewish Committee at Belsen and they continued to draw rations for the "infiltrees" illegally. In August, a further instruction from Headquarters of the Prisoner-of-War and Displaced Persons Division of the Control Commission ordered that from then on the ration strengths of all DP camps would remain at July 2 levels. At the same time it was explained to the inmates of Hohne (Belsen) that ordinary German ration cards would be available to all those living in the camp who were not registered DPs (provided that they complied with the regulation for the issue of ration cards, that is, lived with the civilian German population outside of the camps). The British received no positive response from the camp. From this time onward, as far as the authorities were concerned, the Jewish Committee was solely responsible for the presence in Hohne of the 2,000 ille-

[20]PRO FO 371/46959/4162: FO to WO, November 6, 1945.

[21]Y. Bauer, Flight and Rescue (New York: Random House, 1970), intro.; Sacher, Redemption, 149–51; M. Joyce Harrison, "Note: United States-British Collaboration on Illegal Immigration to Palestine, 1945–1947," Jewish Social Studies (1980–81) 42–43: 177. See Reilly, Belsen, 102–104.

[22]Yad Vashem, Rosensaft papers, 0-70/6: Technical Instruction No. 6: Status and Treatment of DPs Living Outside Assembly Centres.

[23]PRO FO 1049/417/95: Top secret telegram, CONCOMB to BERCOMB, August 1, 1946.

gals. If they were starving to death, as alleged by a Swedish Zionist organization in the press in December, then it was not the result of any military government policy but because of the choice of the Belsen committee to disobey orders.[24]

The British discussed a policy of forcible ejection and repatriation but rejected the idea in 1946. More than the fact that it would have been difficult to implement for relatively little reward, the negative publicity generated by such a policy would have caused terrific embarrassment. A year later, following a deterioration of the situation in Palestine, the British did indeed opt for extreme measures with regard to the *Exodus* passengers.[25]

To conclude, during the final two years in the life of the Belsen DP camp, as one would expect, relations between the British authorities and the Central Jewish Committee had improved a great deal, indeed, enough for Rosensaft to concede later that the British had shown them "much good will." In the years immediately after the war, tensions were far more apparent. Despite the attempts by a powerful Zionist lobby to link the Palestine question with the issues of the Jewish DP question, British policy was often shortsighted and insensitive and, in their attempt to be nondiscriminatory and follow predetermined policy guidelines, the British authorities refused to see the particularity of the Jewish tragedy in the Second World War story.

On the Palestine question Bevin had assumed that there would be a continuing British-American consensus on the need to resolve the problem in a way that would preserve Western interests in the Middle East—communications, oil, and strategic bases—especially in view of the postwar Soviet threat. Yet his repeated attempts at coordination with Washington were frustrated. As Alan Bullock, Bevin's biographer has written, "The Jewish demands and the Arab reaction were predictable; direct intervention by the American President was not."[26]

[24] *PRO FO 1049/417: Top secret telegram, BERCOMB to CONFOIK, August 2, 1946.*

[25] *See Reilly,* Belsen, *114–15.*

[26] *See Sela, "Britain and the Palestine Questions," 225. Bullock,* Ernest Bevin, *48.*

Soviet Policy

David Engel

Maurice Goldberg Professor of Holocaust Studies, New York University; Fellow, Diaspora Institute, Tel Aviv University

Initially I was asked to speak at this session on Soviet policy toward the DPs, a subject about which, I must confess, I know absolutely nothing. Of course I can take some comfort in the fact that no one knows anything about this subject, because no one has examined the relevant (and evidently copious) documents in the archives of the former Soviet Union that constitute the tangible traces of that policy. Of course, for many years there was no possibility of gaining access to those documents—a situation that left room for all sorts of speculation.

Today, however, historians are in a curious position: The archives, or at least a portion of them, are open, but both the volume of the materials they contain and the rather Byzantine conditions that still prevail in them mean that it is liable to take a good many years of work by more than a single scholar before anyone will be able to say much based upon them that is reliable. So we can no longer speculate, but we cannot yet speak responsibly on the basis of sustained research. We are in something of a temporary blackout zone like the one experienced by astronauts upon reentry into the earth's atmosphere, but until we escape it we have to treat requests such as the one made of me by the organizers of this conference with the utmost circumspection.

That is unfortunate not only because we are naturally curious to uncover what has been hidden from us for so many years, but also because what we have learned thus far about the policies of the British and U.S. governments toward the DPs has raised a number of tantalizing questions that, if they can be answered at all, can be so only on the basis of documents from the former Soviet archives. Many of these questions have to do with how the diplomatic context of the immediate postwar years—the context of the incipient Cold War and the concomitant bipolar geopolitical realignment—influenced the fate of the surviving remnant of European Jewry. In particular, they concern how that context might have contributed to the creation of a critical mass of DPs in the American zones of occupation in the first place. In my remarks today I shall try to outline what the nature of this influence might possibly have been and to explain how documentation from the Soviet side might illuminate the thinking and behavior of all of the principal Allies regarding DP matters.

To illustrate what I am talking about, I shall begin with a passage from a confidential memorandum written by a man named Reginald Manningham-Buller, a conservative MP and one of the British members of a body known as the Anglo-American Committee of Inquiry into the Problems of European Jewry and Palestine. The memorandum summarized Manningham-Buller's impressions immediately upon returning from a six-day official mission to Poland in February 1946:

> We visited one reception centre at Lodz. It was supposed to be run by the Jewish Committee, but the manager spoke only Russian. It would have been a brave man or woman who said anything to us, which conflicted with Russian desires. All Jewish organizations in Poland, not only the Zionists, are infected with the Palestine bug. It would be natural for them to indoctrinate their fellows. Two of those we saw in the shel-

ter began their conversation with precisely the same phrase: "We came from Central Asia; we are not [staying] in Poland; we are going on to Palestine." The Russians may want this migration because it will create difficulties for the British and Americans in Europe and accentuate the situation with regard to Palestine, and because they fear the influence and propaganda in Poland of a large number of Jews who have seen the inside of the USSR.

Some background will aid in interpreting these comments. The body under whose auspices Manningham-Buller found himself in Europe in February 1946—the Anglo-American Committee of Inquiry into the Problems of European Jewry and Palestine—had been established three months earlier. Its mission, as stated in the terms of reference that formally constituted it, was "to examine the position of the Jews in those countries in Europe where they have been the victims of Nazi and Fascist persecution, and the practical measures taken or contemplated to be taken in those countries to enable them to live free from discrimination and oppression, and to make estimates of those who wish or will be impelled by their conditions to migrate to Palestine or other countries outside Europe." The committee was formed largely as a reaction to President Truman's counsel to Prime Minister Attlee on August 31, 1945, that Britain could make a significant contribution to relieving the distress of Jewish DPs by issuing 100,000 new Palestine immigration certificates and using them to facilitate "the quick evacuation of as many as possible of the non-repatriable Jews [in the DP camps] as wish it." This American intervention into the Palestine problem had placed Britain, anxious to shore up its strategic position in the Middle East, in a quandary: it could hardly afford to disavow (or even to ignore) the public position of the government of what was clearly by then its senior ally, but on the other hand its grand geopolitical game plan in the rapidly changing postwar world was liable to be severely upset by a step bound to antagonize Arab interests in Palestine. British Foreign Minister Ernest Bevin thus proposed a tried and true political tactic: He would form a committee and co-opt the Americans onto it. The committee would have a threefold aim: to investigate all aspects of the situation of European Jewry, to find out what level of Jewish immigration into Palestine might be acceptable to the various parties with a stake in the region, and to "examine the possibility of relieving the position in Europe by immigration into other countries, including the United States and the Dominions."

Believing that the U.S. position was mainly the result of domestic political pressure, Bevin hoped that a blue-ribbon panel sanctioned in advance by the Truman administration would generate an effective counterweight to the force of American public opinion, and compel the United States to assume an equal measure of the responsibility for the European refugee problem that it, he felt, was trying to cast entirely on the British. This hope, to be sure, was eventually to be disappointed, as the committee ended up recommending that the 100,000 certificates be issued; but in November 1945 Bevin thought that he could control matters to a much greater extent than he could in fact.

The United States, of course, could not reject this ostensibly constructive British proposal—which did not unequivocally negate Truman's suggestion to Attlee—out of hand; but at the same time it could not accept the British formulation of the committee's mission without appearing to abandon the president's earlier stated position. Thus, U.S. Secretary of State James Byrnes insisted that the committee also be mandated "to examine political, economic and social conditions in Palestine as they bear upon the problem of Jewish immigration and settlement therein, and the well-being of the peoples now living therein." And he also insisted that the specific reference to the United States as a possible destination for Jewish DPs be stricken. Bevin was not happy with the changes, which linked the Palestine and the DP problems far more closely than he would have liked, but he feared that were he not to agree to them, the Americans would pull out of the project altogether. The result was that what might have seemed on the surface as a display of common Anglo-American purpose in relieving the plight of Jewish DPs was actually a product of Anglo-American friction and a vehicle for its expression.

Just as the committee was beginning its work, moreover, an additional source of friction emerged. In December 1945 lengthy articles appeared in leading British and American newspapers describing a phenomenon that must have appeared shocking to ordinary readers in those countries: Every month for the past half year, thousands of Jews who had survived the Holocaust in Poland, or who had returned there after being liberated from a Nazi camp or death march in Germany or Austria, had been leaving their native country, for the most part illegally, and infiltrating into the DP camps, mainly in the American zone of occupation. These Jews, who quickly came to make up a sizable proportion of the Jewish DP population, were presented in the press as double victims, not only of the Nazis but of Polish anti-Jewish violence, who had fled Poland out of a well-grounded fear for their lives. Since most of these Jews sought shelter in American-run facilities, the question of their ultimate destination was placed squarely in the Americans' lap. In thinking about this issue, however, the Truman administration had to take note of strong public opposition to expanding existing U.S. immigration quotas—opposition that was reiterated along with sympathy for the refugees when the newspaper reports describing their plight were published.

Responding to heightened public discussion of the issue, Truman issued an official statement from the White House on December 22, 1945, urging that "everything possible should be done . . . to facilitate the entrance of some of these displaced persons and refugees into the United States," but promising that he would not ask Congress to relax any existing immigration restrictions. The practical effect of this statement was to return public attention to Palestine, now not only as a destination for current DPs but as a safe haven for Polish Jews (including, according to estimates in British and U.S. hands at the time, anywhere between 120,000–250,000 who had survived the war in the Soviet Union and whose imminent return to Poland was anticipated in accordance with the Polish-Soviet repatriation agreement of July 1945). For Britain this development, which emphasized how its interests diverged from those of the United States precisely when it was hoping to project a common Anglo-American front, was hardly welcome.

The British government hoped, therefore, that, among other things, the Anglo-American Committee would bring to light information that might temper public sympathy for Jews leaving Poland for the DP camps; in any event, the committee would have to look into the matter in order to determine what was driving the Jewish migration. If it could be shown that that exodus was not a spontaneous flight from persecution, but the result of a calculated attempt by some group to obtain a political or economic benefit at British or American expense, then this source of pressure upon Britain to modify its Palestine policy might be eliminated. Thus it came to pass that immediately upon its arrival in Europe the committee dispatched a small delegation to explore the Polish situation. And thus it was that Manningham-Buller found himself in Lodz in the second week of February 1946.

The working hypothesis of at least some of the committee's members and of the British and American officials who briefed them was that the entire situation in Poland was the product of a well-organized Zionist plot, but none of the members of the delegation found as a result of their visit any compelling reason to believe that this was the case. It was in this context that conjectures about the Soviet Union's possible role in facilitating and perhaps even fostering the

Jewish migration for its own nefarious political purposes entered the reports of Manningham-Buller and of his British colleague, an official of the Midland Bank named Wilfrid Crick. Interestingly it did not enter the reports of the American delegate Frank Buxton, editor of the *Boston Herald,* or of the American staff member who accompanied the delegation, Leslie Rood. But the British delegates presented a picture of a Soviet Union trying to turn the anxieties of Jewish Holocaust survivors into a wedge to split the two Western allies and a spearhead against Britain's position in the Middle East, all in the hope of extending its own sphere of influence in that part of the world at British and American expense.

What grounds did the two Britons adduce for their speculations? To be sure, they were not the first people to have thought along such lines. Since the early fall of 1945, Stanislaw Mikolajczyk, the former premier of the Polish government-in-exile, and other leading Polish anti-Communists had been bending the ears of senior American and British diplomats with the suggestion that the Soviets were actively encouraging Jews not only to leave Poland but to spread rumors that the reason for the flight was the hostility of the Polish population, fanned by the anti-Communist opposition. Mikolajczyk's remonstrances were sufficient to persuade Elbridge Durbrow, chief of the State Department's Division of East European Affairs, that, as he put it in a memorandum to Undersecretary of State Dean Acheson on December 20, 1945, "there is a very strong probability that this entire movement is being planned [by the Soviets as] . . . part of a scheme to further complicate the Arab-Jewish situation in the Near East by forcing us to insist that the large number of Polish Jews in our zone in Germany should be sent into Palestine . . . , [which] will of course further complicate Anglo-American relations." Yet as it turned out the delegation of the Anglo-American Committee to Poland appears to have uncovered virtually no hard evidence to substantiate this thought. Manningham-Buller cited only the presence of a Russian-speaking supervisor at a shelter for homeless Jews in Lodz, who, he thought, was intimidating the residents into demanding entry into Palestine, while Crick cited the prominence of soldiers "in Polish army uniform and wearing Russian decorations" among the 2,500 demonstrators who protested outside the hotel where the Anglo-American representatives were quartered. Manningham-Buller also found it curious that the Polish government was not permitting UNRRA to offer relief to Jewish repatriants. "This may not be due," he wrote, "to just stupidity, hardheartedness or inefficiency on the part of the [Polish] Government, but a part of deliberate Russian-inspired policy." These were not, by themselves, terribly telling proofs, and none of the British, American, Polish, or Jewish observers with whom the delegation met appears to have offered anything more substantial. Indeed, the lack of confirmation led the American Rood to conclude in his summary of the mission that "whether the Soviet Government attempts to exercise influence on the Jewish migration . . . is doubtful." On the contrary, Rood believed that there was evidence that actually negated the conclusions of the two Englishmen. True, he acknowledged, "in the transient shelter at Lodz the wishes of the Jews for Palestine were clearly induced in part by the Russian speaking staff . . . , [and] while Russian soldiers are commonplace in Poland, Russians in a charity shelter were not easily explainable"; but on the other hand he noted that "reliable witnesses state that Jews of the [anti-Zionist] leftist elements . . . which have returned from Russia advocate that Jews remain in Poland to participate in the rebuilding."

Rood's counterevidence, however, was not much stronger than the proofs Manningham-Buller and Crick offered for their assessments. Actually, his final comment indicated just how ignorant not only the Anglo-American observers but their so-called expert informants were of what was happening around them. In any event, the first repatriation transport carrying Jews from the Soviet Union arrived in Poland only on February 8 (that is, while the delegation was actually visiting); there is no evidence to suggest that "anti-Zionist leftist elements" were dominant among the first arrivals; and in any case, Zionist groups in Poland had already managed to smuggle some 500 activists from the USSR into the country before the official transports departed, in order to meet the new arrivals and, they hoped, to direct them toward Zionist institutions. There were also additional facts of which not only they but the highest echelons of the British and American policy-making establishments appear to have been unaware. For example, in November 1945 the Polish government had increased surveillance along its western and southern borders with a mind to stopping the illegal exodus of Jews.

By the time the Anglo-American Committee delegation reached Poland, that campaign had reduced traffic across the frontier to a small fraction of what it had been but a few months before. Yet still, in February 1946, Foreign Office and State Department officials continued to discuss whether it might not be advisable to make a joint Anglo-American approach to the Poles demanding that they do precisely what they had already done three months before. And one of the major factors that militated against such an approach to the Poles was the apprehension that somewhere, somehow, the Soviets might be lurking in the background. As Burke Elbrick, assistant chief of the State Department's Division of Eastern European Affairs, asked Sir Arthur Tandy, first secretary of the British Embassy in Washington, on February 5, "[Have you] given any thought to the fact that Polish Jews reaching the British and American zones in Germany must cross the Soviet zone of occupation?" Elbrick's knowledge of geography does not appear to have been terribly strong, because there were routes that bypassed the Soviet zone; but if that fact meant that the Soviet Union was indeed interested in abetting the exodus of Jews from Poland, then, he feared, any American or British misstep might carry unwanted diplomatic consequences extending far beyond the immediate problem at hand.

In other words, a major aspect of U.S. and British policies toward Jewish DPs in their occupation zones appears to have been formulated, to at least some measure, with an eye toward the USSR, yet without any reliable knowledge of what Soviet policymakers were thinking about the matter. That situation raises many questions, but in light of my mission here today, I shall mention only those that might yield to research in Soviet archives. To begin with, of course, it would be useful to know whether people like Manningham-Buller, Crick, Durbrow, and Elbrick were on to something or not. This is not to suggest that Soviet agents could have put the idea of flight to the American zone into the heads of masses of Jews who wouldn't have gotten the idea otherwise. But the Soviet Union was in a position to influence the rate of flow of Jews both into and out of Poland. So there is room to ask: Did the Soviets think at all about the possible implications of the Jewish flight from Poland for their confrontation with their estranged Western allies? If so, did they apply any pressure upon the Polish government to help the flight along? Did they adjust their repatriation policies or practices to serve that goal? What did they think were likely or liable to be the benefits and risks of trying to manipulate the situation?

Other questions are more subtle. To what extent, for example, were the Soviets aware of British and American suspicions about their involvement in the Jewish exodus and of the evidentiary basis for them? Were they interested in encouraging those suspicions or in discouraging them? How did they use the controls over information flow that were at their disposal to influence British and American thinking? Was their repeated refusal to maintain services for Jewish DPs in their own zones of occupation, to permit UNRRA to operate freely in Eastern Europe, or to allow delegations from the Anglo-American Committee into most of their other East European satellites aimed at making a particular impression upon the British and Americans that would be useful to them in this context? In what ways, in other words, were

Jewish DPs in Europe and Jewish Holocaust survivors behind what was soon to become the iron curtain looked upon by the Soviets as potential pawns in one of the first instances of Cold War gamesmanship?

Only now are we in a position to begin the arduous, painstaking work of locating and piecing together documents that may eventually suggest answers to these questions—answers that are essential for understanding how the conditions in which Jewish life was reborn after the Holocaust came to be created. The scholars who will undertake that labor will be engaged in anything but a trivial pursuit.

RESPONDING TO OUR LEGACY

OVERVIEW

Jean Bloch Rosensaft

National Director for Public Affairs and Institutional Planning, Hebrew Union College—Jewish Institute of Religion; Second Generation Advisory Group, United States Holocaust Memorial Council

Good morning. I am a member of the Second Generation Advisory Group of the United States Holocaust Memorial Council, and I serve as exhibitions chair of the *Life Reborn* conference. It is an honor and a privilege to welcome you to this morning's closing plenary in which we will explore the subject of our legacy.

The displaced persons camp of Bergen-Belsen lies at the heart of my identity as a daughter of Holocaust survivors. Fate brought my parents to Belsen from disparate parts of Europe—my mother, Lilly, and my grandparents, Rose and David Czaban, from Western Galicia; and my father, Sam Bloch, together with my grandmother, Sonia, and uncle, Martin, from Bielorussia. They had endured the annihilation of their extended families, including the killing of my paternal grandfather, Joshua Bloch, the distinguished educator and communal leader after whom I am named. At Belsen, my family emerged from the destruction of the Shoah with courage and strength to rebuild their lives among the Sh'erit ha-Pletah, the "surviving remnant" of European Jewry. Their vitality and optimism have been a source of inspiration throughout my life.

My father, at the age of 22, became the youngest member of the Jewish Committee that governed the Bergen-Belsen DP camp. In that capacity, he administered cultural activities, food and clothing distribution, and security, and was a key organizer of youth activities, including the Zionist youth organizations and kibbutzim in the DP camp. As a member of the Aliya Committee, he organized legal and illegal immigration to Palestine. He was a member of the local command of the Haganah, charged with flight and rescue operations to bring survivors to Palestine, and responsible for acquiring vital defense supplies for the Haganah in Palestine.

My 18-year-old mother was encouraged by my grandparents to pursue her dreams of a medical career. While they remained in Belsen, she attended the University of Bonn's medical school and lived in the home of the head of the Bonn Jewish community. It was during a school holiday that my mother returned to Belsen, where she met my father on a double date, and they fell in love. At their wedding on June 8, 1949, my father was brought to the *hupah* by Hadassah and Josef Rosensaft, leaders of the Central Jewish Committee in the British Zone of Germany and esteemed friends with whom my father worked closely. Their lifelong friendship yielded unexpected but delightful fruits when, a generation later, Menachem, their son, and I would marry and have a daughter, Jodi, linking our families together forever.

Throughout our childhood years, my sister, Gloria, and I grew up in the orbit of the Belsen survivors. Although dispersed throughout the United States, Canada, and Israel, the friendships forged in the DP camp were perpetuated through memorable reunions and significant projects memorializing the Holocaust. During the 1950s, 1960s, and 1970s, when most of the world wanted to forget the Holocaust and the American Jewish community was disinterested in learning too much about it, my parents were always in the forefront of the survivor leadership—establishing the first Yom HaShoah commemorations, memorial sites and museums, and Holocaust publications. Some of the formative memories of my childhood are centered on the anniversary events when hundreds of "Belseners" would gather in New York, Israel, Montreal, and Toronto, and in pilgrimages to the memorial site of the Bergen-Belsen concentration camp, to remember the *kedoshim,* recall the miracle of liberation on April 15, 1945, and affirm that the Jewish people lives and endures.

While never forgetting the loss and pain of the Shoah, my parents and their friends would reminisce with humor and nostalgia about their memorable experiences in the Belsen DP camp, where they met, married, were educated, began new families, and prepared for a future of freedom and hope. Their reminiscences were, for me, the positive, life-affirming lens through which I first encountered the subject of the Holocaust—a lens through which I could assimilate the tragic realities of my family's wartime experiences.

I have vivid memories of my father spending hours poring over documents, photographs, and film footage for his extraordinary book, *Holocaust and Rebirth: Bergen-Belsen 1945–50,* published in 1965. This unique volume presents the definitive pictorial documentation of the political, social, educational, and cultural activities of the Belsen survivors after liberation. At a time when American publishers declined to publish Holocaust-related books as commercially unviable, my father's book was the first in a series of many volumes of survivor testimony and Holocaust history, which he edited and were published by the Bergen-Belsen Memorial Press.

As secretary-general of the International Remembrance Award for Distinction and Excellence in Literature of the Holocaust—chaired by Elie Wiesel—he, Professor Wiesel, and my parents-in-law established an international literary jury, an innovative program of international literary conferences, and visits to Belsen led by the Belsen survivor leadership, through which celebrated American and European novelists, poets, and essayists ranging from George Steiner and Chaim Grade to Arthur Morse and Andre Schwarz-Bart were encouraged to explore the subject of the Holocaust in their work.

My parents' odyssey from Belsen to today has been characterized by a zest for life, a delight in community and friendship, and an indomitable spirit of pride and strength that I have strived to emulate. I am privileged to be my parents' daughter and to be imbued with their values and commitments. My involvement in the *Life Reborn* project is a tribute to my parents and their enduring legacy to Jewish history and the Jewish people. Their example has certainly influenced and inspired my professional and communal life.

My parents' example conditioned me to understand that, when it came to the Holocaust, to be introspective and retrospective, while important, was not enough. Their experiences in the DP camp and afterward taught me the importance of activism in the cause of Holocaust remembrance and education.

And so, as an art historian at the Museum of Modern Art in New York, I soon came to the realization that while I could succeed in teaching millions of people to truly appreciate Picasso and Pissarro, the greater fulfillment in my life would come from a professional commitment to Jewish life.

Thus, I joined the Jewish Museum in New York as a curator and educator, where the intersection of my family history and 4,000 years of Jewish spiritual and cultural life would enable me to contribute as a builder of Jewish continuity. This is an effort that has intensified through my work at Hebrew Union College, Jewish Institute of Religion, where I help to strengthen the viability of that institution's mission: to train the rabbis, cantors, educators, Jewish communal professionals, and scholars for world Jewry.

As a curator and museum director, I've had the opportunity to organize the first exhibitions of art by survivor artists and children of survivor artists in the early 1980s; to curate the Jewish Museum's traveling exhibition of *Justice in Jerusalem Revisited: The Eichmann Trial* as well as *Chagall and the Bible;* to present the creativity of scores of contemporary artists who are exploring Jewish identity and experience; and, most recently, to co-curate with my father, *Rebirth After the Holocaust: The Bergen-Belsen Displaced Persons Camp, 1945–1950,* presented at the B'nai B'rith Klutznick National Jewish Museum in Washington, D.C., as part of the *Life Reborn* project.

It has been a unique privilege to be closely associated with the United States Holocaust Memorial Museum from its very inception—as a member of the initial Museum Committee, the Collections and Acquisitions Committee, and the Second Generation Advisory Group. How proud we all are of the Museum's development and impact as a thriving center of documentation and memory—educating millions of people of all faiths about the ultimate consequences of intolerance and injustice.

Our role in the chain in the transmission of Holocaust memory comes into sharpest focus, however, as parents. When our daughter was born, we grappled with the challenge of how could we condition in our own child the commitment to Holocaust remembrance and education that we had received from our survivor parents. It was a natural process of osmosis—as our home served as the central staging ground for the development of Second Generation in New York, and for the creation of the International Network of Children of Jewish Holocaust Survivors. Our daughter was exposed to an extensive circle of our friends who were actively absorbed in organizing conferences and gatherings; as well as traveling to Belsen to demonstrate against President Reagan's defamation of the martyrs of Belsen with his immoral equation of the victims of the Holocaust with the Waffen-SS dead buried at Bitburg.

But our daughter has also grown up with the values of her grandparents and great-grandparents through an immersion in Jewish education and observance and a sensitization to the cause of human rights. For I believe that our legacy extends beyond perpetuating the memory of the destruction of the Holocaust, to a commitment to the vitality of our Jewish heritage and faith, to the security and strengthening of the State of Israel, and to fighting all forms of prejudice and persecution.

We, who are the witnesses to the witnesses, bear a special privilege and a special responsibility. We have been privileged to be our parents' children, to fulfill their hopes and aspirations in the rebirth of the Jewish people out of destruction, and to absorb their memories, their insights, and their wisdom as the essence of our very being. As we look to the future, our responsibility calls upon us to emulate their vision and strength and to exert our own leadership in the intergenerational transmission of memory.

At a time when the Holocaust has become all too fashionable—subject to exploitation, trivialization, commodification, and universalization, we must exert our vigilance as guardians of the integrity of Holocaust memory. Elie Wiesel spoke yesterday about the difference between knowledge and understanding. This, I believe, is where the Second and Third Generations bear a crucial responsibility and imperative for leadership, for our relationship with our parents and grandparents transcends mere knowledge of the Holocaust through a profound understanding of their pain, their loss, their courage, and their hope.

Today, we affirm our parents' legacy to perpetuate Holocaust commemoration and education, so that present and future generations will understand the dangers of indifference in the face of intolerance and injustice. All of us sitting here today share this responsibility, within our personal, communal, and professional lives.

Each of us can make a difference, by supporting the United States Holocaust Memorial Museum, by bringing groups to visit the Museum, by bringing the Museum's exhibitions to our own cities, by establishing Holocaust curricula in our schools, and by organizing *Yom HaShoah* commemorations and Holocaust education programs in our own communities. Each of us can demonstrate the leadership that will sustain Holocaust education and commemoration into the future.

We, who bear the names of grandparents we never knew, and whose children affirm that the Jewish people lives, pledge to you, our parents, that we will continue your work and ensure your values and commitment for the generations to come.

We are privileged that a panel of distinguished members of the Second Generation will now explore the scope and imperatives of our legacy. They bring to this panel a diversity of life experiences and points of view that will illuminate their own unique understanding of the enduring impact of the Holocaust on our lives and its implications for the future.

To explore the meaning and impact of our legacy, we have with us Thane Rosenbaum, adjunct professor of law at Fordham University. Thane is a novelist and the author of *Elijah Visible* and *Second Hand Smoke*. Debbie Teicholz-Guedalia is a photographer and artist whose work for the last 15 years has described the impact of the Holocaust. Dr. Gary John Schiller is associate professor of medicine, Division of Hematology-Oncology, UCLA School of Medicine, and the president of Second Generation Los Angeles, Sons and Daughters of Jewish Holocaust Survivors. We also want to express the profound regrets of Elan Steinberg, executive director of the World Jewish Congress, who is unfortunately unable to be with us today because of illness.

Second Generation Perspectives

Thane Rosenbaum

Novelist; Adjunct Professor of Law, Fordham University

Thank you, Jeanie, for those moving words.

What I plan to do now is read two very short passages from my latest novel, *Second Hand Smoke*. And sandwiched in between each reading I'll talk for a few minutes about some of the ideas that this conference has inspired.

In walking around the conference I am flattered by the many people who have actually read this book, but I think I should still do a very brief synopsis of what the novel is about.

It is the story of Mila Katz, who was an Auschwitz-Birkenau survivor. In 1947 she abandons her young son, a six-month-old child, Isaac Borowski, in Warsaw, Poland, and makes her way to Frankfurt, and then Miami Beach, Florida. There, she befriends Jewish mobsters, and becomes the confidante of the Jewish syndicate in Florida. She also has another son, Duncan Katz, when she marries another survivor, Yankee Katz.

Duncan is raised in the spirit of a Jewish Golem, a Frankenstein monster, a prisoner of his own inherited rage. Shall we say, he's a very large, imposing Jewish man. He was a black belt karate master at the age of nine, where he makes an appearance on the Johnny Carson show. He was also an all-American linebacker at Yale University. He then becomes a lawyer for the Justice Department, in their Office of Special Investigations, where he obtains, what would be for him a dream job: a prosecutor of Nazi war criminals.

But Duncan is very much a monster himself, an unfeeling creature, a creation out of the ashes of Auschwitz, and determined entirely to vindicate the crimes committed against his parents. It is only through the loss of his job and his return to Poland, reclaiming and revisiting the steps of his now dead parents, that he begins to soften, heal, and come to terms with his legacy. And in some ways, he learns to breathe again after having choked for so long on *Second Hand Smoke*, which is where the title of the book comes from.

And in doing so, in returning to Poland, he reunites with his brother, whom he had never met, a man who is the caretaker of the Warsaw Jewish cemetery, as well as a yoga master and Christlike figure in Catholic Poland.

So I thought I would begin by reading the prologue for the novel, which is very short. After that I would speak for a few minutes about some thoughts I had about this conference, as well as where my work fits in the context of the Second Generation experience.

Then I'll finish up with a little piece about Mila, who throughout the novel is making a series of deathbed confessions about the terrible truths of her life, which she expresses to her three African American, round-the-clock nurses at Mount Sinai Hospital in Miami Beach. They become the caretakers of her story: the abandoning of Isaac in Poland, and something else she does to him, and the emotional scarring of Duncan in America.

This is the prologue from *Second Hand Smoke:*

He was a child of trauma, not of love, or happiness, or exceptional wealth, just trauma. And nightmare too; wouldn't want to leave that out. As a young man, he seemed to have come equipped with all the right credentials.

Primed for loss, consigned to his fate, but what kind of a career exploits such talents, and who would want such a job?

He certainly wasn't pleased by the hand dealt to him, the straw that he nervously drew from the lot of random legacies, only to wish that he could immediately pick again.

This wasn't a badge of honor, not the sort of thing that registered, even in his own morbid vision of the world, as a source of personal pride.

But the circumstances of his birth were much like everyone else's; he hadn't been given much of a choice in the matter. He couldn't help who his parents were, where they had been, what they had seen, what they might have done.

Without the workings of a will, or a bequest, he had received an inheritance that he would have rather done without. The kind of legacy he'd just as soon give back.

But it doesn't work that way. What his parents gave him, he couldn't pass off on someone else, he couldn't even explain or understand what it was that he even had.

Splintered, disembodied memories that once belonged to them, were now his alone, as though their two lives couldn't exhaust the outrage. The pain lived on as a family heirloom of unknown origins.

What he saw he couldn't exactly identify, and what he remembered was not something he actually ever knew. It was all interior, like a prison, like a cage.

Duncan had not been a witness to the Holocaust, only to its aftermath. His testimony was merely secondhand. Yet, the staggering reality of the cattle cars, the gas chambers, and the crematoria, did not feel remote to him, either, even though a half century of years, and an ocean of water, separated him from the actual crime. But crimes don't just end with the immediate injuries; the mind, alas, does not allow for that, and this was a special crime. The dreams of his parents—actually, their nightmares—kept it all alive. What he saw firsthand was the damage that could never be undone, the true legacy of the Shoah.

Lives that were supposed to start all over, but couldn't. Halting first steps, then the stumbles. The inexhaustible sorrow of the parents; the imminent recognition of the children.

A father rendered impotent by the violence done to his life, a mother who would not, could not mother.

What to expect from such pedigrees, such mis-breeds. Children of smoke and skeletons. The heirs of those who once had shaved heads and still had numbered arms.

What chance did their parents have? And what chance did they? The Holocaust shaped those who were survivors of survivors, inexorably, cruelly, and unfairly so.

The choices and compromises made, the relationships cultivated and broken, the psychic demons and grotesque muses that mockingly interfered with everyday life.

That was the prologue from *Second Hand Smoke*.

I should say that I was really honored when Menachem Rosensaft invited me to speak at this conference. But in being here, I must also confess to you that it has been very intimidating for me. Because, in some strange way, I actually don't feel like I belong, or fit in that well. You think so?

I'll tell you why I feel this way. I didn't realize when Menachem called to invite me to appear here, and it was very palpable on the first night, that these sessions, which were very powerful and profound, felt very much to me like pep rallies. They have been very spirited experiences all connected to themes about renaissance, about renewal, rebirth—essentially the very title of this conference.

But my fictional landscapes arise very much out of the perspective, and aesthetic, of damage and spiritual injury and loss and grief and martyrdom and paralysis and trauma—essentially, the mass extermination of Europe's Jews.

And so within these sessions, which were so poignant in its spirit and animation about the celebration of life in the DP camps, my work doesn't really seem to fit in because my novels, while regarded as comic and dark and very contemporary at their center, are really about the sense of loss, and the transmission of grief and trauma to the survivors and their children.

So there were moments here, within this impressive celebration, within the real joyousness of the occasion, that it was remarkable for me to witness it all given the darker, starker qualities of my fiction.

For this reason, I was pleased when Elie Wiesel reminded us yesterday, that those who were once tortured remain so.

Because I really do write from that aesthetic. To me, that feels emotionally true. Despite the spirit of the repair and renewal of this conference, there is still this incredible, palpable, tangible sense that most people in this room still have more in common with loss than anything else, either in their First Generational elements, or in their Second Generational elements. I don't want to in any way put a damper on the final phase of this session, but I think that it is something I felt that I needed to say. I hope that within the spiritual power of moving forward into the next millennium, that we never lose sight of that fact that we really all are born out of the ashes of Auschwitz.

And yes, it is indeed a miracle, and yes, it is a powerful statement of Jewish continuity and self-preservation that we are here today. But it is also true that there is a legacy here, as Jeanie quite correctly pointed out, that is deep within us, so deep that even the broader culture oftentimes needs to exploit it. And we need to remember, and guard against that, as well.

I would also like to say, that unlike the Rosensafts, as an example, and you know, Romana, and Rositta, Eva Fogelman, and some other organizers of the conference, I was born in 1960 and my parents, who died many years ago, were not in DP camps.

So again, in this way as well, I don't feel connected to this conference. I am a novelist whose focus is more on death and loss than on life and renewal. My parents were in concentration camps but not in displaced persons camps. And my parents never spoke to me or others about the Holocaust.

I never heard a word about it in my home. It's the mystery of art, to me, that I would leave a corporate law firm after having been a lawyer for a number of years, to go off and write novels with post-Holocaust themes given what little presence the Holocaust had in my childhood.

And when I left corporate law to write post-Holocaust fiction, I didn't know that these kinds of books would come out.

And if my parents were alive today, I think they would be shocked, totally shocked that Elie Wiesel would mention my name in a room such as this, and also shocked, that I would be here with Menachem Rosensaft and other leaders of the Second Generation because this was not my world. My parents did everything in their power to conceal their dark past.

In some ways they were successful. But in other ways, parents always fail in trying to conceal their darkest fears from their children.

No matter how hard they try, children pick it up, whether it's money troubles, or whether it's Birkenau; they pick it up. They understand what frightens their parents most, even when their parents never speak of it.

And living in Miami Beach in what was very much an idyllic childhood as a small boy, I was processing something that my parents were transmitting even through their silence.

Because as I already said, my parents never spoke about the Holocaust, either in its traumatic or comedic elements.

Given all that silence, this is what I would call the mysterious, spooky elements to my fiction.

And, when I do readings around the country, it always shocks me that invariably a person in the audience who is a child of Holocaust survivors—there's always one, if not more—comes to see me and says, "You have no idea how much your writing resonates with me."

When this happens I am always completely dumbfounded, because 90 percent of what takes place in my books didn't happen to me.

And so how it is that my fictions come out this way is really mysterious to me, and I think it speaks to this idea of the enormity of Auschwitz, that was so great, the magnitude of horror was so great that the outrage could not have been canceled or exhausted in just one generation. You cannot, in fact, expect 11 million ghosts, 6 million Jewish ghosts to go away that easily.

They must penetrate and perpetuate themselves somewhere—within the soul or within the body and spirit of all of us. That is what inspires this kind of mystical artistic experience that winds up as one of the books.

Now I'll just read a few paragraphs. This is when Mila is in the hospital, about to make another confession.

It really was my nod not necessarily to the DP experience, but to the immediate postwar experience:

> Before Mila, not one of these nurses had ever heard of Auschwitz or Birkenau, and why should they have? Even most American Jews thought of camps only as places to send children during the summer.

But now, weeks into her care, the nurses would forever know the words. It was more than just that death had occurred at Auschwitz; it was at least for their patient, the place where life became twisted and deviant.

After liberation, from that point forward, every decision Mila made was shadowed by Auschwtiz. At the age of fifteen, Mila had been taken from the Warsaw Ghetto and brought to Birkenau. Her parents were sent to Treblinka, and she never saw them again.

One died from starvation, the other gas. Once the privileged child of a prosperous Jewish family, she became almost overnight an orphan, and, after her experience in the ghetto and the camp, a seasoned scavenger.

Survival came to her naturally, the same fingers that once tapped piano keys now learned the sleight of a grabbing hand. She made the right allies in the camp, avoided the harshest work detail, got hold of essential provisions, made her cheeks appear more robust with contraband rouge enabling her to pass through selections and live another day. She had returned home knowing that no other member of her family had survived. A new set of drastic measures was necessary.

She would now live without moderation. Not quite seventeen years old, she began to smoke and drink heavily, as if she were Marlene Dietrich.

She spent many nights in makeshift Polish nightclubs, listening to American jazz, dancing to American bee-bop and swing, seduced by life in whatever imperfect form the world after Auschwitz could offer.

And there were many men. Their names were unimportant, so were their pasts, which had been obliterated anyway.

Only the syntax on the forearms was unerasable. They could look to no one but to each other, and when they looked to each other, they knew that nothing further had to be said.

Nobody else was waiting, and their confiscated homes did not expect their return, nor would such homecomings have been welcome by those who now occupied them.

What they shared in common was the poisonous knowledge of the camps, and that was more than enough. All other dating rituals were superfluous, conversation was itself a waste of time, silence was the most reliable language of all.

Foreplay was foolish, cheap thrills were precious, attractions had little to do with love. Mila's circle made love wildly, with total abandon, and sometimes silently, with orgasms of anguish, mournful and true.

Second Generation Perspectives

Debbie Teicholz-Guedalia

Photographer and artist

Good morning. I'm a photographer. My feelings about the legacy of the Holocaust have always been positive, productive, and a vital part of my and the rest of my world's existence.

My parents were vocal about their experiences and were Jewish activists during and after the war. That's not to say that the Holocaust did not traumatize them, and that they, in their very special way, did not pass their trauma down to their children.

But, unlike the theory proposed by Helen Epstein in the late '70s, that the Second Generation—as children of survivors were now being referred to—are all severely repressed, nonproductive, sheltered inmates of the psychological trauma of the Holocaust, all of my parents' friends and their children are productive, family oriented, usually community-minded, happy people. Imagine.

For me personally, it is always the greatest source of inspiration, as it has been this weekend, to hear Holocaust survivors tell their stories, and for me to do whatever I am able to do to respect their personal experiences. Through my photography, I hope to translate the memory of that experience to my generation, and to the generations to follow.

I grew up in New York City, where everybody is a survivor of something. I grew up exposed to different kinds of cultures, religions, economic levels, and sexual orientations. The difference between my experience and that of other immigrant children is that I was not allowed to take my freedom or my religious background for granted. I was forbidden to forget, but I was also well educated in the art of assimilation.

I am among a handful of photographers of my generation who tries to address the Holocaust as a non-documentarian issue. Firstly, the archival images that we all know, belong to our collective consciousness: like the entrance gate to Auschwitz, the faces hanging from the cattle cars, the mass graves. These already have a major historical impact. The viewers can walk by them and dismiss the pictures emotionally; they can say, I don't need to deal with that picture, I've seen it a thousand times.

Secondly, I feel this is a personal journey that I'm leading the viewer through, so I want to use firsthand images, I mean images that I make myself, not appropriated ones to describe my interpretation of the Holocaust legacy. As a photographer, I am present with the reality that presents itself before me. As a child of Holocaust survivors, I am trying to picture an experience from which I am once removed. After all, I did not survive the Holocaust, but had my parents not survived, I wouldn't be here to speak to you today.

My father, Bruce Teicholz, was a Jewish activist during and after World War II. In 1942 he escaped from his hometown of Lvov, Poland, where he left his mother, father, and 12 brothers and sisters to lose their lives at the hand of the Third Reich. Rather than serve the Nazis as president of the *Judenrat,* the Jewish council, he became a partisan fighter.

Escaping into Hungary, he became a hero of the Jewish underground in Budapest. He was the leader of 120 resistance fighters, young men and women who fought the Nazis until liberation in April 1945.

It was in Budapest that he worked with a young Swedish diplomat, Raoul Wallenberg. Wallenberg heard that my father was fabricating forged identity papers for the Jews. Working together they saved thousands of Hungarian Jews. My father last saw Wallenberg two days before he disappeared. He was one of the few who worked directly with, and was a witness to, Wallenberg's heroism. In 1945, after the war, my father convinced the four powers occupying Vienna to turn the Rothschild Hospital into a shelter center for all persons displaced by the Holocaust. As president of the Rothschild Hospital, with the aid of The American Joint Distribution Committee, he was able to provide shelter and a gathering place to reunite thousands of other Eastern European Holocaust survivors. Also, using the Rothschild Hospital as a cover, he was active in the Bricha, the clandestine flight of Jews out of Eastern Europe. Both my parents continued to be community leaders with Jewish organizations such as the Joint, ORT, and Reuth.

For me, the memory and the memorializing of the Holocaust are fraught with the difficulty of our displacement of time and place. Fifty years have passed, and unfortunately, the voices of survivors are being silenced by the passing of time. It is left up to communities to raise their own voices to protect whatever physical and emotional history we have.

We must preserve the artifacts of survivors and their testimony in serious institutions and museums as we have already started to do.

Like the United States Holocaust Memorial Museum in Washington, the Museum of Jewish Heritage in New York, and Yad Vashem, we must protect the sites of destruction from vandalism and physical revisionism, because the Eastern Europeans are still trying to cover up the camps and the mass grave sites, by trying to transform them into farmland, or erecting churches on the sites of destruction.

And when I say "we," I mean you and me. We must encourage artists to explore the effects of the Holocaust on society, and on themselves. And we must demand that society integrate Holocaust history into the education system, in order to teach not only the children, but also the parents of those children.

But it is also up to us to be vigilant, to be watchful and attentive to what is being taught.

Holocaust education is about teaching my children about their family history, and about making them understand that antisemitism, and other forms of ethnic cleansing existed not only at the time of the pharaohs, but they exist today, as we walk through the earth.
Thank you.

Debbie Teicholz-Guedalia's presentation also included an extensive and sensitive discussion of her powerful photography, and the interrelationship of her art and her identity as the daughter of Holocaust survivors. Unfortunately, we are unable to reproduce these outstanding photographs together with Ms. Teicholz-Guedalia's commentaries thereon.

Second Generation Perspectives

Gary John Schiller

Associate Professor of Medicine, Division of Hematology/Oncology, Department of Medicine, UCLA School of Medicine; President, Second Generation Los Angeles, Sons and Daughters of Jewish Holocaust Survivors

First of all, I'd like to thank the organizers for generously inviting me to this conference. I found it very interesting, and the conference has encouraged me personally to seek out more knowledge.

Because of the sensitivity we have, because of the knowledge and the information we require, I now come to you from a very different perspective.

Before coming up to the speaker's podium, Thane said that I, as a physician, come with a certain amount of moral responsibility. That is not what society usually confers upon doctors, not nowadays, not certainly after the Holocaust. Physicians come forward with a certain amount of contempt, perhaps, but not a lot of moral responsibility. I am a doctor, I'm a professor, and my research is quite particular. I'm a particularist, a typical university academic. And so I'm used to speaking about very esoteric or arcane subjects, specifically in the treatment of cancer. I am not a professional Holocaust historian, and so in some ways, I feel here as a poseur, as an impostor, trying to speak before you.

And yet, I intend to use my oncology background to create an analogy. In my business, the business of rendering care for cancer, who are our greatest activists? Who are the people who establish foundations? Who are the people who encourage research? Who are the people who go before Congress, before insurance companies, before the courts, to establish rights for cancer patients? It is the survivors, sadly to say, the few survivors of mortal illness, and their family members, because their family members are witnesses to the devastation of that disease.

And so I want to speak to you about being a witness. A witness, a recipient of transmitted memory. Now the Bible acknowledges that there is such a thing as transmitted memory. All of you know the *Shema,*[1] the watchword of our people. And most of you know, to whom the *Shema* is addressed. Now you hear *Shema Yisrael* in the Elizabethan translation: "Hear, harken oh Community of Israel." But of course, it is possible that it is Jacob individually to whom the *Shema* is addressed.

Shema Yisrael, Hear O Israel, but Israel is another name for Jacob. And I will make a connection to that individual address to Jacob in my little *D'var Torah* in a moment. But the *ayin* and the *daled*[2] of the *Shema* are usually enlarged, to represent the concept of witness.

And so even in this watchword of our people, an address to Jacob, who will be the progenitor of the Jewish people, there is the command to bear witness: all the Jewish people for generations are hearkened to the call of being witness to the oneness of God.

---

[1]*Fundamental prayer of Judaism: "Hear oh Israel, the Lord is our God, the Lord is one."—Editor's note*

[2]*Hebrew letters in the* Shema Yisrael *prayer. Together the letters spell the Hebrew word, "witness."—Editor's note*

And so, we too, like the descendants of our forefather Jacob, are given a legacy of bearing witness. We are bequeathed a responsibility of bearing witness. Now, being a doctor, I believe not only in the wisdom of the Divine but also in rational thought. As children of the Enlightenment, we are students of the scientific method and we need to define the millennial charge to bear witness.

Even with respect to the Shoah, no matter how stochastic, no matter how random survival was, we have no choice but to believe in a certain amount of reason—rational thinking which determined the course of events that led to the Shoah.

And so it is our responsibility and it's our job, to try to determine the elements essential to the concept of bearing witness. What is the concept of transmitted memory? Is it biologic? Is it psychological? Is it neurochemical? Is it electrophysiological? Well, those of you who have studied the Second Generation literature know that it's all of those things. Being a witness, receiving a legacy from your parents, is not merely a conceptual thing, it is a biological thing.

Now what I propose to do with you, in the few moments that I have, is to try to give you the charge, and the challenge, to do something concrete with the biologic heritage of transmitted memory.

Now there are Second Generation groups all over the country. Ours in Los Angeles is a large one; ours has a thousand members. Sometimes we have a general meeting and only ten people show up. But, for the most part, these thousand members periodically send in their dues, and they keep us afloat. What is the history of such an association?

The history of Second Generation stems from an attempt to deal with transmitted trauma. Quite clearly, there are those among the Second Generation who believe that their legacy is traumatic. And these members of the Second Generation try to negotiate their way through life, by considering this trauma, a trauma which has a legitimate biblical counterpart as well. The Second Generation after all is the generation of Yitzhak.

Abraham, our parents, managed to leave their homeland amidst great turbulence and establish a new life and a New World. However traumatized they may have been, they left their countries of origin to establish a new existence. We, having sensed the fire, are dealt with somewhat more transitionally. Hopefully, we will usher in a generation more solid and more secure in who they are, as Jews, as recipients of this legacy, than we are. But that is one of our charges as witness, and that is the history of the formation of Second Generation groups all around the country, dating back about 20 years.

What are the objectives of a Second Generation group today? Well, the main objective is to act as witness, as I said, in the *Shema*, that *ayin daled*, a purity of witness, something that Elie Wiesel talked to us about before.

The Jewish community has established a good model for communicating transmitted memory. The Jewish community has established a model in which organizations are run by lay leadership, and the professional personnel take their marching orders from the lay leadership.

Why is that? Because the lay leadership is felt to have a more pure role as witness and advocates. Clearly the role of teaching, of educating, is one of the objectives we have as Second Generation.

One objective should be involvement in Holocaust study, education, and transmission of information, not for academic purposes, not for financial purposes, not for political purposes—but purely because we bear a role as transmitted witnesses and as teachers. The second objective we have is remembrance. We are compelled by our parents to remember.

Now, does memory have to serve a purpose? An analogy in the natural sciences comes from the purpose of scientific inquiry. Do you need to study the segmentation of the body habitus of a fruit fly, because it has implications for human beings?

I would say that the answer is, no. The purpose of study and the development of memory is sufficient. We don't need to remember for the sake of immediately useful purpose. We don't need to remember in order to raise money for Israel Bonds. We don't need to remember for the sake of motivating Congress to do something about Bosnia, good though that might be. We don't need to remember in order to keep financially afloat the Jewish Federation in our town. We just need to remember, pure and simple.

Another major objective for Second Generation is to be Jewish. Many of us are motivated to our Judaism as a result of that memory. We fulfill Emil Fackenheim's[3] commandment not to grant Hitler a posthumous victory. Thus, we remain Jewish, and in part, that Judaism is informed by our heritage of memory.

And our final objective is commemorative. So we have these objectives as witness among the Second Generation: education, remembrance, the revival of Judaism, in perhaps a different form.

Also, being a child of the Enlightenment, I believe in the concrete implementation of these objectives. Now how do you do this? You've heard artists who use their Holocaust heritage, their Second Generation heritage, to create something.

How about the rest of us who are not artistic? Well, I give you the following tools to implement the charge to memory and to education.

One, form a Second Generation group in your community. Interact with the Second Generation Advisory Group of the United States Holocaust Memorial Museum. Interact with the Ghetto Fighters House in Israel, which seems to have a large role in Second Generation work in Israel. Join a network with Second Generation groups throughout the United States. Serve your community, in terms of their psychosocial needs, become active in your *Yom HaShoah* commemorations.

Get yourself educated so that you can teach the children, so that you can go out into the community. Be active in your memorials, and in your museums. Become a tax-exempt organization. Write bylaws, become a credible organization, in the pattern of many of the survivors, because we will be the ones to receive their legacy.

The other part that we have to do, in terms of implementation, is to make ourselves serious and recognizable by our Jewish Federations. Show the Jewish community that we are the ones who carry the torch of memory.

---

[3] *Emil Fackenheim is a prominent contemporary Jewish philosopher.—Editor's note*

And that's something very difficult to do, something that you have to interact with your own communities to do, but by organizing, you have a chance to do it.

In Los Angeles, the survivor organizations are very credible. One of them, the 1939 Club, has a Holocaust chair at UCLA that they fund. They also fund educational projects, so they have very concrete goals.

One of our future challenges is to struggle against complacency. It has been the goal of our parents to normalize us, and I think they have been very successful. We are not really victims, we are actually beneficiaries of a legacy that informs our Jewish identity, and that can stimulate our revival and our purpose.

For me, obviously, that's why I'm a cancer doctor. For others, it's art, or literature. This legacy is one of action, not of inaction. And yet, the challenge for us is to struggle against complacency. Because we see around us the popularization of the Holocaust, and this popularization encourages our complacency. We see the Shoah taken up by professionals, and they do a very credible job of generalizing the Shoah. We see it taken up by the entertainment industry, we see it taken up by fund-raising organizations and so on.

So, what is our role given this professionalization of the Shoah? What is our purpose? Well, I gave you some of the reasons for our purpose, and the most salient one is the purity of vision, the purity of transmitted memory from survivors.

That purity should be reason enough to stimulate our interest, our activism, and our purpose. And it will take many forms. It will take a psychosocial form, it will take an educational form, it will take a political activism form.

There are many ways for us to respond. We just need to be organized to do it.

Now finally, some personal reflections. My colleagues here on the panel spoke a lot about where they come from, I don't usually do that.

For whatever reason, maybe I'm guarded or whatever—you know, that's what "they" say about us, we are guarded, trouble with intimacy, all these things "they" talk about.

I just want to say that I come from a family where the idea of transmitted history is important. The one person who can vouch for that is Yehuda Bauer, who went to primary school under the name of Martin in those prewar days, with my father in Prague.

My father never had trouble talking about his Holocaust experiences. He viewed it as history that had to be transmitted much like his father transmitted his history of fighting in World War I in the trenches to his kids.

That transmitted history I value as a significant component in stimulating me to action. And I hope that I have in turn, passed that purpose, that action, on to you, that I have given you the energy, determination, and vision to be witnesses out there in the public as well.

CONFERENCE ADJOURNMENT

Romana Strochlitz Primus

As chair of *Life Reborn*, I have had the privilege of working with some extraordinary people: Miles Lerman, whose faith in the Second Generation never falters; Menachem Rosensaft, who spoke yesterday so eloquently of his parents; Rositta Kenigsberg, who chaired last night's musical tribute—an evening that moved us to cry and to dance; Felicia Anchor, Ritalynne Brechner, Eva Fogelman, Jean Rosensaft, and the rest of the Second Generation Advisory Group; and Sam Norich, who has been an invaluable consultant.

It is a pleasure to thank the donors who gave so generously and the speakers who brought us their knowledge, their insights, and their stories.

The planners, the donors, and the speakers; these names are recorded in your programs. But *Life Reborn* also depended on many people whose names are not in the program: Sara Bloomfield and the dedicated volunteers and staff of the Museum. When we attend conferences, we rarely think about the work involved in tasks such as designing signage and printed material, assembling registration kits, coordinating travel arrangements for speakers, or supervising the catering. You probably noticed all the people who monitored the meeting rooms and the halls to help us find a session or solve a problem.

We are profoundly grateful to all the staff and volunteers:

- The Center for Advanced Holocaust Studies and Severin Hochberg

- Steve Luckert and Suzy Snyder, curators of the *Life Reborn* exhibition at the Museum, and their staff

- Diane Saltzman and the staff of Collections, Photo Archives, and the Meed Survivors' Registry

- Musicologist Bret Werb

- Mel Hecker, Mariah Keller, and the Publishing Division

- Stacy Riggs and the Finance Office

- Arnie Kramer and the staff who developed the DP website

- Jerry Rehm and the Museum Shop

- Sue Grant and the Development Office

- Kris Donly and Museum Services

- Kathleen Parke

- Sylvia Kaye

- Mary Morrison and the Communications Division. In addition to her responsibilities as director of communications, two months ago Mary assumed a leadership position in this project.

- Martin Goldman, Betsy Anthony, and the entire staff of Survivor Affairs. Martin has been with this project from the beginning and has been devoted to its success.

- And, of course, the Museum's dedicated volunteers, including survivors, children of survivors, and grandchildren of survivors. Daniel Feldman, a grandchild of survivors, has spent many weeks working full time for *Life Reborn*.

Thank you all. The project would have been impossible without you.

As we conclude this conference, let us remember that history is never simple. Even the history of apparently simple subjects is complex.

Who is telling the story? What are his sources? How did she choose her material? What is his perspective, her thesis? Is there a hidden agenda?

This weekend we have tried to offer many sources and to present multiple perspectives:

- The historian and the witness

- The DP and the welfare worker

- The army officer and the politically active DP

- The poet and the journalist

- Those who worked within the bureaucracy and those who circumvented it

- The child and the adult, woman and man, the Second Generation

- The concentration camp survivor, the hidden survivor, and the survivor who returned from exile in the Soviet Union

- The religious, the secular, and the Zionist

- The people and the music

All of them have something to tell us. Together, they begin to shape the lens through which we view the DP era.

For those of us who are children of survivors, the DP period adds a critical facet to the prism through which we see our parents. Once, in prewar Europe, they were cobblers or doctors, *yeshiva bukherim* or farmers, mothers or children. Then they became the hunted, those marked for extermination. And somehow they survived. They became the Sh'erit ha-Pletah, the Surviving Remnant *and* the Saving Remnant, the builders.

I hope we leave here today with a clearer picture of the DP era, some of us with a richer portrait of our parents and all of us with a commitment. We must preserve the essential Jewishness of the Holocaust, advance Holocaust remembrance and education, and champion human rights and dignity.

Life Reborn is an energizing project. The United States Holocaust Memorial Museum is an awesome institution. Thank you all for participating. The end.

Glossary of Hebrew, Yiddish, and German Terms

A gutten Shabbes.   Traditional Yiddish Friday night greeting

Am Yisrael khai   The Jewish people lives.

Aliya Bet   Illegal immigration of Jews into Palestine under the British Mandate

Aussenkommandos   Subsidiary camps, part of the German concentration camp system

Bricha   Organized, clandestine rescue and escape of Jews out of Eastern European countries, mainly into Jewish DP camps in Germany and Austria, in the aftermath of the Holocaust

Brith Milah   Circumcision ritual

Dorf   Village

D'var Torah   Commentary on Scriptures

Haganah   Clandestine military arm of the organized Jewish leadership in Palestine before the establishment of the State of Israel

Hatikva   Zionist anthem that became the national anthem of Israel

Hochdeutsch   High German

Hupah   Wedding canopy

Kedoshim   Holy ones; martyrs

Kishkes   Guts

Maapilim   Illegal immigrants

Machzorim   High Holy Day prayer books

Matzoth   Unleavened bread eaten during Passover

Meine tayere kinder   My dear children

Menshlichkeit   Human decency

Minyan   Quorum of ten required for a Jewish religious service

Moshav	Cooperative settlement
Olim	Immigrants
Oneg Shabbat	A joyful, spiritual celebration of the Sabbath
Shlichim	Emissaries
Shloshim	Thirtieth-day observance following a person's death
Shtetl	Village; Yiddish term for largely self-contained 19th- and early 20th-century Jewish communities in eastern European villages and towns
Talitot	Prayer shawls
Tefillin	Phylacteries
Tsu lange yor	May he have a long life.
Volksdeutsche	Ethnic Germans who were citizens of countries other than Germany
Yeshiva bukherim	Yeshiva students
Yiddishe kinder	Jewish children
Yiddishe Neshume	Jewish soul, a spirit
Yishuv	Organized Jewish community in Palestine before the establishment of the State of Israel
Yizkor service	Memorial service
Yom HaShoah	Day of Holocaust remembrance

Bauer, Yehuda. *Flight and Rescue: Bricha*. New York: Random House, 1970.

> History of the clandestine organized escape of Jews out of Eastern Europe following the Holocaust. The book also describes the smuggling of survivors into Palestine, their clashes with occupying forces, and the Jewish DPs' role in the creation of the State of Israel.

Bauer, Yehuda. *Out of the Ashes*. Oxford: Pergamon Press, 1989.

> This book discusses the impact of American Jews on Jewish Holocaust survivors. Bauer begins with the details of liberation in Eastern and Western Europe, and continues with a description of the creation of DP camps in 1945 and 1946; the pivotal roles that UNRRA and the JDC played in the camps; interagency problems; the migration of the survivors; and the disbanding of the camps.

Belsen. Tel Aviv: Irgun Sheerit Hapleita Me'Haezor Habriti, 1957.

> A comprehensive overview of all aspects of life in the Bergen-Belsen DP camp between 1945 and 1950. The book includes personal narratives by the camp's Jewish leaders, British military personnel, senior officials of the World Jewish Congress, and others. The authors discuss a wide range of topics, including political issues, liberation, the children of Belsen, health care, education, the Belsen theater, religious life, and the 1945 Belsen trial.

Bloch, Sam E., ed. *Holocaust and Rebirth: Bergen-Belsen 1945–1965*. New York: Bergen-Belsen Memorial Press, 1965.

> Using pictures, flyers, and posters of the era, this book provides the history of the Bergen-Belsen concentration camp from liberation through its time as a DP camp. The photographs depict the rebirth of the survivors, the educational and cultural programs that developed in the DP camp, the Zionist demonstrations that took place, and the Belsen survivors' eventual immigration to Israel, the United States, and Canada.

Brenner, Michael. *After the Holocaust: Rebuilding Jewish Lives in Postwar Germany*. Princeton University Press, 1997.

> Comprehensive account of Jewish life and communities in Germany after the Holocaust, emphasizing the tension between Jews and their former oppressors. The work analyzes the psychological, spiritual, and material challenges that confronted the Jewish survivors as they began to rebuild their lives in the DP camps.

Dinnerstein, Leonard. *America and the Survivors of the Holocaust.* Columbia University Press, 1982.

Historical study of how the American political climate immediately following World War II affected U.S. legislation and policy regarding the DPs. The book contains a useful statistical appendix and complete copies of several historical documents, including the Harrison Report.

Grobman, Alex. *Rekindling the Flame: American Jewish Chaplains and the Survivors of European Jewry, 1944–1948.* Wayne State University Press, 1993.

Account of the roles and activities of American Jewish chaplains in the DP camps, with special emphasis on the months following the end of the war and the impact of the Harrison Report.

Halamish, Aviva. *The* Exodus *Affair: Holocaust Survivors and the Struggle for Palestine.* Syracuse University Press, 1998.

A detailed, thoroughly researched account of the *Exodus 1947*—the illegal immigration ship that was intercepted by British warships off the coast of Palestine in 1947 with 4,515 Holocaust survivors on board, culminating in the subsequent international controversy over the British authorities' decision to forcibly return the survivors to Germany.

Heymont, Irving. *Among the Survivors—The Landsberg DP Camp Letters of Major Irving Heymont, United States Army.* Cincinnati: American Jewish Archives, 1982.

This compilation of 34 letters written by Major Heymont to his wife in the United States between September 19 and December 6, 1945, recounts the events at Landsberg DP camp as seen by the American-Jewish officer in command. While primarily attempting to describe the refugees' anxieties, Heymont also weighs the broader policies of the U.S. Army's governance of the camp's day-to-day administration.

Hilliard, Robert L. *Surviving the Americans, the Continued Struggle of the Jews after Liberation.* New York: Seven Stories Press, 1997.

The author's personal memoir of the time he spent as a soldier in the St. Ottilien DP camp. The book deals with life in the camp, as well as politics and their effect on those inside the camp. A compelling insight into the rebirth and renewal of the DPs.

Hyman, Abraham S. *The Undefeated*. Jerusalem: Gefen Publishing House, 1993.

> Comprehensive account of the Jewish DP experience by the acting advisor on Jewish affairs at U.S. Army headquarters in Germany, including the logistics of the DP issue for the Allied armies in 1945; DP demographics after the influx of Polish and Romanian DPs in 1946 and 1947; and renewal of life in the DP camps.

Levy, Isaac. *Witness to Evil: Bergen-Belsen, 1945*. London: Peter Halban Publishers, Ltd., 1995.

> A memoir of the first months after liberation in the Bergen-Belsen DP camp by the senior Jewish chaplain to the British liberation army, including moving contemporaneous letters describing conditions in the camp, relations between the survivors and the British military authorities, and the beginning of self-government by the Central Jewish Committee in the British Zone of Germany.

Nadich, Judah. *Eisenhower and the Jews*. New York: Twayne Publishers, 1953.

> Rabbi Nadich, an American army chaplain who served as advisor on Jewish affairs to General Eisenhower discusses the general's attitude toward the Jewish survivors of the Holocaust during the DP era, as well as Eisenhower's visits to liberated concentration camps and DP camps.

Reilly, Jo, David Cesarini, Tony Kushner, and Colin Richmond, eds. *Belsen in History and Memory*. London: Frank Cass, 1997.

> The history of the Bergen-Belsen camp from the Nazi era to liberation to its eventual conversion into the DP camp that became the center of Jewish religious and political life in the British zone. The book also discusses the roles that women played in liberation as well as the treatment of other individuals during the liberation process.

Reilly, Joanne. *Belsen: The Liberation of a Concentration Camp*. London and New York: Routledge, 1998.

> Using Bergen-Belsen as a paradigm, Reilly discusses British responses to the Holocaust and how they were affected by British domestic and Middle Eastern policies during the postwar period; Anglo-Jewish relief efforts; and the political issues facing liberated Jewish survivors in the Belsen DP camp—a camp that witnessed a rebirth of Jewish culture and national sentiment.

Schwarz, Leo W. *The Redeemers: A Saga of the Years 1945–1952.*
New York: Farrar, Straus, and Young, 1953.

The story of the Jewish survivors of the Holocaust in Germany as they rebuilt their lives and culture in the DP camps. One of the earliest accounts of the DP era, written by a senior JDC official of the period.

United Nations Relief and Rehabilitation Administration. *Summary of Displaced Persons Population: UNRRA Assembly Centers in the United States Zone 24 August 1946.* Statistics and Reports Branch, UNRRA Headquarters, U.S. Zone.

The statistical UNRRA report on the DP camps administered by that relief agency. In graph form, the report provides primary data about the DP camps, including population figures, relief team numbers, camp locations, assembly center numbers, and camp names and capacities.

Wyman, Mark. *DP: Europe's Displaced Persons.* Ithaca and London: Cornell University Press, 1998.

Examination of life in both the Jewish and non-Jewish DP camps, which uses historical documents and primary source depictions of the camps to give a history of the activities and concerns of DP camp residents.

ARTICLES

PUBLISHED 1945–52

Bernstein, David. "Europe's Jews: Summer 1947." *Commentary* 4 (1947): 101–09.

Friedman, Paul. "The Road Back for DPs." *Commentary* 6 (December 1948): 502–10.

Genêt. "Letter from Aschaffenburg." *New Yorker* 24 (30 October 1948): 86–91.

Gringauz, Samuel. "Jewish Destiny as the DPs See It." *Commentary* 4 (1947): 501–09.

"The Harrison Report." *The Department of State Bulletin* 13 (30 September 1945): 456–63; also included as Appendix B in Leonard Dinnerstein, *America and the Survivors of the Holocaust* (Columbia University Press: 1982).

Pinson, Koppel S. "Jewish Life in Liberated Germany: A Study of the Jewish DPs." *Jewish Social Studies* 9 (1947): 101–26.

Baumel, Judith Tydor. "Kibbutz Buchenwald and Kibbutz Hafetz Hayyim: Two Experiments in the Rehabilitation of Jewish Survivors in Germany." *Holocaust and Genocide Studies* 9 (1995): 231–49.

Benz, Wolfgang. "Germans, Jews and Anti-Semitism in Germany After 1945." *Journal of Politics and History* 41 (1995): 118–29.

Dawidowicz, Lucy. "Belsen Remembered." *Commentary* (March 1966): 82–85.

Friedlander, Henry. "Darkness and Dawn in 1945: The Nazis, the Allies, and the Survivors." In *1945: The Year of Liberation*, 11–35. United States Holocaust Memorial Museum, 1995.

Lavsky, Hagit. "British Jewry and the Jews in Post Holocaust Germany: The Jewish Relief Unit, 1945–50." *Journal of Holocaust Education* 4 (1995): 29–40.

Peck, Abraham J. "The Displaced." *Dimensions* 9 (1995): 11–14.

Webster, Ronald. "American Relief and Jews in Germany, 1945–60." *Diverging Perspectives—Leo Baeck Institute Yearbook* 38 (1993): 293–321.

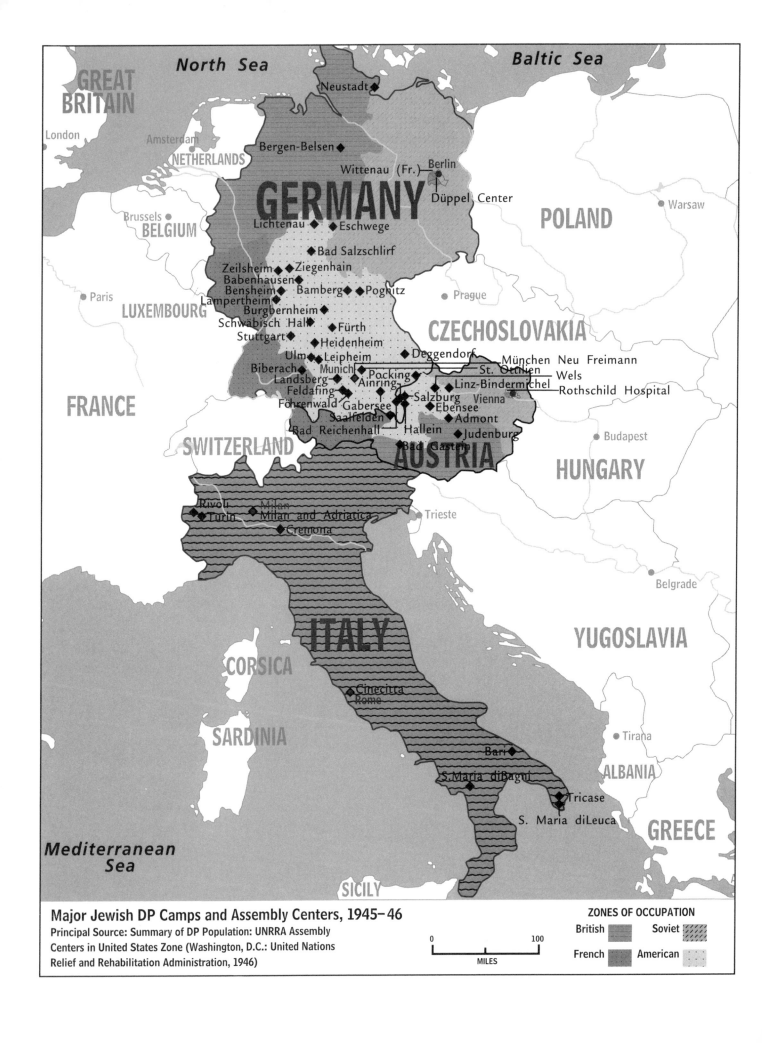

North Sea

Baltic Sea

GREAT BRITAIN

London

Amsterdam

NETHERLANDS

BELGIUM

Brussels

Paris

LUXEMBOURG

FRANCE

SWITZERLAND

Neustadt ◆

Bergen-Belsen ◆

Wittenau (Fr.) Berlin
Düppel Center

GERMANY

POLAND

Warsaw

Lichtenau ◆ ◆ Eschwege

Bad Salzschlirf ◆

Zeilsheim ◆ ◆ Ziegenhain
Babenhausen ◆
Bensheim ◆ ◆ Bamberg ◆ ◆ Pognitz
Lampertheim ◆
Burgbernheim ◆
Schwäbisch Hall ◆ ◆ Fürth
Stuttgart ◆ ◆ Heidenheim
Ulm ◆ ◆ Leipheim ◆ Deggendorf
Biberach ◆ ◆ Munich
Landsberg ◆ ◆ Ainring
Feldafing ◆
Föhrenwald ◆ Gabersee
Saalfelden ◆
Bad Reichenhall ◆ Hallein
Bad Gastein

Prague

CZECHOSLOVAKIA

München Neu Freimann
St. Ottilien
Wels
Pocking
Linz-Bindermichel
Rothschild Hospital
Salzburg Vienna
◆ Ebensee
◆ Admont
◆ Judenburg

AUSTRIA

HUNGARY

Budapest

Rivoli ◆ Milan
Turin ◆ ◆ Milan and Adriatica
◆ Cremona

Trieste

Belgrade

ITALY

YUGOSLAVIA

CORSICA

SARDINIA

Cinecittà ◆
Rome

Bari ◆

S.Maria diBagni ◆

Tricase
S. Maria diLeuca

ALBANIA

Tirana

GREECE

Mediterranean Sea

SICILY

Major Jewish DP Camps and Assembly Centers, 1945–46

Principal Source: Summary of DP Population: UNRRA Assembly
Centers in United States Zone (Washington, D.C.: United Nations
Relief and Rehabilitation Administration, 1946)

0   100

MILES

ZONES OF OCCUPATION

British   Soviet

French   American

Conference Program

6–7:30 P.M.

OPENING SESSION

Welcome
Sara J. Bloomfield
Director, United States Holocaust Memorial Museum

Remarks
Rositta Ehrlich Kenigsberg
Executive Vice President, Holocaust Documentation and Education Center, Florida International University; Chairperson, Second Generation Advisory Group; member, United States Holocaust Memorial Council; born Bindermichel DP camp

Opening Address
Miles Lerman
Chairperson, United States Holocaust Memorial Council

7:45 P.M.

FRAMING THE CONFERENCE AND ONEG SHABBAT

CHAIRPERSON

Romana Strochlitz Primus
Chairperson, *Life Reborn* Project, Second Generation Advisory Group; member, United States Holocaust Memorial Council; born Bergen-Belsen DP camp

The DP Period in History
Yehuda Bauer
Director, International Institute for Holocaust Research, Yad Vashem

Oneg Shabbat
PERSONAL RECOLLECTIONS

Rabbi Mayer Abramowitz
U.S. Military Chaplain, Germany and Austria; JDC emigration director in Italy

Cantor Moshe Kraus
First Chief Cantor of the Israel Defense Forces; Holocaust survivor; General Secretary of the Chief Rabbinate of the British Zone of Germany; cantor, Bergen-Belsen DP camp

Cantor Isaac Goodfriend
Cantor Emeritus, Ahavath Achim Synagogue, Atlanta; Holocaust survivor; choir member, Feldafing DP camp

SONG LEADERS

Cantor Moshe Kraus

Adrienne Cooper
Singer/songwriter; Director of Program Development for the Workmens Circle/Arbeter Ring

Cantor Isaac Goodfriend

Saturday, January 15, 2000

9 A.M.

VISITS TO THE UNITED STATES HOLOCAUST MEMORIAL MUSEUM
(optional)

SHABBAT SERVICES AVAILABLE AT THE MARRIOTT WARDMAN PARK HOTEL

NOON–2 P.M.

LUNCH PLENARY: THE JOINT DISTRIBUTION COMMITTEE

Introduction
Sara J. Bloomfield
Director, United States Holocaust Memorial Museum

CHAIRPERSON
Jonathan W. Kolker
President, The American Jewish Joint Distribution Committee

Tribute to the Memory of Dr. Joseph J. Schwartz
Michael Schneider
Executive Vice President, JDC

Life in the DP Camps: The Special Role of the JDC
Ted Feder
Missions and VIP Coordinator, JDC; Deputy Director, JDC Program, American Zone of Germany

Isaac Norich
Holocaust survivor; Feldafing DP camp; JDC official in Foehrenwald and Munich Office

Closing
Theodore Comet
Honorary Associate Executive Vice-President, JDC; student volunteer, JDC program to rehabilitate war orphans in France

2:30–3:45 P.M.   TEXT STUDY SESSIONS

Appeal for Aid to the American Jewish Community
The Harrison Report
Robert L. Hilliard
Dean, Emerson College, Boston; U.S. Army, St. Ottilien DP camp

Ben Gurion's Speech to the DPs
Samuel Norich
General Manager, Forward Association; born Feldafing DP camp

Directives from the *Yishuv* to Its Emissaries
Dina Porat
Professor of Jewish History, Tel Aviv University

Editorial from a DP Newspaper
Aron Hirt-Manheimer
Editor, *Reform Judaism;* born Feldafing DP camp

Faith and Observance after the *Khurbn*
Gershon Greenberg
Research Fellow, Institute for Holocaust Research, Bar Ilan University;
Professor of Philosophy and Religion, American University

First Steps: Encounters, Strategies, and Rituals
after Liberation
Toby Blum Dobkin
Folklorist; born Landsberg DP camp

JDC Field Reports
Ted Feder
Missions and VIP Coordinator, JDC; Deputy Director, JDC Program,
American Zone of Germany

Jewish Students in Munich
Emanuel Tanay
Clinical Professor of Psychiatry, Wayne State University; child
survivor, Landsberg and Foehrenwald DP camps

Justice
Joseph Harmatz
Former director general, World ORT Union; Holocaust survivor; *Bricha*
leader

Landsberger Lagercajtung
Abraham Peck
Director, Academic Research and Institutional Operations, American
Jewish Historical Society; born Landsberg DP camp

Selections from the American Press
Ruth Gruber
Author; U.S. journalist covering DP camps and the *Exodus*

2:30–3:45 P.M. (continued)	**Sephardim in the DP Camps** *Yitzhak Kerem* Professor, Hebrew University; Editor, *Sefarad*, the Sephardic newsletter

Parshat Bo: Waiting to Enter the Promised Land, a Chaplain and the *Bricha*
Rabbi Mayer Abramowitz
U.S. Military Chaplain, Germany and Austria; JDC emigration director in Italy

Yiddish Expository Prose *(in Yiddish)*
Miriam Isaacs
Assistant Professor, Meyerhoff Center for Jewish Studies, University of Maryland; born Leipheim DP camp

Yiddish Poetry
Anita Norich
Associate Professor, English Language and Literature Department, University of Michigan; daughter of Holocaust survivors; born in Munich

4:30–6:30 P.M. **AFFINITY GROUP RECEPTIONS**
JDC RECEPTION

8:15–9:30 P.M. **EVENING PROGRAM**
CHAIRPERSON
Felicia Figlarz Anchor
Vice President, National Council of Jewish Women; Second Generation Advisory Group, United States Holocaust Memorial Council; born Bergen-Belsen DP camp

Choosing Life: Our Parents, Ourselves
Samuel Norich
General Manager, Forward Association; born Feldafing DP camp

Address
The Honorable Sam Gejdenson
Member of Congress (Democrat—Connecticut); born Eschwege DP camp; first child of survivors elected to the U.S. House of Representatives

Nothing Makes You Free
Melvin Jules Bukiet
Novelist; Professor, Sarah Lawrence College; son of Holocaust survivors

The DP Experience in Film
Aviva Kempner
Filmmaker; daughter of Holocaust survivor

9:45–11 P.M. *LONG IS THE WAY* FILM SCREENING

Sunday, January 16, 2000

8:45–10:30 A.M. **MORNING PLENARY: THE DP EXPERIENCE**
OVERVIEW
Romana Strochlitz Primus
Chairperson, Life Reborn Project, Second Generation Advisory Group;
member, United States Holocaust Memorial Council;
born Bergen-Belsen DP camp

RECOLLECTIONS
Sam E. Bloch
President, World Federation of Bergen-Belsen Survivors Associations;
Holocaust survivor; member, Jewish Committee, Bergen-Belsen DP camp

Rabbi Herbert Friedman
Executive Director, Wexner Heritage Foundation; Military Assistant to
the Advisor on Jewish Affairs, U.S. Military Authorities in Germany and
Austria

HISTORICAL ISSUES
Henry Friedlander
Professor of History, Department of Judaic Studies, Brooklyn College;
Holocaust survivor

10:45 A.M. **FORUMS 1: SELF-DETERMINATION**
–12:30 P.M. **After Liberation**
MODERATOR
Ruth B. Mandel
Vice Chairperson, United States Holocaust Memorial Council; Director
and Professor, Eagleton Institute of Politics, Rutgers University

OVERVIEW
Henry Friedlander
Professor of History, Department of Judaic Studies, Brooklyn College;
Holocaust survivor

RECOLLECTIONS
Alvin Corwin
First Vice President, Solomon, Smith, Barney; U.S. Army Captain in
charge of six DP camps, including two Jewish DP camps (Lampertheim
and Bensheim) from August 1945 to April 1946

Tzvi Rosenwein
Holocaust survivor; staff, Central Jewish Committee, American Zone of
Germany

**10:45 A.M.
–12:30 P.M.
(continued)**

Bergen-Belsen and the British Zone

MODERATOR

Sigmund Strochlitz
Former National Chairman, Days of Remembrance Committee, United
States Holocaust Memorial Council; Bergen-Belsen DP camp

OVERVIEW

Jo Reilly
Education and Outreach Officer, Wiener Library; lecturer in
history, Southampton University

RECOLLECTIONS

Sam E. Bloch
President, World Federation of Bergen-Belsen Survivors Associations;
member, Jewish Committee, Bergen-Belsen DP camp

Tania Rozmaryn
United States Holocaust Memorial Museum survivor volunteer; Bergen-
Belsen DP camp

PHOTOS

Eric Nooter
Director of Archives and Records, JDC

Bricha and Emigration

MODERATOR

Sam Knobler
Past President, The Combined Generations of the Holocaust, Cincinnati;
Second Generation Advisory Group, United States Holocaust Memorial
Council

OVERVIEW

Yehuda Bauer
Director, International Institute for Holocaust Research,
Yad Vashem

RECOLLECTIONS

Rabbi Mayer Abramowitz
U.S. Military Chaplain, Germany and Austria; JDC emigration
director in Italy

Samuel Ron
Holocaust survivor; organized survivor escapes from Eastern Europe;
brought child survivors to Palestine

Child Survivors

MODERATOR

Stefanie Seltzer
Holocaust survivor; President, Federation of Jewish Child Survivors of
the Holocaust

**10:45 A.M.
–12:30 P.M.
(continued)**

OVERVIEW

Robert Krell
Professor Emeritus, Department of Psychiatry, The University of British Columbia; survived in hiding in Holland

RECOLLECTIONS

George Schwab
President, National Committee on American Foreign Policy; Holocaust survivor, Blankenese Children's Home

Paula Goldberg
Holocaust survivor; Foehrenwald and other DP camps

Italy and Austria

MODERATOR

George Rich
Chair, JDC Committee for Eastern Europe; DP in Vienna camp

OVERVIEW

Yitzhak Kerem
Professor, Hebrew University; Editor, *Sefarad,* the Sephardic newsletter

RECOLLECTIONS

Jacob Trobe
Founding producer, Telecommunications & Information Revolution; JDC Country Director for Germany and Italy

Hyman Silberstrom
Holocaust survivor; DP in Puch, Hallain, and Salzburg, Austria

Non-Jewish DPs

MODERATOR

Rev. John T. Pawlikowski
Professor, Catholic Theological Union; member, United States Holocaust Memorial Council

OVERVIEW

Mark Wyman
Professor of History, Illinois State University

RECOLLECTIONS

Vladimir Pregelj
Trade and finance specialist, Congressional Research Service; Slovenian DP in Pagani and Senigallia DP camps

Guntis Sraders
Retired from the Office of the Secretary of Defense; Latvian DP in Haunstetten DP camp

10:45 A.M. –12:30 P.M. (continued)	## Self-Government **MODERATOR** *Alan Silver* Attorney; son of Holocaust survivors **OVERVIEW** *Abraham Peck* Director, Academic Research and Institutional Operations, American Jewish Historical Society; born Landsberg DP camp **RECOLLECTIONS** *Stanley Abramovitch* JDC education office, Europe, Iran, North Africa, Israel; JDC director Foehrenwald/Windsheim DP camps, JDC Frankfurt Regional Office *Marion Pritchard* UNRRA worker, Foehrenwald, Kloster-Indesdorf, and Windsheim DP camps *Kalman Sultanik* Vice President, World Jewish Congress; member, Central Jewish Committee, American Zone of Germany

The U.S. Army, the Germans, and the DPs
MODERATOR
Jacqueline Giere
Education Department, Fritz Bauer Institute, Germany

OVERVIEW
Severin Hochberg
Center for Advanced Holocaust Studies, United States Holocaust Memorial Museum

RECOLLECTIONS
Rabbi Herbert Friedman
Executive Director, Wexner Heritage Foundation; Military Assistant to the Advisor on Jewish Affairs, U.S. Military Authorities in Germany and Austria

Col. (ret) Irving Heymont
U.S. Army officer responsible for Landsberg DP camp

Robert L. Hilliard
Dean, Emerson College, Boston; U.S. Army, St. Ottilien DP camp

12:45–2:15 P.M.	## LUNCH PLENARY: REMEMBRANCE **CHAIRPERSON** *Menachem Z. Rosensaft* Founding Chairman, International Network of Children of Jewish Holocaust Survivors; past chairperson, Second Generation Advisory Group; member, United States Holocaust Memorial Council; born Bergen-Belsen DP camp

My Father: A Model for Empowerment
Menachem Z. Rosensaft

Keynote Address
Elie Wiesel
Founding Chairman, United States Holocaust Memorial Council; Nobel
Peace Prize Laureate; OSE *(Oeuvre de Secours aux Enfants)* schools,
France

2:45–4:30 P.M.   FORUMS 2: FAMILY, WORK, AND CULTURE
Artistic Creativity
MODERATOR
Debbie Teicholz-Guedalia
Photographer-artist; daughter of Holocaust survivors

OVERVIEW AND RECOLLECTIONS
Samuel Bak
Artist; Holocaust survivor, Landsberg DP camp

David Rogow
Staff, YIVO; Holocaust survivor, actor, *Minkhner Yidisher Teater* (DP
theater company)

Henny Durmashkin-Gurko
Vocal soloist; Holocaust survivor, member of all-DP St. Ottilien
Orchestra

Coping with the Psychological Aftermath of Survival and Extreme Trauma
MODERATOR
Sheila Erlich
Psychologist; daughter of Holocaust survivors

OVERVIEW
Eva Fogelman
Psychologist; Second Generation Advisory Group, United States
Holocaust Memorial Council; born Kassel DP camp

RECOLLECTIONS
Henry Krystal
Psychiatrist; Holocaust survivor, Neustadt DP camp

Maria Rosenbloom
Associate Professor, Hunter College; Holocaust survivor, UNRRA and
JDC official

2:45–4:30 P.M.
(continued)

Courtship, Marriage, and Children

MODERATOR
Aletta Schaap
Member, United States Holocaust Memorial Council

OVERVIEW
Toby Blum-Dobkin
Folklorist; born Landsberg DP camp

RECOLLECTIONS
Minna Aspler
Holocaust survivor; Landsberg DP camp

Regina Spiegel
United States Holocaust Memorial Museum survivor volunteer;
Foehrenwald DP camp

Donia Gold Schwartzstein
Holocaust survivor; Schlachtensee DP camp

Education, Training, Employment, and *Hakhshara* (kibbutz training)

MODERATOR
Abraham Peck
Director, Academic Research and Institutional Operations,
American Jewish Historical Society; born Landsberg DP camp

OVERVIEW
Jacqueline Giere
Education Department, Fritz Bauer Institute, Germany

RECOLLECTIONS
Solomon Goldman
Director Emeritus, Jewish National Fund of America;
Holocaust survivor, Feldafing DP camp

Helen Luksenberg
United States Holocaust Memorial Museum survivor volunteer;
ORT trainee

Justice

MODERATOR
Lanny A. Breuer
Attorney; member, United States Holocaust Memorial Council

OVERVIEW
Dina Porat
Professor, Department of Jewish History, Tel Aviv University

RECOLLECTIONS
Joseph Harmatz
Former director, World ORT Union; Holocaust survivor; *Bricha* leader

Boleslaw Brodecki
Holocaust survivor; police officer, Landsberg DP camp

**2:45–4:30 P.M.
(continued)**

The Multiple Roles of Women

MODERATOR

Ritalynne Brechner
Second Generation Advisory Group, United States Holocaust Memorial
Council; daughter of Holocaust survivors, born in Stuttgart

OVERVIEW

Margarete Myers Feinstein
Professor of History, Indiana University at South Bend

RECOLLECTIONS

Nesse Godin
United States Holocaust Memorial Museum survivor volunteer;
Feldafing DP camp

Tonia Rotkopf Blair
Holocaust survivor; nurse, Lodz Ghetto Hospital; nurse, Landsberg DP
camp hospital

The Press and Book Publishing

MODERATOR

Aron Hirt-Manheimer
Editor, *Reform Judaism;* born Feldafing DP camp

OVERVIEW

Zachary Baker
Reinhard Family Curator of Judaica and Hebraica Collections, Stanford
University Libraries

Miriam Isaacs
Assistant Professor, Meyerhoff Center for Jewish Studies,
University of Maryland, College Park; born Leipheim DP camp

RECOLLECTIONS

Ruth Gruber
Author; journalist covering DP camps and the *Exodus*

Michael Baran
Holocaust survivor; editorial staff, Foehrenwald DP camp newspaper

Religious Observance

MODERATOR

Rella Feldman
Second Generation Advisory Group, United States
Holocaust Memorial Council; born Bindermichel DP camp

OVERVIEW

Gershon Greenberg
Research Fellow, Institute for Holocaust Research, Bar Ilan University;
Professor of Philosophy and Religion, American University

2:45–4:30 P.M. (continued)	**RECOLLECTIONS**
	Rabbi Emanuel Rackman
	Chancellor Emeritus, Bar Ilan University; Military Assistant to the Advisor on Jewish Affairs, U.S. Military Authorities in Germany and Austria

Cantor Moshe Kraus
First Chief Cantor of the Israel Defense Forces; Holocaust survivor; General Secretary of the Chief Rabbinate of the British Zone of Germany; cantor, Bergen-Belsen DP camp

8:30–10:30 P.M.

L'CHAIM—TO LIFE!

An evening performance drawn from the DP period and dedicated to our parents, the survivors of the Holocaust.

CHAIRPERSON

Rositta Ehrlich Kenigsberg
Executive Vice President, Holocaust Documentation and Education Center, Florida International University; Chairperson, Second Generation Advisory Group; member, United States Holocaust Memorial Council; born Bindermichel DP camp

FEATURING

Adrienne Cooper, Frieda Enoch Ensemble, Robyn Helzner Trio, Zalmen Mlotek, and Herman and Susan Taube

RESPONSE TO DEDICATION

Benjamin Meed
President, American Gathering of Jewish Holocaust Survivors; Chairperson, Days of Remembrance Committee, United States Holocaust Memorial Council

Monday, January 17, 2000

8:45–10:15 A.M.

MORNING PLENARY: ALLIED POLICY TOWARD THE DPS

CHAIRPERSON

Dina Porat
Professor of Jewish History, Tel Aviv University

PANELISTS

Leonard Dinnerstein
Director of Judaic Studies, University of Arizona

David Engel
Maurice Goldberg Professor of Holocaust Studies, New York University; Fellow, Diaspora Institute, Tel Aviv University

Jo Reilly
Education and Outreach Officer, Wiener Library; Lecturer in History, Southampton University

10:45 A.M.
–12:45 P.M.

CLOSING PLENARY: THE LEGACY CHAIRPERSON AND OVERVIEW

Jean Bloch Rosensaft
National Director for Public Affairs and Institutional Planning, Hebrew Union College—Jewish Institute of Religion; Second Generation Advisory Group, United States Holocaust Memorial Council

Responding to Our Legacy: A Panel of Children of Holocaust Survivors

Thane Rosenbaum
Novelist; Adjunct Professor of Law, Fordham University

Gary John Schiller
Associate Professor of Medicine, Division of Hematology/Oncology, Department of Medicine, UCLA School of Medicine; President, Second Generation Los Angeles, Sons and Daughters of Jewish Holocaust Survivors

Debbie Teicholz-Guedalia
Photographer and artist

Conference Adjournment

Romana Strochlitz Primus
Chairperson, *Life Reborn* Project, Second Generation Advisory Group; member, United States Holocaust Memorial Council; born Bergen-Belsen DP camp

Life Reborn *Steering Committee*

Romana Strochlitz Primus
Waterford, CT
Chairperson, *Life Reborn* Project
Member, United States Holocaust Memorial Council

Felicia Figlarz Anchor
Nashville, TN
Chairperson, Arrangements Committee

Ritalynne Brechner
New York, NY
Chairperson, Products Committee

Eva Fogelman
New York, NY
Chairperson, Academic Publications Committee

Rositta Ehrlich Kenigsberg
Miami, FL
Chairperson, Second Generation Advisory Group
Member, United States Holocaust Memorial Council

Jean Bloch Rosensaft
New York, NY
Chairperson, Exhibitions Committee

Menachem Z. Rosensaft
New York, NY
Chairperson, Collections and Acquisition Committee,
United States Holocaust Memorial Council

Second Generation Advisory Group of the United States Holocaust Memorial Council

Rositta Ehrlich Kenigsberg,*
Chairperson
Miami, FL

Romana Strochlitz Primus*
Waterford, CT

Menachem Z. Rosensaft*
New York, NY

Felicia Figlarz Anchor
Nashville, TN

Ritalynne Brechner
New York, NY

Rella Feldman
Teaneck, NJ

Eva Fogelman
New York, NY

David Halpern
Woodbridge, NJ

Sam Knobler
Cincinnati, OH

Howard Konar
Rochester, NY

Abraham Krieger
Great Neck, NY

Linda Laulicht
West Orange, NJ

Jean Bloch Rosensaft
New York, NY

Paul Steinfeld
Atlanta, GA

Ann Weiss
Bryn Mawr, PA

Henry Welt
New York, NY

Cheryl Zoller
Los Angeles, CA

Wayne Zuckerman
Union, NJ

*Member, United States Holocaust Memorial Council

Donors to the Life Reborn Conference

The Museum gratefully acknowledges the generous support of the following donors to the Life Reborn Conference.

The American Jewish Joint Distribution Committee

Theodore and Renee Weiler Foundation, Inc.
The Harry and Jeanette Weinberg Foundation, Inc.

Projekt
Jewish Community Endowment Fund of the Jewish Community
    Federation of San Francisco, the Peninsula, Marin and Sonoma Counties

American Gathering of Jewish Holocaust Survivors
Felicia and Kenneth Anchor
Bertram Associates
Wallace Chavkin
Haron Dahan Foundation
Rella and Dr. Charles Feldman
Gold Family Foundation
Sharon and David Halpern
The Hebrew Immigrant Aid Society
Gershon Kekst
Konar Family Foundation
Harvey Krueger
Charles Kushner
Kushner Family Foundation
Esther and Joseph Lumer
Louise and Murray Pantirer
The Louis and Harold Price Foundation, Inc.
Romana Strochlitz Primus and Charles Primus
Wardynski & Partners
Leonard Wilf
Wilmer, Cutler & Pickering
Millie and Abraham Zuckerman
Wayne Zuckerman

Vivian and Daniel Bernstein
Dora Butnick Charitable Trust
Chicago Mercantile Exchange
Congregation Emanu-El of the City of New York
Simona and Hart Hasten
Jesselson Foundation
Amos and Floy Kaminski
Renée and Abe Krieger

Rose and Sigmund Strochlitz
Michael B. Trencher
Cheryl and Henry Welt
Joseph Wilf

Combined Generations of the Holocaust
Andrew Gaspar
Irwin Kruger
The Rita Poretsky Foundation
Jean and Menachem Rosensaft
Axel Stawski

Anonymous
Amivest Corporation
Walter Baker
Martin Bloch
George Blumenthal
Debra Braverman and David Rosensaft
Dora Brechner
Ritalynne Brechner
Diana and Robert Cohen
The Coleman Foundation
David Ben Gurion Cultural Club
Nancy, Ross, Rachel, and Jill Delston, in memory
    of Irma Z. Baker and Kenneth A. Baker
Louis Detz
James Elkind
Fagenson Family Foundation
Doug Feith
Eva Fogelman
Susie and Michael Gelman
Bernard Goldberg
International Network of Children of Jewish Holocaust Survivors
Ezra Katz
Rositta Ehrlich Kenigsberg
Susan and Sam Knobler
Simon Konover
The Henry and Rose Moskowitz Foundation
The New American Jewish Social Club
Samuel Norich
Pick Family Foundation
Sheila Erlich Pruzansky
Arthur and Jane Rosenbloom
The Rosenthal Family Foundation
Mannes and Malka Schwarz
Stella and Samuel Skura

Sperber and Steinfeld Families'
   Charitable Trust
Transcon Builders, Inc.
Stephanie and Julius Trump
William Ungar
Florence and Robert Werner
Women's American ORT and
   American ORT Federation, Inc.
Cheryl, Martine, and Barry Zoller

———

Rae Benjamin
Liselotte Boehm
Bogen and Sperling Children
Johanna Brainin
Bruce T. Brown
Joseph Bukiet
Sylvan Dubow
Lola Eisenberg
Mona Feldman
Helene Frankle
Matthew Geller
Patricia and Steven Goldman, in honor of the
   birthday of Mrs. Bertha Goldman
Vasile Iszakovits
Roman Kent
Linda Klein
Donald E. Lefton
Hershel Lipow
Irene Lozowski
Andrea and Steven Mandelsberg
Linda and Curt Mankoff
Sylvia and Chuck Meyers
Frances and Ber Nisenbaum, in memory
   of Louis Goldstein
Robert Oberlender
Mitchel H. Perkiel
Richard Primus
Jill and Barry Shiffman
Marla and Michael Solarz
Adam Starkopf
Marlene Eva Stern
Stephen Tencer
The Thaler Family Foundation
Ann Weiss
Mr. and Mrs. Natan Wekselbaum
Francine Werdinger
Ruth Wiseman
Alicia and Vladimir Zwass